THE FOURTH WORLD

SAM HALL

The Fourth World

The Heritage of the Arctic and its Destruction

ALFRED A. KNOPF
NEW YORK 1987

THIS IS A BORZOI BOOK
PUBLISHED BY ALFRED A. KNOPF, INC.

Copyright © 1987 by Sam Hall

Maps copyright © 1987 by The Bodley Head

All rights reserved under International and Pan-American
Copyright Conventions.
Published in the United States by Alfred A. Knopf, Inc., New York.
Distributed by Random House, Inc., New York.
Published in Great Britain by The Bodley Head, Ltd., London, in 1987.

Library of Congress Cataloging-in-Publication Data

Hall, Sam
The fourth world.
Bibliography: p.
Includes index.
1. Arctic regions.   I. Title.
G606.H35   1987   919.8   86-46121
ISBN 0-394-55942-8

Manufactured in the United States of America

First American Edition

To Susanna

'... as the peoples and nations of the world have come to recognize the existence and rights of those peoples who make up the Third World, the day must come, and will come, when the nations of the Fourth World will come to be recognized and respected ...'

The Dene Declaration, 1975

Notes on Temperature Conversion

In the text, temperatures are given in Celsius. Readers more familiar with the Fahrenheit thermometer may remember that five Celsius degrees are the equivalent of nine Fahrenheit degrees, while freezing is 0° Celsius and 32° Fahrenheit. Some equivalents are listed below:

C	F
−70°	−94°
−50°	−58°
−40°	−40°
−35°	−31°
0°	+32°
+ 5°	+41°
+10°	+50°
+15°	+59°
+35°	+95°

CONTENTS

Contents

Maps

Maps drawn by Swanston Graphics

INTRODUCTION

For five thousand years, the Eskimos, or *Inuit*, have survived in one of the harshest environments in the world, the Arctic. Here, at the top of the world, hardship and suffering go hand in hand with fortitude and courage. A mere fifty years ago, starvation, cannibalism and female infanticide were as much a part of their lives as hamburgers and electronic arcade games are today.

This transition from Stone Age to Space Age living, and its implications for the future, have passed almost unnoticed in the south. Although hundreds of books have been written about the Arctic, the majority allude to the courage of explorers, and by inference to that of their authors, who have consistently portrayed the Eskimo as 'Nanook of the North', the happy hunter living with his family and a litter of husky puppies in an igloo. *The Fourth World* is an attempt to destroy this outdated image.

Today, the old hunting culture is theatened by hydro-electric plants, oil pipelines, offshore oil rigs, western consumer goods and fall-out from military and political manoeuvring. In the next decade, and during the early years of the twenty-first century, industrial man will build new towns, roads, railways and airports in the frozen wastelands. Crops will be grown where previously there was only ice and snow. Ships, escorted by nuclear icebreakers, will regularly ply the Northwest and Northeast Passages, for centuries the dream of European merchants. On the polar ice cap, oil men will drill to a depth of 20,000 feet, while beneath them nuclear submarines bristling with missiles patrol the ocean darkness.

If, in the future, the Arctic is to be developed responsibly, it is important to review the effects on Eskimo culture of the developed world. This can be achieved only by studying and understanding the reasons for ancient Eskimo customs. To this end, Part One traces the Eskimo migrations from Siberia to Alaska, Canada and Greenland, and from the reports of the earliest travellers from the 'civilised' world shows how the Eskimos lived, and pieces together the fundamental reasons for their ability to survive.

The attitudes of the explorers, missionaries, whalers, hunters, trappers and traders, whose incursions contributed directly to the erosion of the Eskimo culture, are discussed in Part Two. This goes on to describe from personal observation the realities of the Arctic today, and to compare the plight of the Eskimos with that of the Sami (Lapps) of Scandinavia. Part Three deals with the new political awareness that is emerging among minority groups in the North, and looks at the future dangers and challenges in the Arctic.

Progress in all areas has been rapid and unchecked. Governments and business interests have exploited the region without thought for the land or the sea, or for the peoples of the north. In the scramble to exploit arctic riches, the Eskimos have been swept aside, to become second-class citizens in their own territory. Since the Arctic was opened up during the 1940s, ignorance and greed have jeopardised the equilibrium not only of the delicate arctic environment, but of the entire northern hemisphere. Yet, once the wheels of the industrial mono-culture begin to turn, they are difficult to stop. They must, however, be brought under control at once if the Arctic is to be saved.

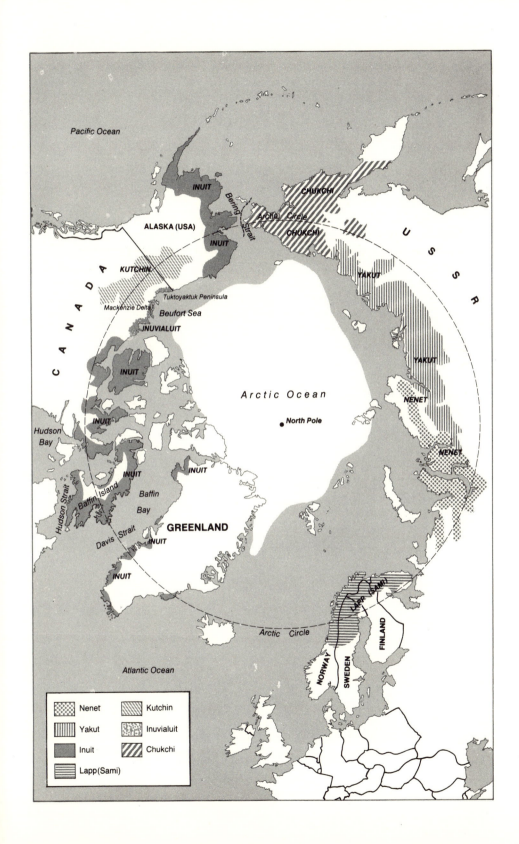

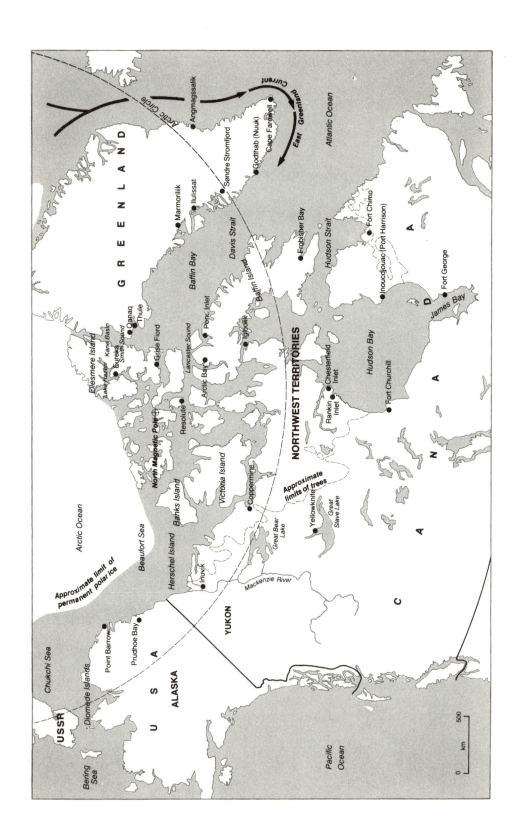

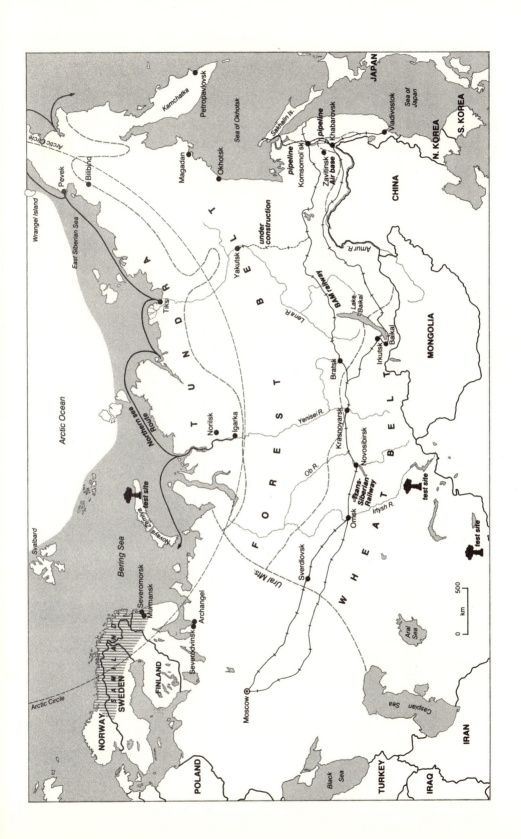

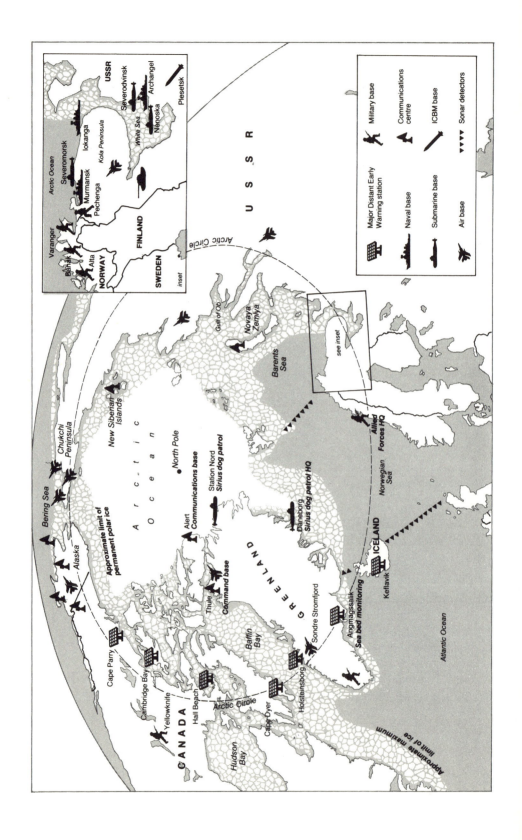

Map legend:

Military base
Communications centre
ICBM base
Sonar detectors

Major Distant Early Warning station
Naval base
Submarine base
Air base

Inset (USSR):

Arctic Ocean
Severomorsk
Severodvinsk
Murmansk
Iokanga
Archangel
Pechenga
White Sea
Kola Peninsula
Nenoksa
Plesetsk
USSR
Varanger
Alta
NORWAY
FINLAND
SWEDEN
Arctic Circle
inset

Main map:

USSR
Gulf of Ob
Novaya Zemlya
Barents Sea
see inset
New Siberian Islands
Chukchi Peninsula
Bering Sea
Alaska
Approximate limit of permanent polar ice
Arctic Ocean
North Pole
Station Nord
Sirius dog patrol
Alert
Communications base
Danneborg
Sirius dog patrol HQ
Norwegian Sea
Allied Forces HQ
ICELAND
Keflavik
Angmagssalik
Sea bed monitoring
Thule
Command base
Baffin Bay
GREENLAND
Sondre Stromfjord
Holsteinsborg
Cape Dyer
Hall Beach
Arctic Circle
Yellowknife
Cambridge Bay
Cape Parry
CANADA
Hudson Bay
Atlantic Ocean
Approximate maximum limit of ice

PART ONE

Life on the Ice

CHAPTER 1

The White Desert

In the depths of an arctic winter, there is only the darkness and the cold, a glacial, bone-chilling cold so intense that it seems the dry air will split apart with the slightest movement. The hostile expanse of velvety-white snow emits clouds of white fog, which in the stillness, is transformed instantly into millions of tiny ice particles, each one needle-sharp on exposed skin. The atmosphere feels alive, as if charged with static electricity. A solitary raven flying overhead will leave behind an icy vapour trail as its cumbersome wing beats fill the taut, silent air with the sound of tearing silk. It is a cold in which exhaled breath freezes instantly, forming ice on the eyebrows and in the nose. If Hell freezes over, it must surely be in this wintry grave of Nature, for here is a cold that freezes mercury, that can plunge to −70°C. So efficiently does it freeze the northern seas, that a thin skein of ice in August will be four feet thick by April.

For eight months of the year there is no sun, and for twenty days of each winter month the moon remains below the horizon. Yet, even at such times it is never completely dark because clouds reflect the rays of the hidden moon onto the ice. At such times, the frozen desert is bathed in a pale and haunting half-light. Sometimes, the heavens are kindled with the lurid fires and ghostly streamers of the *Aurora Borealis*, the Northern Lights, a fascinating, still unexplained canopy of light hanging in a huge arc across the sky. Usually, the display is phosphorescent green, but in the highest latitudes the phenomenon washes the polar night with all the colours of the rainbow. There is a weird, almost supernatural quality about it, redolent of evil spirits and witchcraft. After a few days of this eternal semi-darkness, a strange weariness sets in. Moodiness and depression follow, and a deep yearning for the moon's return.

At other times, when the moon is high, the disappearing clouds reveal a coal-black sky, studded with myriads of gloriously intense and radiant stars. In this eerie, colourless world, the lack of dust in the atmosphere makes it possible to see scores of miles across the icefields and fissured glaciers to the mountains washed by moonlight in the distance. Occasionally, a wisp of cottonwool cloud floats across the brilliant moon, the only movement in a world serene as a still-life.

Imperceptibly, the gentlest of breezes materialises, a mere brush of icy air against the cheek. Within minutes and without warning, it can grow to a dry, piercing wind which shatters the peace of the ghostly landscape. The wind strengthens, its howl rising to a shriek as it rips across the icefields at more than eighty miles an hour, sweeping down into the valleys in violent blasts and sucking up the snow in a whirling commotion that shakes the very ground itself. Off the coast, a turbulent sea agitates the heaving icepack. The arctic night creaks with the sound of grinding, breaking ice. For days, the wind howls and moans and whistles, but eventually it fades away, and the muffled silence returns.

The winds gusting in from the southern oceans bring snow and fog, but the dry winds from the north and east are more violent and dangerous. It is then that the careless become susceptible to frostbite, their unprotected skin whitening and freezing. The hands, feet, nose and ears are most at risk. Exposure for as little as one or two minutes is enough to induce the symptoms: hard, cold patches of skin insensitive to touch. Icy winds can transform a moderately cold temperature into one of bitter severity, a factor known as windchill. A 30-M.P.H. wind can reduce a temperature of $-35°C$. to $-70°C$. Forward movement into the wind increases the relative windspeed, and reduces the temperature still further.

The Arctic is a rugged expanse of treacherous, yet ineffably beautiful icefields, glaciers, mountains and fjords, and frozen seas. When the freezing fog around the arctic coastline lifts, it reveals a profusion of icebergs. Their translucent pinnacles wreathed in mist, these huge cathedrals of ice drift silently in the open sea like enchanted crystalline monuments. This vast, brittle world of iridescent blues, greens and blinding white takes its name from one of the brightest stars in the northern heavens, *Arcturus*, an arctic beacon which is part of the constellation known as 'The Herdsman', and was once thought to be the closest star to Earth.

There is no official definition for the Arctic. To some, it is that area of the globe beyond the northern limit of the trees. To others it is the region north of the Arctic Circle, an imaginary line on 66.32° N. which separates the top of the world from the rest of the globe as a knife might slice open a breakfast egg. It cuts across the northernmost tracts of Alaska and Canada, contains three-quarters of Greenland, a quarter of Scandinavia and twenty per cent of the Soviet Union. Yet, strangely, no part of Iceland lies within it.

For several months during high summer, the sun does not drop below the horizon. The short summers are uniformly cool because the sun so low in the sky gives little heat. The four months of summer daylight are offset by eight months of perpetual semi-darkness during the bleak, polar winter. Only the Gulf Stream alleviates this pattern by markedly raising the temperatures in those parts of the region east of the Atlantic Ocean. The residents of Narvik on Norway's northwest coast, for example, could be sitting outdoors with an ice cream enjoying the late September sunshine while the people of Abisko, just 35 miles inland across the mountainous border with Sweden, might be digging themselves out of the first winter snowdrifts in fifteen degrees of frost.

Nowadays, it is generally agreed that the most effective definition of the Arctic is that region in which the mean temperature for the warmest month is not greater 10°C. This line of temperature, or isotherm, roughly follows the northern line, and is a particularly suitable definition because it incorporates various regions with a similar climate and, consequently, much the same flora and fauna.

In March, as if shrugging off a great burden, the arctic world begins to stir. The winter sky brightens, revealing the austere magnificence of the landscape in a continual blend of morning and evening twilight. Small flocks of chirping snow buntings, the heralds of spring, arrive with empty, shrunken stomachs, battered by blizzards and gales during their long migration from the south. They are followed by an abundance of seabirds: first the fulmars, then kittiwakes, glaucous gulls, razorbills and other auks.

As the light intensifies, the animals awaken. The ground squirrel, one of the few animals to hibernate in the Arctic, digs through the snow concealing the entrance to his burrow. Nose twitching, he darts fifty yards or so to another tunnel to search for a mate. The weasels, too, are mating. So are the lemmings, bears and seals. Gradually, the whole region comes alive. Foxes bark in the snow of the mountains. On the plains and tundra of Canada's Low Arctic, a great multitude of caribou begin their annual trek north and thunder across the barren lands, a dense confusion of antlers. From the forests in which they have spent the winter grazing on grasses and lichens, they race northwards to new grazing lands along the shores of the polar seas as if drawn by a magnet. Nothing can stop them, neither the deepest rivers nor the sudden blizzards. In their wake come the wolves, their traditional enemies.

Gradually, the nocturnal pallor of winter yields to spring. The morning sky whitens. As the light becomes more intense, there is a sense of growing expectancy. For the first time in several months, a narrow rim of sun shows above the horizon, staining the grey-blue ice deep orange. As the sun rises, the ice glistens with the hues of opal and mother-of-pearl. Beams of sunlight caress the glaciers and the great inland plateaux, slowly flooding the valleys and sandstone cliffs with gradations of soft yellows and fiery reds. Soon, the shadowy world of winter and the oppressive darkness are forgotten. The surface of the ice moistens, each droplet suffused in rays of crimson and gold. By contrast, the open sea remains a black void, and should anyone fall into it, he would die within minutes. The reality is harsh, but it is easily forgotten in the enchantment of the moment.

Offshore, fleets of icebergs gleam like burnished metal in the new light. They glide past, a dazzling array of strange shapes and colours: proud, floating monoliths, magical castles, fairy-tale palaces of emeralds and diamonds, and sparkling minsters with grotesque gargoyles of opaline glass.

The rising of the sun is by far the most important event in the arctic calendar. Invoking the miracle of spring, the weak light warms the air. The ice begins to melt, enabling the light to penetrate into the sea. This action creates carbon dioxide, which permits the annual, vigorous growth of plankton, microscopic organisms upon which all animal life in the sea depends.

Plankton is the only source of food for the minute crustaceans known as krill. Both develop rapidly, forming a crucial food source for the capelin, a small fish similar to herring. Within days, the coastal bays, creeks and fjords are alive with the fish, itself easy prey for the larger arctic char, a salmonoid which also feeds off plankton and krill. Together, the crustaceans and small fish provide the diet for cod and other fish. Eventually, the sea ice breaks up, and the abundance of food attracts seals, walrus, whales and a confusion of seabirds.

May is the month of migration. Skeins of a hundred or more honking geese sail overhead bound for Alaska and the Northwest Passage. Stately eider ducks glide into the pebbly bays searching for molluscs. For the first time, the daytime temperature rises above zero. On the remaining icefields, the awesome emptiness is filled with the sounds of thawing ice groaning and cracking. Glaciers calve their icebergs thunderously. The sound of water is everywhere. Streams gurgle. Melting snow cascades down the dark valleys and ravines. On flatter terrain, the water seeps into the depressions along the rocky, coastal plains and waterlogs the vast, barren tundras.

As the sun thaws the upper layer of soil, the water from the melting ice and snow is prevented from draining away by the permafrost. This is the rock, sand, gravel and mud which remains permanently frozen to a depth of thousands of feet. In many areas, particularly in Canada's Northwest

Territories and along the coastal fringe of Greenland, the land is too flat for streams to run to the sea, so the water remains on the surface, forming bogs and hundreds of thousands of pools and lakes.

Warmed by the sun for the ten to twelve brief weeks of summer, the topsoil and these innumerable shallow reservoirs of fresh water become a natural incubator for plants and insects. Mites, flies, beetles and mosquitoes multiply in such profusion that arctic travellers must frequently use headnets and insect-proof tents to protect themselves from the bites. The swarms can be so dense that it is often impossible to see through them. Many a wayfarer has been deceived by a cloud of insects, believing it to be the smoke of a friendly encampment. Mosquitoes can be so numerous, huge and vicious as to drive the unaccustomed traveller insane. In certain areas, the swarms are so populous that a single slap on the arm may reveal the bodies of more than a hundred dead insects. Yet this profusion of insect and plant life is a vital part of the ecological food chain that ensures survival for dozens of species of bird and animal.

In the few inches of soggy topsoil above the layer of permafrost, a tangled forest of roots takes hold. May and June bring an explosion of arctic flowers, which fill the landscape with colour. Melting snow reveals clusters of grey-green and orange lichen. Tiny purple and white saxifrages and yellow cinquefoil burgeon in the low heathlands. Abundant grasses, heathers, arctic poppies, buttercups and cotton plants bloom everywhere in sudden floral display. Botanists have identified nearly five hundred species of wild flowers in the Arctic, a hundred of them in regions like Lake Hazen on Ellesmere Island in the extreme North.

Willow shrubs sprout their buds sunwards. Stunted pine and dwarf birch bend to the high winds, twisting and creeping close to the exposed ground. Plants grow slowly. So precarious is arctic life, that a pine more than a hundred years old may have a girth of less than three inches. On the steep rocks guarding the coastlines, only the mosses and lichens can survive. Yet, where tawny screes sweep down from buttresses of naked rock to the hard, cracked earth and pebbled beaches, small tufts of dry, yellow grass may be found sheltering in protective hollows.

By early June in the Far North, wolves, wolverines, foxes, arctic hares, ermine, weasels and lemmings have all ushered their young into the perilous arctic world. Musk oxen with their wide, curving horns have calved on Devon Island and Ellesmere and begun to shed their shaggy, ankle-length coats of wool in preparation for the summer. Clouds of butterflies flutter across the heathlands. Ringed seals and their pups bask in the sun beside their blowholes. The great Greenland whales swim up the centre of Davis Strait and Baffin Bay until they are halted by unbroken ice. Here, the huge mammals wait and play, leaping high out of the dark waters and crashing back onto the surface to disappear again in a deluge of water. Afterwards, when the ice breaks up, they move northwards again to their traditional feeding and breeding grounds.

As the days lengthen, the summer moves northwards, followed by the fish and the birds. Arctic terns reappear after a journey of nearly 25,000 miles to the southern oceans and back. Soon the precarious ledges on the steep cliffs are alive with squawking seabirds: guillemots, razorbills, little auks, puffins and kittiwakes. Little auks are so numerous that a breeding colony can contain millions of birds. Almost as numerous are the larger seabirds: the fulmars and glaucous gulls.

Even in summer, conditions in the Arctic are harsh and unpredictable. All life hangs by a thread. In order to survive, each living creature must mesh together with all the others in mutual dependence. The ecological balance is so delicate, so precise, that the slightest interruption in the life-cycle of one species can lead to the decimation of several others. Just as plankton and krill feed crustaceans, and both, in turn, nourish fish and mammals, so Nature produces copious numbers of little auks as a primary source of food for arctic foxes, ravens, glaucous gulls and skuas. They in turn eat the eggs and young of other small seabirds. Similarly, the ptarmigan becomes the staple diet of the gyrfalcon.

This inter-dependence can be seen right across the Arctic. When the polar bear waits with infinite patience for the seal to appear through a blowhole in the ice, the fox bides his time nearby in the sure knowledge that there will be some discarded scraps. Caribou and reindeer rely on lichens for their survival. The lichens grow slowly, so the herds migrate to give them a chance to recover. Caribou have a legendary pact with the wolves which follow their migration. The wolves pick off the old, weak and sick members of the herd, and ensure their own survival, each depending on the other. Convocations of eagles circle overhead. Ravens, and skulks of foxes whose subsistence depends on the wolves' leftovers, trail the herd.

When the caribou cross the tundra on their way to the arctic coast, they are attacked by warble flies, which lay their eggs in the animals' fur. The larvae penetrate the skin and remain there until the following year when they have developed. At this time, the parasites bore their way out of the caribou's body, causing so much pain that the infested caribou shakes itself vigorously to expel the flies. Hardly an adult escapes. Yet, warble flies *never* settle on the calves, which could not tolerate the pain and would undoubtedly die, thus endangering the continued existence of the species.

Lemmings are another major source of food in the Arctic and they, too, multiply according to Nature's laws of supply and demand. The furry, mouselike creatures are equipped with long claws used rather like a garden fork to grub for food among the mass of roots in the topsoil. In winter when the snow falls, their claws change and take the form of flat pads which are particularly useful for burrowing.

Living in a maze of subterranean tunnels, the lemmings are well protected from predators. Reproducing frequently, their numbers grow at an alarming rate, until there are too many for the food source. Suddenly, after a few years, one will break out, heading for new feeding grounds. Others take his cue, and soon thousands more follow. This phenomenon has given rise to the myth of a suicidal migration to the sea. Although some lemmings may drown in lakes, most die from attacks by predators.

The migration is an essential part of the ecological food chain, providing pickings for thousands of birds, foxes, wolves and wolverines. Snowy owls, hawks and skuas, which depend on the tiny creatures, wheel overhead. Eventually, as many as three-quarters of the lemmings die. Yet, there are always enough left in the burrows to replenish the stock. The tragic animals have no choice in the matter. If their compulsive search for a new food source were not re-enacted every three or four years, there would be mass starvation in the burrows, a disaster for themselves, and ultimately for their predators.

This fluid meshing of animal, mammal and bird life would be no different from that of the other regions in the world were it not for the harsh, often life-denying conditions of the Arctic. No sooner has mid-summer arrived than the sun once more begins to gravitate towards the horizon. The short, hectic season allows no time for mistakes.

All species can cope with the occasional loss of adults and a proportion of the young. One or two trouble-free seasons usually ensure complete recovery, but few birds and animals can sustain massive losses of breeding adults, and it is vital that the nesting colonies remain undisturbed. The arctic schedule is so tight that there is often no time for courtship and some birds must mate *before* they find a nest. For others, breeding must take place at precisely the right time, for the early production of young could result in their death from sudden storms and blizzards. Tardiness can be equally devastating, with unpredictable weather trapping the fleeing birds as they migrate southwards, or reducing their ability to survive the fierce winds and blinding showers of sleet in the autumn.

Slowly, the fragile summer recedes. The streams cease to run. The fjords and bays freeze. Soon a crust of ice spreads across the sea and snow blankets the hills and valleys. The last birds fly southwards. The sun retreats, and in the waning light the polar world is given once more to the silent loneliness and terrible weight of winter.

CHAPTER 2

Real People

The first humans to penetrate the fissured world of arctic ice were the Eskimos. No one knows with certainty whence they came, nor what prompted them to settle in such uncompromising terrain. It is unlikely that they evolved in the arctic wilderness. More probably, they emerged from the tropics, the birthplace of earliest man. Primitive families and hunting communities living in Africa 300,000 years ago began to disperse across the continent and in the world's first great migration moved into Egypt, Israel and Syria. Later, they advanced further, into Europe and southern Asia.

The move north continued for another 90,000 years as the primeval tribes multiplied and settled in Scandinavia, central Russia and China. During this wave of human expansion, the polar icecap had been inching relentlessly southwards until the hunter-gatherers were stopped in their tracks on the edge of the frost line. The colder climate had hardened them, but it was only the discovery of fire, and ingenuity born of necessity, which helped them to exist in such harsh conditions.

Toughened by nature, these early tribesmen were forced to build their homes underground to protect themselves from the arctic winds sweeping in across the plains and lowlands of northeastern Siberia. The remains of some of these dwellings, which had central fire pits and are the world's oldest subterranean houses, have been found on the shores of Lake Baikal, and on the banks of the Upper Yenisei River north of Mongolia. Here the migrants lived for thousands of years, until the glacial advance was halted and the Ice Age came to an end. With infinite slowness, the ice receded and the hunting communities once more began to spread northwards, as if drawn by a polar magnet.

This prolonged migration probably followed the banks of the Yenisei River north to the Kara Sea on the Soviet arctic coast, a distance of some 2,000 miles. Other hunters would have moved from the Black and Caspian Seas west of the Urals to the same coast. Eventually, the primitive vanguard conquered all the Asian lands north of the Arctic Circle. The last areas to be settled, northeastern Siberia and the

Kamchatka Peninsula, were those in which the most appalling weather in the known world prevailed. When the leathery, weather-beaten Chukchi, Koryak and Kamchadal tribesmen reached these forbidding regions, they found the Eskimos already there. They were probably the spearhead of the northbound tribes, which, after reaching the arctic shoreline, turned eastwards along the coast towards Siberia. Almost certainly, they were the remnants of an earlier migration from the Asian continent to North America.

The arctic icecap in those post-glacial days was not centred on the North Pole as it is today, but somewhere between Hudson Bay, in eastern Canada, and Greenland. This meant that vast areas of the Asian coastline and Alaska were free of ice. As the sea level was a good deal lower than it is now, the continents of Asia and America were linked by a continuous stretch of barren tundra called Beringia. Today, it is known as Bering Strait, one of the stormiest seas in the world. Ten thousand years ago, it was a land bridge approximately 700 miles wide from north to south. Although the ice had receded and the climate was reasonably equable, the low-lying land offered no resistance to the ferocious polar winds, which carried the seeds of grasses, poppies and other plants for hundreds of miles. The animals followed. Musk oxen, mammoths and mastodons roamed freely over the windswept flatlands, and with them small groups of hunters.

The ancestors of the American Indians passed this way between 10,000 and 5,000 BC, spreading south through Alaska, down the Canadian west coast to California, and on to the new world of the American continent. A study of language similarities shows that two of the tribes emigrating from the Soviet Arctic became the forebears of nineteen separate Californian Indian tribes, including the 'Wintu-an' of Sacramento Valley and the 'Costanoans' from the region south of San Francisco. The Californian tribes are long since extinct.

The Soviet tribes, the Mansi and Khant, still live in the Sverdlovsk region west of the Urals, approximately 4,000 miles from the Beringian land bridge. When Professor Otto von Sadovszky, an anthropologist of California State College at Fullerton, studied the Vogul and Ostiak languages spoken by the two tribes, he found that many words used by the Californian Indians were strikingly similar and that some 10,000 words were identical. The similarities include place names. The Indians called San Francisco 'Awas-te', which in the Vogul language means 'Place of the bay'. Similarly, 'Petaluma', the name of a northern Californian city meaning 'the flat back of a hill', would be understood by the Soviet tribes to this day. The hunting methods, weapons, magic, beliefs and group customs also show extraordinary similarities.

The development of the Siberian Eskimos took a completely different path from that of the American Indians. They relied less on bows and arrows for hunting, and the tiny, half-wild reindeer for food, but fashioned new tools more suitable for coastal life. They developed kayaks, hooks and detachable, toggle-headed harpoons so that they could fish and hunt seal, walrus and, much later, whales. The kayak, one of most elegant boat designs in the world, was probably their most important piece of equipment as it allowed the hunters to take to the sea and paddle within a few feet of their prey. They were primarily inshore fishermen and it was their quest for seal and walrus 6,000 years ago that attracted them to the coasts of Beringia and ultimately across to Alaska.

These early Eskimo hunters did not shun the land completely. They based their existence not only on sea mammals but also on caribou, musk oxen, mammoth and the other animals and birds of the tundra. The climate was reasonably temperate and by the time they reached Alaska, the Eskimos had evolved a distinctive culture which came to be known as the Arctic Small Tool Tradition.

Their achievements were considerable. They made tools of stone: bird arrows, knives, scrapers with which to flense the sea mammals, and lamps in which to burn sea oil. There were bone fish-hooks. Harpoon heads were made with iron blades held in ivory sockets, which were bound with braided sinew and painted with resin. Ivory needles were used to sew skin and fur clothing, tents, and sealskin covers for kayaks. The hair on the dorsal ridge of the caribou provided excellent thread. The Eskimos also used needles to tattoo their faces, a popular form of decoration among adult women until the nineteenth century. Illustrations of animal life were etched into the handles of knives and spoons, and adorned quivers, clothes and headbands, elaborate lip ornaments and face masks.

Some of the Eskimos populated the chain of Aleutian islands, colonizing one island at a time, but they were to become geographically and culturally isolated from the rest of the tribe. Other Eskimos moved eastwards along the north coast of Alaska to Greenland, and down the Mackenzie valley and across the barren lands of Canada's Northwest Territories to Labrador. By the time they arrived at their destinations, a separate, virtually independent culture had evolved. This was called the Dorset culture, which flourished between 1000 BC and 1200 AD.

The Dorset Eskimos were eventually overrun, probably by the third and the hardiest group of the Beringian migrants. Wave after wave of these intrepid hunters defied the relentlessly hostile environment as they advanced along the Northwest Passage, towards Baffin Island, Ellesmere Island, and finally Greenland. Archaeological evidence shows that they had crossed the Smith Sound and were living along the northwestern coast of Greenland at least 4,000 years ago. In the process they evolved another cultural aberration, the Northern Maritime Tradition, and it was this branch of the culture which eventually formed the basis of the traditional Eskimo life we know today.

Unlike the Siberian and north Alaskan coasts, the north American coast at that time was icebound, the climate considerably more testing than in Beringia. The unremitting storms, the numbing cold and the constant search for scanty sustenance exhausted the Eskimos, who suffered the most appalling privation. Their hands became malformed, blackened and as hard as ebony from constant exposure to temperatures of −40°C. or lower. They suffered bone disorders. There was little food or fuel. The lack of driftwood forced them to burn seal and whale oil in small soapstone lamps. These gave off so much smoke that their bodies became riddled with black lung disease. Yet the hardy Eskimos continued eastwards, scratching a frugal existence from the white desert, gradually adapting to the awesome conditions. The first changes, over several thousand years, were physical.

The Eskimos are almost Lilliputian, with a mean stature of 5ft 4 in. Their faces are flat, the bridge of their noses is low, and their high cheekbones are padded with fatty tissue. Successive generations developed uniquely eskimoid features, the most striking of which were their tiny noses and remarkably short limbs. Another extraordinary characteristic, which developed as the Eskimos moved deeper into the polar regions, was a shortening of the arm below the elbow, and the leg below the knee. In proportion to their bodies, these extremities are stubbier than in any other race in the world. The reason is simple. In such excruciating cold the body was forced to adapt in order to survive. The shorter the distance to the extremities, the greater the chances of survival.

The change was achieved by the heart pumping blood more quickly to exposed parts of the body such as the hands and feet. Chemical changes in the fundamental body processes ensured that the temperature of the blood stayed within acceptable limits. Another ingenious adaptation to climatic conditions was the body's ability to transfuse blood from one artery to another, and warm the blood in the veins of the hands and feet, before it returned to the heart. The internal heating system enabled the Eskimo to work with bare hands in extreme sub-zero temperatures, and on frozen ground, for longer periods without chilled blood affecting other vital parts of the body such as the heart and the brain. Today, when temperatures rise above +5°C., and most travellers are still wrapped up in sweaters and windproof jackets, the Eskimo is quite likely to strip to the waist and complain of the oppressive heat.

Inclement weather also brought cultural changes. It was customary for

Eskimo men from Beringia to the Mackenzie River to perforate their lower lip, studding it with ivory, or buttons of blue and green quartz. Some Eskimos inserted quills and shells into their noses and fashioned necklaces from the teeth of musk ox, wolves, foxes and seals. The lip and other ornaments were among the first to be discarded. A lack of driftwood and other materials resulted in more utilitarian, though less decorative tools. Although many cultural changes were enforced upon them over the centuries, they managed to retain both their language and the fundamental ingredients of their culture and, in time, they mastered the harsh environment and became the only people ever to make the Arctic a permanent home.

Their closest neighbours were the Naskapi and Cree Indians. Although the Indians never ventured north of the tree line, the relationship between the two groups was always acrimonious. The Indians contemptuously called the Eskimos 'Eskimantsies', a word meaning 'eaters of raw flesh'. This label is as hurtful today as it was then. Now, an Eskimo prefers to be called an 'Inuk'. His language is 'Inuktitut', and his people the 'Inuit', which means 'Real People'.

This name is singularly apt. Unparalleled physical toughness, moral fortitude and ferocious heroism were common qualities among the Inuit, whose quiet pride, compassion and self-effacing humour helped them to overcome adversity. There is no better example of this than the last migration in 1864, when a group of about forty Inuit abandoned their encampment at Arctic Bay on the shores of Admiralty Inlet, a long finger of water extending south from the Lancaster Sound into Baffin Island, to travel by dog sled to Greenland.

The story of their trek did not emerge until nearly forty years later, when members of an expedition to Cape York in the Melville Bay area of north Greenland in 1903 discovered an old man, deeply scarred around the eyes. He told the explorers that his name was Mequsaq, the younger of two brothers, and the only survivor of the migration.

Listening to the account, as it has been handed down and retold in the cafés and bars of Greenland, it is not difficult to imagine the wind howling across the headland at Arctic Bay, drifts of deep snow sloping down from the low cliffs to the shoreline. In the darkness of the polar night, it would have been difficult for Mequsaq and his companions to see where the land ended and the sea began. Everything would have been cloaked in a shroud of filmy white, the cold dry air crackling with the slightest movement, blackening the toughest skin. The birds and animals the Inuit might have hunted would long since have fled southwards. The winter of 1864, Mequsaq explained, had been particularly harsh, with poor hunting and little food. Huddled miserably in their houses of stone and turf the Inuit faced starvation.

The shaman, or wise man of the settlement, at the time was the most powerful the Inuit could remember. When the worried settlers crawled from their subterranean houses to consult him, the shaman prepared himself so that he might commune with the spirits. Emerging from his trance some days later, he announced that the spirits had advised him that they must leave the settlement, and trek north to join other Inuit living on the far side of Baffin Bay, a prophecy too remarkable for an Inuk to dismiss.

Such a journey could not be undertaken lightly. Fearfully, the Inuit hunters and their families packed their meagre belongings and food supplies, loaded their bows and arrows and kayaks onto the sleds and assembled the dog teams. Setting off across the coastal ice, the whalebone runners of their sleds hissing on the ice, they would have turned right past the headland, and swept up the long, frozen fjord towards Lancaster Sound. Rather than following the smooth curve of cliffs along the western bank of the fjord, they would have hugged the foot of the higher cliffs, which towered nearly 2,000 ft above them on the eastern shore, protecting them from the high winds roaring in from the northeast.

Eventually, the dogs crossed the mouth of the fjord and headed towards the deeply dissected northern plateau of Cape Crauford. Over the centuries, the Inuit had inherited an unerring sense of direction. Mequsaq described how they had been beset by gales. As they drove across the exposed wastes of Lancaster Sound, the northern coast of Baffin Island falling away behind them, the Inuit and their huskies were forced to haul the sleds through vast fields of ice hummocks and high pressure ridges, the dogs straining and standing on their hind legs as they tried to surmount the obstacles.

Ice hummocks in this part of the world can be as high as two-storey houses. A sled will frequently overturn or become wedged, as if caught in a giant ice-encrusted vice. At other times, when the ice is smooth and unbroken, the dogs will race ahead enthusiastically, so that clouds of snow trail like smoke behind them. Mequsaq explained how the Inuit had been overtaken by violent storms and black nights of hunger. The temperature sank to −50°C., so that thick layers of rime frost formed on their clothes. For weeks on end, they saw no trace of animal or bird. Gradually, despite rationing, their meagre stocks of blubber and raw meat dwindled.

Defying hazardous conditions, the old shaman urged the Inuit onwards. Time and again, he called on the spirits for guidance, and always they told him to continue northwards. The wise man's powers were unlimited. When he drove far in front of the other dog teams and the *Aurora Borealis* illuminated the sky, the Inuit believed that fire was bursting from his head, a sign from the spirits and sure proof of his infallibility. For two winters, the small band of Inuit travelled, stopping in the summer months to hunt and replenish their supplies. They crossed to Devon Island and struggled on, across Jones Sound to Ellesmere Island.

Conditions during their second winter were so harsh and debilitating that the group inevitably quarrelled. The shaman's powers were brought into question. One disgruntled group opted to return home. The others, their faith unshaken, continued the journey, taking three more winters before they crossed Smith Sound, that frozen gateway to the North Pole which, in winter, links Ellesmere Island to the north Greenland coast.

The journey ended at what is now Etah in northernmost Greenland and there, just as the shaman had promised, was a tribe of about forty families. These were the Polar, or Thule, Inuit who lived in complete isolation further north than any other human beings, and whose only contact with white man had been nearly fifty years earlier, when in 1818 Commander James Ross introduced them to coffee, ships' biscuits and firewood. The Baffin Islanders stayed with the Polar Inuit for several years, but this was difficult terrain and the food base was barely sufficient for the sudden increase in population. When the hunting was poor, relations between the two groups were strained. Eventually, the old shaman was again obliged to consult the spirits.

This time, the spirits told him that the group must return to Baffin Island, so once more the tiny band of travellers packed their sledges, and started out across the ice in the direction from which they had come. Conditions on the return leg of the journey were, if anything, worse than those they had endured before. They were beset by blinding snowstorms. The grinding ice churned up huge, almost impassable ridges. Hunting failed again for lack of animals.

Owing to a shortage of food on their previous journey, they had been unable to lay caches of food for emergencies. When their stomachs became cramped from starvation, the group reluctantly began to eat their dogs. No Inuk does so willingly. Each dog eaten makes the distribution of weight greater for the remaining dogs to haul, and their speed across the ice is proportionately slower. The intense cold and lack of food soon took its toll. One by one, the Inuit succumbed. One day, they were distraught to find that their shaman had died, too.

Exhausted and leaderless, the Inuit pushed onwards, struggling desperately homeward. The lack of game forced them to kill yet more dogs, and they were left with scarcely enough to continue the journey. Crazed from hunger, two brothers in the group conspired to attack the others and eat them in order to survive. The two Inuit burst into a shelter occupied by a woman and her three children. After a fierce fight, during which Mequsaq nearly lost an eye from a knife wound, the older men stabbed the mother and daughter and carried their bodies away. Mequsaq and his brother, battered and bleeding, followed at a distance and watched the men gorge themselves on their meal of human flesh. The youths feared that as the only witnesses they would be the next victims, and decided to leave the group. They turned and headed back to Etah, scratching what sustenance they could from the frozen wastes until, more than a year later, they reached the Greenland coast exhausted, starving and barely able to walk.

The Thule Inuit were not overjoyed to see them. In the depths of the winter darkness where food supplies were low or non-existent, it was their custom to hibernate. They slept under a cover of skins, not moving but breathing as slowly as possible, until the sun rose above the horizon and they could drag themselves out to hunt again. The arrival of the runaway brothers was an intrusion into this soporific existence, but when spring came, the boys helped them to build kayaks, and gave them further instruction on how to use them to hunt seals, a technique the Thule Inuit had forgotten during their long migration from Beringia and Alaska. Until the Baffin Islanders arrived, the Thule Inuit had used the same technique as polar bears for hunting seal, waiting close to a blowhole until a seal came up for air.

The Baffin Islanders also showed their hosts how to make bows and arrows, and for the first time in more than a thousand years, the Thule Inuit were able to hunt and kill mountain reindeer. Having proved their worth, the boys were accepted into the community, and stayed with the Polar Inuit for the rest of their days.

Hovering directly above the North Pole, facing south in every direction, it would be possible, if one were high enough, to view the whole of the white wilderness contained within the Arctic Circle. Those who live within this region number less than 200,000, and of these about 60,000 are Inuit from Alaska, Canada and Greenland. There are between 45,000 and 50,000 Lapps, who prefer to be called Sami. The remainder live in the Eurasian-Siberian Arctic, or are whites from the south.

Despite national and political boundaries, the vast tracts of land between Siberia and Greenland comprise a region in which physical appearance, language and traditions coalesce into a single, cultural area. For all their wanderings over tens of thousands of years, the Inuit can still understand each other, albeit sometimes with difficulty. Separation from each other during such an enormous time span obviously spawned many new dialects. Yet, incredibly, several Inuit of Greenland were recently able to understand and converse with Inuit in Alaska, with whom their tribe had had no contact for 4,000 years.

In Asia, nineteen separate tribes inhabit the Soviet Arctic and Scandinavia. These tribes all resemble the Inuit in that they are uniformly small in stature, are toughened by nature and have retained similar customs. Bone tools decorated with pictures of seals and caribou discovered in Eurasia have been found to be identical to utensils excavated from the Canadian Arctic. In west Greenland, flint chips were fashioned in exactly the same way as microliths unearthed in northern Scandinavia, Mongolia and Siberia.

Naturally, huge differences have evolved. Neither the Inuit nor the Indians of the Western Cultural Area adopted reindeer breeding which, together with fishing, was the principal means of livelihood throughout the Soviet Arctic and among the Lapps, or Sami, of northern Scandinavia. The Inuit in eastern Canada and Greenland customarily harnessed their dog teams on separate traces, in a fan formation, whereas in Alaska, Scandinavia and Eurasia, where there are more trees, they were – and still are – assembled with tandem traces. Lip ornaments, face masks, grave monuments, basketry and pottery found to the west of the Mackenzie Delta were inherited from the Soviet Arctic, perhaps even as far west as the Urals, although many of these were discarded as the Inuit migrated into colder regions. The semi-subterranean houses first used 100,000 years ago, when the primitive tribes reached Lake Baikal, were in use until quite recently in the Eurasian region. Only the Chukchi, Koryak and Kamchadal tribes of Siberia, however, have adopted a lifestyle similar to that of the Inuit.

The demands of life in the Arctic moulded the Inuit into an adaptable and innovative people who were at the same time warm, gregarious and hospitable. They were essentially monogamous, but for practical reasons which are discussed later, wife-swapping was common. Occasionally, a successful hunter would have two wives, but this was unusual, one difficulty being the shortage of women after a famine. At such times, the Inuit were frequently obliged to kill young girls in order to ensure the survival of the group.

The harshness of life in the Arctic seems to have left its mark. Although softened in recent years by an imported lifestyle from the south, the Inuit at first sight appear to be ferocious, as cold and cruel as their environment. Squat, stubby and immensely strong, their torsos and muscles are highly developed from hunting, and with the heavy clothes of winter, they appear to have exceptionally broad shoulders. Their ability to cope with the austere world in which they live gives them an air of formidable superiority. Unkempt, jet-black hair, often kept in check with a narrow headband, frames limpid, brown eyes, which stare with unashamed curiosity, and sometimes hostility, at strangers.

Inuit women seem to possess an innate happiness. They bubble, giggle and sparkle, their smiles revealing strong, even white teeth, their humorous, black eyes hinting at hidden passion. Despite a sensual zest for life, they are graceful and essentially docile. In former times, an Inuk could not hunt successfully without an industrious wife. She had to be a superb seamstress, with strong teeth to chew and soften the skins, which she would make into clothing and summer tents. When her man returned exhausted and frozen from a hunting expedition, perhaps after sitting motionless for many hours by a seal's blowhole, the catch had to be prepared and cooked. The gentler, neater and more talented the wife, the greater was her ability to command respect.

So difficult was the Inuit way of life, that when an Inuk woman reached her mid-thirties, her clear complexion matured into a dark quilt of hair-fine wrinkles engrained with the soot of countless whale-oil lamps. Years of chewing skins wore her teeth to the gums. When she served a meal of boiled seal, raw blubber and blood soup to friends, she would declare that, alas, it was a great pity that the visitors had the misfortune to come to the house of a poor woman who could not cook. 'A poor body can but try,' she might say, 'but clearly the meat is ruined. It is quite disgusting and it would be a great blessing should you refuse it.' At that, the guests would set to enthusiastically. An Inuk woman, similarly feigning a lack of ability, might still serve such a meal in parts of the Arctic, especially in northwestern and eastern Greenland, where despite the influence of southern living, hunting traditions have remained largely unchanged. Inuit seldom reveal their thoughts. Self-effacement is as much a part of their character as the pride of achievement, although few of them would admit it to a stranger whatever their accomplishments.

The oppressive darkness of the Arctic winter inevitably affected Inuit thinking. They lived in fear of the nightmares induced by the long, polar night. They were fearful of the blizzards, the souls of the dead and the unknown, though never of death itself. Even today, worry and superstition are an integral part of their lives. For this reason, the Inuit sometimes appear elusive and morose, constantly masking their innermost thoughts and feelings. In winter, they become indolent and restless. They sleep and eat and sleep again, sometimes in a state of virtual hibernation.

When the pressure of the night is too much, they become irritable, and occasionally hysterical, but with the coming of spring, such dark uncertainties explode into euphoria as life returns to the winter-deadened regions. The torrent of vitality brought by the return of the sun fills the Inuit with a sense of release. At such times, they are cheerful, good-tempered, humorous and generous. Not surprisingly, many travellers to the Arctic find the Inuit a complex and unpredictable people, but this is understandable, for the Inuit are truly at one with an environment which is itself notoriously capricious.

CHAPTER 3

Hunters and Game

Throughout their history, the Inuit were aboriginal hunters who could not have survived the Arctic had it not been for the game and the sparse vegetation. Hunting was an essential part of community life. Wise hunters laid down caches of food for the long winter months when the game was scarce. They replenished their food stocks and regained their health and strength during the twelve weeks of spring and summer.

Hunting seals in winter was a miserable occupation which demanded extraordinary endurance and patience. For hours, the Inuk hunter would squat motionless in the polar darkness beside one of the small, dome-shaped mounds of ice where the seal surfaced for air. Normally, the seal can hold its breath under water for only seven or eight minutes. In an emergency, this can be extended to about quarter of an hour. In order to guarantee a constant supply of air within his territorial boundaries, the sensitive, wary creature swims beneath the surface of the icefield, which may be more than four feet thick, scooping as many as two dozen bell-shaped breathing holes with the sharp claws on each flipper. The entrance to these blowholes must be large enough to contain the seal's tapered body, but the opening on the surface must be as small as possible so that he can remain undetected. The seal visits the blowholes regularly not only to breathe but to maintain them, and ensure unrestricted access.

Fully aware of the seal's circumspect nature, an Inuk was scrupulously careful to avoid detection. Nowadays, he hunts with a rifle rather than a harpoon, but it is not difficult to imagine him, at the beginning of the twentieth century, approaching the blowhole, treading gingerly onto pieces of bear or caribou skin so that his footsteps would make no sound on the crunchy surface. The accounts of the nineteenth-century explorers describe how an Inuk, scarcely moving, would insert several forked sticks into the snow beside him. On these he rested his knife, lines and other equipment so that when the time came to move them, he could do so in complete silence. The hunter was so intent on not making a noise that he tied thongs of skin round his legs and arms so that his clothes would not rustle.

Above the surface, the seal's blowhole looks like a molehill. The hunter would probably have built a small wall of ice around it, as a shelter from the wind. Here, he waited, a shapeless huddle of white, his clothing encrusted with a thin film of rime frost and his face, eyebrows, moustache and beard glittering in the moonlight with the frozen moisture of his breath. His eyes, mere slits in the freezing cold, would lock onto a thin rod of tapered bone which he had previously inserted into the small opening.

If the 'float' quivered, it meant that a seal was about to surface. Holding his harpoon gently in his right hand, the hunter settled down to wait. From that moment onwards, the seal was doomed. Once the Inuk had taken up his post he would remain there, with infinite patience, for as long as necessary, no matter how pitiless the weather. In the darkness and the mind-numbing cold, it was easy to fall into a semi-comatose state, so he would force himself to concentrate and stay awake. When the little bone indicator moved, there was no time to spare. If the seal, always timid, was uneasy, he would poke his whiskered nose above the surface for only a few seconds.

As the hours passed, the icy wind would penetrate the hunter's fur and skin clothing, but not once would his gaze waver. Now and again, he would allow his hand to fall carefully to his leg, to remind himself that he had secured the harpoon line to his ankle. This kind of movement seemed to take an eternity because the slightest crackling of the ice crystals on his clothes could betray his presence. When the indicator trembled, the hunter exploded into action, stretching to his full height and plunging the harpoon as powerfully as he could into the rim of the breathing hole.

The Inuk could not see the seal beneath the suface, but he knew its position exactly from his knowledge of the angle and shape of the hole beneath the ice. A spreading stain of red told him that his aim had been precise, that the barbed harpoon had struck the seal in the nape of the neck, and killed it with a single blow. An accurate kill was gratifying because a hunter could easily widen the blowhole with his broad-bladed knife, and haul the slippery seal onto the ice. Struggling with an injured seal weighing as much as a hundred pounds was more difficult.

The Inuit still hunt all the animals, mammals and birds of the Arctic. In summer, they would fish with tridents for arctic char and salmon, but the seal has always been by far the most important. It provided them not only with one of the few available sources of fresh meat in winter, but with heat, light, clothing and equipment. The hunters and their families favoured seal fat for cooking, and as fuel for their lamps, because it burned more brightly than that of walrus.

A typical lamp was a small, stone dish which was filled with blubber. A twist of dried moss was inserted as a wick, and ignited with the help of a flint chip, or more usually, a bow drill. This was a pointed stick, held vertically between the knees, its sharpened point resting on a piece of wood at the Inuk's feet, close to a handful of dried grass. Holding the bow horizontally, the hunter wrapped the bowstring round the stick, and by rapidly moving the bow from side to side, caused the stick to revolve and create enough friction and heat to light the kindling.

The hunters also used the seal skins, which were prized for their suppleness, to make sacks for collecting birds and birds' eggs, and as a basic material for boots, gloves and anoraks (the word 'anorak' is derived from the Inuktitut word 'anaraq', meaning a hooded, waterproof jacket). They cut strips of seal skin for the thongs of driving whips, and as traces for dog teams, a custom still practised widely in Greenland. If the hunting season was successful, an Inuk woman might stitch together as many as twenty-five skins to provide the covering for a summer tent. The Inuit also stretched the skins over the wood or bone frames of their kayaks, which are still used in Greenland for hunting seal, narwhal and walrus in the summer.

Hunting was the only occupation available to the Inuit. Thousands of years of dependence on game for their subsistence instilled in them a highly developed hunting instinct. A lack of polar bears, which feed on seals, might indicate that the blowholes had been deserted. A skulk of foxes, waiting to scavenge a carcass, would call attention to the presence of polar bears. An abundance of arctic hares could signal a lack of their predators, the foxes.

The arctic landscape abounded with signs which were essential to the hunter, whose very survival depended on being able to recognise them. The most insignificant animal was important to those who lived in such difficult conditions. The Inuit killed arctic hares for their fur, which was used for socks and the insides of sealskin boots. They snared the fox for its warm, supple fur which the women prized as material with which to line the hoods and cuffs of their jackets, or to make panties for themselves of blue foxskin. In the depths of winter, the fox and the occasional seal provided the only form of fresh meat available to the Inuit. Raw fox meat, like that of the polar bear, tends to be infested with parasitic worms, and had to be boiled, a process which, according to the Danish explorer, Peter Freuchen, and others who have lived with the Inuit, made it utterly tasteless.

While the hunter sat patiently by the seal's blowhole, his wife set the fox traps, perhaps a dozen or more along as many miles of coastline. Foxes were snared in winter when their fur was at its prime. Every few days, the Inuk woman visited the snares, which were built of stone and disguised with snow, either to empty them or to replenish them with bait of strong-smelling meat. When the fox, itself often starving, wriggled into the cave-like trap, hidden stones were dislodged. These could kill him or block the entrance so that the wretched animal expired from hunger and cold.

An Inuk hunter observed not only the habits and spoor of animals, but cloud formations, and the speed and direction of the wind, important factors when navigating a way through the arctic desert. Leaden clouds ahead might signal open water. A warm, gentle wind blowing down from the interior icecap of Greenland could herald terrible storms. The vast emptiness of the region tended to exaggerate the smallest factor. Yet, nothing could be overlooked. Travelling over the ice of Jones Sound, south of Ellesmere, recently, two hunters, Elijah Nutara and Tony Manik, noticed from a distance of several hundred yards the corpse of a seabird. Examining the body, they discussed for more than an hour its likely flight path, the time it had lain there and the possible causes of its death, all potential sources of information which might have had a bearing on their own safety. To an Inuk hundreds of miles from the nearest settlement, there is much to be learned from the clarity of the air, the type and size of the sun's halo, the crispness of the snow or dryness of the ice. The Inuit's knowledge of snow and ice conditions is reflected in the Inuktitut language, in which seventeen different words describe varying shades of white, and more than fifty words the type and consistency of frost and snow.

Breezes, winds and gales form different patterns in the snow. In mountainous areas, these snow 'waves' tend to lie along the valleys, so by following them it is possible to keep to a specific course, even in poor visibility. This is particularly true when the intended direction runs parallel to the snow ridges. In most of the Arctic, on open ground, lakes and sea ice, these wavelets are remarkably consistent, their direction usually lying between north-northwest and west-northwest. Aware of this, an Inuk was able to steer a course with uncanny accuracy by keeping the wind on the same quarter of his body, by dragging his feet across the ridges, and by checking his direction against the sun, or in the case of fog and blizzards, against his instinctive feeling for the direction of north, south, east and west.

Tracks radiating from settlements to hunting grounds were another important source of information. Driving his dog team in the general direction of a settlement, a hunter would eventually cross a track leading directly to it. The condition of the snow told him not only when the track was made, but perhaps that the sledge was narrow and heavily loaded, that it was pulled by ten dogs, and that the driver was accompanied by his wife and small child. Depending on the hunter's local knowledge, such information could reveal who made the tracks, and consequently which settlement lay ahead. Additionally, the Inuit gave to the islands, peninsulas, headlands and cliffs names which reflected their character, so that the hunter could easily recognise them.

In determining how far he had travelled, a hunter relied on a standard rule. This was the time taken to travel a known distance with a strong team of ten dogs and a moderate load, in perfect conditions. The time required for the journey was measured by the number of times he needed to sleep during it. If ten sleeps were required in standard conditions, he might have to provision for sixteen sleeps if he had only eight dogs and a heavy load, or twenty sleeps if the ice conditions were poor. A correct estimate was vital because, in the Arctic, errors cost lives.

On the ice, the hunter's senses were keyed to the highest pitch of awareness. It was as if he was not a human individual at all, but a medium of supernormal sensibility, charged with the essence of every living being around him. It is the same today. A modern hunter caught a hundred miles from the nearest shore in a white-out (when light reflected from low cloud obliterates the horizon and gauging distance becomes impossible) will climb to the top of an iceberg or hummock, and gaze motionless into the white void, sensing his whereabouts. An inexperienced traveller accompanying him may feel a rising panic at the thought of being hopelessly lost, but after a few minutes the hunter will climb down and, with an apparent lack of concern, head unerringly for his destination. After a week on the ice, the traveller learns to relax and he, too, finds that his awareness of his surroundings has sharpened.

In the mid-nineteenth century, British navigators and explorers returned to Britain and described how the Inuit's understanding of Nature was so great that a hunter could draw a seal skin over his shoulders and in it creep across the ice, imitating the seal's appearance and mannerisms so exactly that he could creep within harpoon range before his disguise was detected. Inuit hunters learned the various calls of seagulls, guillemots and razorbills, kittiwakes and puffins, ducks and geese, all an important source of food. The Inuit were particularly skilful at imitating the call of the little auk, which is so prevalent that it could almost be considered the national bird of the Arctic.

These chubby, diving seabirds, with their black upper parts and distinctive white breast, are not much larger than starlings, and congregate in great bazaars along the cliffs and screes of the High Arctic, swarming back and forth, often darkening and sometimes almost blotting out the sky. Their numbers, as they dive for crustaceans and fish, are impossible to record. The arctic navigator, Admiral Frederick William Beechey, claimed to have seen a column of four million auks on the wing, although this was almost certainly an exaggeration. Nevertheless, each breeding place is tenanted by thousands of birds endlessly circling, soaring and diving, sometimes within a few feet above the stones under which they deposit their eggs and hatch their young.

On the fringes of this swirling cloud of screeching birds, whole Inuit communities leapt from rock to rock imitating their calls to attract the birds into their long-handled nets. The nimble hunters were so adept at catching the little auks that one Inuk, darting across the scree, could net one bird a minute. In a full day, a hunter would expect to take home several hundred birds. Once caught, the Inuk jabbed a podgy finger into the bird's breast. The little auk died instantly from heart failure, and was collected later by the women, who tossed the lifeless bodies into sealskin bags tied round their foreheads. Every year, thousands of the birds were taken, yet their numbers never seemed to decrease.

Wearing the skins and feathers of the hunted animals and birds was as natural to the Inuit as enduring the cold. Thousands of years ago, the early wanderers from Beringia had noticed which birds and animals survived where, and learned how various types of bird feathers possessed different thermal qualities. Almost certainly, some of the Inuit suffered from extreme exposure when the experiments proved unsuccessful, but eventually they designed hooded vests, or anoraks, delicately fashioned from the feathers of five species of ducks and geese.

Different kinds of feathers were used for specific purposes according to their thermogenic properties. The Inuit museum at Godthab, Greenland's capital, which in Inuktitut is called Nuuk, has a fascinating display of clothing taken from the bodies of Inuit who lived approximately 500 years ago. The exhibition shows how the inner hood of the Inuk's vest was shaped from the delicate feathers of the red-throated diver. The white-fronted goose provided warm down to protect the neck and shoulders, while the front and back of the garment were made from the less densely-packed feathers of a young cormorant to ensure adequate ventilation. Because the sides of the body are less active, and therefore more likely to chill, protection was given by the down of the king eider duck. The feathers of cormorant and mallard were used for sleeves.

A single warm, sophisticated vest required the feathers of nearly a hundred birds and was extremely delicate. It was worn next to the skin and was modelled in such a way as to retain the warmth while offering the body ample opportunity to breathe, a vital consideration because clothes soaked in perspiration can freeze, and result in death. A vest or coat frozen stiff from perspiration can also be extremely difficult and uncomfortable to put back on again.

Travellers to the Arctic were often surprised to see that the Inuk's jacket appeared too short for the inclement weather, exposing his lower back to the elements. This was normal. From long experience, the Inuk knew the value of aeration and a dry skin, and tended to move with slow deliberation. As a precaution against the weather, drawstrings were sewn into the bottom of the Inuk's jacket, and these, when released, allowed cold, dry air to filter over his body and absorb the warm, damp air. To prevent the body temperature cooling too rapidly, the drawstrings were easily tightened again.

Clothing, whether one is wearing furs or modern, quilted underwear and down-filled parkas, is as critical in the Arctic as housing. From the earliest times, its development was essentially the same among all the arctic tribes, from the Yakuts and Samoyeds of central Eurasia to the Chukchis of Siberia and the Inuit of Alaska, Canada and Greenland. The parka hood was introduced at an early stage. The Inuit discovered long ago that the most effective way to keep out the cold and retain body warmth was to wear the fur of skin clothing on the outside. Before bird feathers were used for under-garments, skins were sewn back to back with one layer of fur on the outside and the other next to the body. Caribou or reindeer skins were chosen when the hairs were at exactly the right stage of development.

The hunter's wife first chewed the fat from the skins, which were then steeped in hot water. When softened, the skins were stretched on a frame and hung out to dry. Later, the cured skins were fashioned with bone needles into jackets, trousers and boots. The sinews of caribou or seal, which were also chewed, were softened to make the thread. The jacket was finished by stitching a fox tail or a strip of reindeer fur onto the hood and cuffs to prevent chaffing. Sewing was difficult because the needles often broke and had be reground on a stone, making them shorter and, consequently, more difficult to manipulate.

The women wore essentially the same clothes as their menfolk, except that the hoods, which lay flat on the head in men's clothing, were made considerably higher to accommodate the women's hair, which was usually tied in a huge bun. Many years ago, Inuit women plaited their black, glossy hair with great care, and tattooed their forehead, cheeks and chin with gently curving lines. They used an extremely painful technique which involved dipping sinew thread in soot and plant juice, and stitching the mixture beneath the skin with needles of bone.

In winter, the women wore overcoats of fox skin which today would be worth a small fortune in the world's southern capitals. These were abandoned in the summer for the cooler, but equally valuable, sealskin coats. If it was very hot, 10°C. or higher, jackets would be replaced by watertight shirts, immaculately stitched and made from the entrails of a seal or walrus. Objectionable as this may seem, fashion was as important to an Inuk woman as to the chic Parisienne. The length and cut of a coat was dictated by the climate and did not alter, but stylish skin anoraks featured narrow open necks, and strips of skin were left dangling like tails from the hems. Inuit women making a pair of pants took great care in choosing the pieces of multi-coloured fur, which they meticulously stitched together so that the pattern matched on each buttock.

An outer coat, which was usually slightly longer than the man's jacket, was frequently fashioned from as many as forty or fifty small pieces of skin with similar markings. In Alaska and the Canadian Arctic, however, the colouring of clothing was dictated as much by a variety of taboos as by the current fashion. The women's outer boots, or *kamiks*, reached the top of their thighs and were sewn tightly enough to be completely watertight. The neatness of the stitching was a source of pride and status. In Labrador, a woman's boots were sewn with a long, pointed flap at the front in which they could carry a new-born baby. (Elsewhere, Inuit women carried their children on their shoulders, or in the hoods of their anoraks.)

The hunters, who were usually subjected to a greater degree of cold for longer periods, wore stockings made from the skin of arctic hare or reindeer, with the fur as a lining. Layers of dried grass within their *kamiks* served as an insole and protected them from the frozen ground. The hunter who forgot to change the grass daily paid dearly, almost always suffering from severe frostbite.

The man's *kamiks*, made from depilated seal skin and waterproofed with seal oil and urine, were just long enough to reach his bearskin trousers, which were tied below the knee and also worn with the fur outside. It took a whole bear skin to make a pair of trousers, which seldom lasted for more than four or five years. In the extreme cold, the Inuk wore additional fox skins tied round his knees inside the trousers.

The polar bear was an indispensable source of clothing for the Inuk. Arctic folklore abounds with the legends of this magnificent and courageous carnivore, the death of which the primitive Inuit mourned for up to a week. Fierce and muscular, the polar bear was the only animal in the Arctic on which the Inuit hunters wasted any sympathy. Yet as little as a hundred years ago in some parts of the Arctic, fighting a bear in hand-to-hand combat was a test of masculinity. This was no mean task for a young Inuk when one considers that a large bear might stand ten feet tall on its hind legs and weigh more than 650 lb., four times the weight of the average man.

The most spectacular of all the arctic animals, the male polar bear can kill a man, and most other beasts, with a single blow of his front paw. The female is intensely maternal and will go to great lengths to defend her young. In winter, she cannot leave her cubs because they need the warmth of her body for survival, so unlike the Inuit, she cannot hunt and has therefore learned to hibernate in a cave hewn from the ice, her heart beating ten times more slowly than in spring. The male plays no part in fostering the cubs, and goes his separate way, roaming freely over the ice hummocks for most of the winter, relying on his blubber rather than his fur for warmth.

At this time of year, the huge animals stir and set off over the ice in search of seals, their primary source of food. Swimming across the open water, they haul themselves onto the icefloes with a lithe and leisurely gait. When alarmed or annoyed, they are surprisingly quick, loping in an ungainly fashion towards the rough ice hummocks where no man or dog can overtake them. Catching such powerful and watchful creatures might seem impossible, but just as elephants may dance in fear at the sight of mice, polar bears can be harassed by dogs, despite their keen sense of smell, acute hearing and superb vision.

The Inuit hunted polar bears, the world's largest carnivores, principally for their fur. The greasy, tasteless meat was eaten only when a family faced starvation. Once the dogs caught the scent, the cry went up: 'Nanuuk! Nanuuk!' ('A bear! A bear!'), and the excited huskies hauled the sleds at such a furious pace that the hunters disappeared in clouds of whirling snow. As the gap between the dogs and the bear narrowed, the drivers would leap off the sleds, bring the impatient animals to a halt, and cut their traces. If the dogs were not released, the cunning and remarkably intelligent bear would catch hold of their harnesses and, like an Olympic athlete in a hammer event, fling them with a deep grunt through the air. The unharnessed dogs would race ahead unchecked, attacking the distressed animal from the right, its weakest side, and force it to a halt. The enraged bear would whirl its paws frenziedly, snapping and snarling at its tormentors while the hunters, perhaps half a mile behind, ran as fast as their short stature and heavy clothing allowed, their spears at the ready.

It was difficult to throw a lance at a bear without killing the dogs holding it at bay. Roaring with rage, the bear would single out one victim after another, taking a dog by the nape of its neck, and hurling it as much as fifty feet against the ice.

The American explorer, Dr Elisha Kane, who wintered in the Smith

Sound in 1854 (ten years before Mequsaq and his companions set out from Arctic Bay), wrote in the report of his expedition that the dogs in Smith Sound were particularly well-educated in bear hunting. He described one fight, in which one of the dogs 'made no exertion whatever when seized, but allowed himself to be flung, with all his muscles relaxed, a really fearful distance: the next instant he rose and renewed the attack'. Though lanced repeatedly, the courageous bear frequently defended itself and often charged the hunters, many of whom bore the scars of such battles for the rest of their lives.

In spring and summer, polar bears search for seal pups, their favourite food. Moving closer inshore, they swim in the open leads between the icefloes with only the tips of their noses showing above the surface. From time to time, a bear will haul its lumbering body onto a large floe to sleep in the sun, and wake up to find that the floe has broken away, and that it is stranded on a small raft of rapidly melting ice. If the weather worsens and the winds blow from the north, the diminishing floe may be buffeted by waves and icy gales, and the marooned bear may be carried further and further south to Baffin Bay and the Davis Straits. It is not unknown for bears to be found drifting on floes a hundred miles from land. Some have been discovered fifty miles offshore, utterly exhausted from swimming after their rafts of ice had finally disappeared.

Although the polar bear is an excellent swimmer and a graceful diver, it is most vulnerable in the water where it is unable to use its powerful front paws to defend itself. Aware of this, the traditional hunter sometimes pursued the bear in his kayak, driving the creature in front of the slender craft with an occasional prod from his paddle, manoeuvring it to a pre-determined spot where he intended to kill it. He would not kill the bear in the water because even when attached to an air-filled buoy, the carcass tended to sink quickly, and was too heavy to tow to the shore. The Inuk much preferred to harpoon the creature immediately it dragged itself onto an icefloe.

Hunting at sea would not have been possible were it not for the kayak, or *baidar* as it was called in Eurasia. Nansen described it as the best one-man boat in existence. The narrow craft, which is still used widely in Greenland, is tailor-made to the measurements of the owner and fits so snugly that the Greenlanders refer to it as an extra pair of trousers, and speak of 'wearing' it. The total length, normally between 15 feet and 17 feet, is exactly three times the height of the kayaker. Depending on the size, five or six waterproofed seal skins, carefully stitched, are stretched over the long, narrow frame, which is usually less than two feet wide, the kayaker sitting in a space as little as eight inches deep from keel to deck.

Drawing the hood of his sealskin anorak tightly round his face, the kayaker buttons the bottom of the anorak onto the cockpit coaming, which fits closely round his waist ensuring that the kayak is completely watertight. Waves hitting the kayaker head-on could break his back, so the sea-going Inuk must be able to overturn the small craft, and right it again when the wave has passed. In heavy seas, this can be an exhausting and dangerous process. A testimonial to the seaworthiness of such craft and the dexterity of the kayaker himself can be found in the Scottish Statistical Accounts, in which the vicar of Orkney, the Rev. James Wallace, wrote that in 1682, and again two years later, men in unsinkable and presumably storm-driven boats were seen off the coasts of Eda and Westra. The churchman added:

> ... they have this advantage, that be the Seas never so boisterous, their boats being made of Fish Skins, are so contrived that he can never sink, but is like a Sea-gull swimming on the top of the water. His shirt he has is so fastned to the Boat, that no water can come into his Boat to do him damage, except when he pleases to untye it, which he never does but to ease nature, or when he comes ashore.

Clearly, kayaking called for a strong bladder as well as endurance. The Orcadians were so intrigued by the strange seafarers that one of the kayaks was sent from Orkney to Edinburgh to be displayed in the Physicians Hall, together with the 'oar and the dart he makes use of for killing Fish'. The kayak, and 'ye shirt of ye barbarous man yt ws in ye boat', was later presented to the Anthropological Museum of Marischal College at Aberdeen University. It was rumoured that one of the unfortunate occupants was captured, killed, and after a visit to the local taxidermist, put on display until the Victorians decided that it was not the most tasteful of exhibits. This rumour, however, remains unconfirmed. According to the Rev. Wallace's account, the kayakers were 'Finnmen'. This seems to indicate that they came from northern Scandinavia, which was then called 'Finnmark'. Certainly the Sami fishermen there made boats of skin, but these were stubbier and wider, and it is more likely that the stray kayakers were storm-driven Inuit hunters from Greenland.

Once the hunter took his seat in the kayak, his legs outstretched in front of him, he placed a pike and a six-foot harpoon with a detachable shaft along the deck. The point of the harpoon, which was also used for inland fishing, was attached to a line which was coiled neatly on a small circular tray in front of him. The other end of the line was tied to an inflatable sealskin buoy. In later years, after the traders came, the hunter would also position a small square of white canvas on the bow to dupe his quarry into believing the kayak was a harmless piece of floating ice.

Once the seal was harpooned, the shaft separated and floated away. If the stricken creature dived, the line was paid out and the inflatable buoy was thrown into the water to tire the seal, and indicate its position. After a few minutes, the exhausted mammal would surface and the hunter moved in for the kill with his pike, retrieving the harpoon shaft later on. The heavy carcass was then secured to the kayak, and towed back to shore.

Most of the seals hunted in Baffin Bay and off the Greenland coast were ringed seals, but the Inuit also prized the great seal, the tough skin of which was especially useful for making whips, boots and harnesses for dog teams. Larger and stronger than the ringed seal, the great seal was less timid, and once harpooned, it put up a vigorous defence, diving fast and deep so that the kayaker was always in danger of being dragged to the depths.

Walrus were hunted for similar reasons and the hazards, if anything, were greater. These ferocious sea monsters can be as much as twelve feet long with a ten-foot girth. The tough skin of a mammal weighing nearly two tons is invaluable. The long curving tusks, which walrus use like grappling irons to haul themselves over steep ricks and hummocks of ice, were an important source of material for tools. The thick layer of blubber, often nearly as thick as a kayak is wide, would keep an Inuk hunter's family in lamp oil for most of the winter, though as we have seen, the Inuit preferred seal oil because of its brighter flame. The meat, normally eaten frozen during hunting trips, was particularly nourishing and would feed a dog team for several months. Surplus meat was hidden away in stone caches, where it remained until needed in the winter.

The walrus is a gregarious creature and assembles in large herds, one bull and several females in small, open pools near the coast or close to the edge of the ice. Unlike the seal, the walrus is unable to claw blowholes from the underside of the ice, and must burst through the ice cover with one charge. Consequently, the ice must be no more than a few inches thick. For the kayaker, the walrus presented a daunting opponent. It was essential that the harpoon struck the head or the nape of the neck. If the hunter missed, the maddened beast was liable to charge the kayak, flipping it out of the water, bringing instant death to the hunter.

No Inuk hunted walrus alone. The kayaker paddled, then drifted silently to within a few feet of the enormous creature, followed closely by the community's *umiak*, a larger sealskin boat seating ten or a dozen men armed with pikes. Once within range, the kayaker hurled his harpoon and back-paddled furiously, the harpoon line uncoiling as he did so. The infuriated beast dived immediately but was soon weakened by the trailing, inflated buoy attached to the line. When the wounded animal finally surfaced, the other hunters in the *umiak* ended his life with their pikes.

The massive carcass was lashed to the sides of the *umiak*, and tubes inserted into the beast's stomach so that it could be inflated and the body towed more easily to the shore. Here, the waiting community helped to drag the carcass onto the beach. Knives were sharpened and the walrus meat was divided up according to strict custom. The harpooner took the choicest joint, known as the 'first harpoon'. Afterwards, the other hunters cut out the second, third and fourth harpoons, and collected the spurting blood for soup.

Another method of killing walrus was from the shore, or on the icefield itself. A group of hunters walked for days until they heard the monotonous baying and barking of the creatures in the distance. Approaching in single file, they would advance carefully, hiding behind knolls of ice and waiting until the walrus dipped below the surface of a pool. Dr Kane records that when the animal re-surfaced, panting and snorting, the lead hunter cast a harpoon fashioned from the heavy tusk of a narwhal, and sprang rapidly away from the scene. Allowing the coiled line to run out behind him, the hunter rushed for safety, plunged a stake into the ice, and wrapped the final loop of his line around it. As the maddened walrus reared high out of the water and laboriously tried to struggle onto the ice, the other Inuit leapt from their hiding places, and from every angle attacked the stricken beast with their pikes.

The Inuit did not always have things their own way. From time to time, a wounded walrus reacted so violently that it jerked the harpoons out of its body, charged the hunters like a crazed bull, and ripped open their bodies with an adroit flip of its huge head. Sometimes, a hunter would be caught between the huge tusks and carried off to sea like a rag doll. If the walrus dived beneath the ice then, the unfortunate Inuk was unlikely to be seen again. Yet, the instinct for self-preservation runs deep among the Inuit, and it was not unknown for a hunter to be dragged to the bottom, free himself, and stagger home only to die of hypothermia. Folklore has it that one hunter, soaking wet after being tossed into the water, was encased in ice as he ran back to his settlement. The unfortunate man is said to have expired when his spine, brittle and frozen, snapped as he bent over to crawl into the entrance of his home.

Not surprisingly, the hunters were respectful, even fearful, of their prey, although there were few animals, mammals or birds that they did not hunt. Only the great killer whale, the unquestioned master of the deep, proved too great a challenge. When its huge fin was seen slicing the deep waters of the open sea or one of the larger fjords, the kayaker immediately headed for the nearest iceberg or spit of land, no doubt terrified should those fearsome jaws catch up with him.

The bowhead whale, a 55ft leviathan which yields as much as twenty tons of oil, is still hunted by Alaskan Inuit. Hunters east of the Mackenzie Delta prefer to seek out the 15ft beluga, or white whale, which is found in shallower water, and can be harpooned more easily. The beluga, harassed and driven inshore by hunters in an *umiak*, is pursued for its meat, blubber and its skin which, like that of the narwhal, is a Vitamin-C- and protein-rich delicacy known as *mattak* or *muktuk*.

Mattak was invaluable as a means of preventing scurvy, which was always a potential threat among a people who, until recently, ate a diet only of meat. Weighing nearly two tons, narwhal was valued not just for its *mattak* and oil, which burned well, but for the huge tusk protruding from the upper lip of the male. This elongated tooth grows to some six feet, and was used as a spear for hunting walrus, or as a tent pole. It was also a strong door support for the semi-subterranean stone and turf houses used in winter. The Inuits' inventiveness was apparently limitless. Over the centuries, they developed their hunting tools and techniques to a fine art, enabling them to survive in a region where human life was all but impossible, and in which danger beset them every hour of the day.

CHAPTER 4

Courage and Cannibals

Death was the daily companion of an Inuk hunter. Each time he lowered himself into his kayak, he masked his anxiety, aware that if he should succumb to fear, disaster would follow. He knew only too well the infinite possibilities with which Nature could test him. If his reactions were slow during a sudden storm, wavelets whipped into heavy walls of water could crush him. He had only to misjudge by one second the moment at which to flip over his kayak, and the full weight of a breaking wave might snap the frail craft apart, or break his back and drown him. Or he might be driven far out to sea and lose his bearings. If the wind was cold, the spray could freeze and numb his body. At such times, knowing that he would not be able to reach the shore, he would flip over his kayak for the last time.

Even inshore, the kayaker was not safe. The weather could change without warning and the sea might dash a hunter onto the low ice-smooth islands of the fjords, or the needle-sharp rocks at the base of the cliffs. From such a catastrophe there was seldom a safe return. Sometimes, the overlapping tongue of the inner icecap would break away from a clifftop without warning, showering the inshore kayaker with a deadly cascade of ice and small rocks. However alert he might be in the fjords and the open sea, he knew that there was always the danger of an iceberg splitting apart and toppling onto him. The modern kayaker, of course, faces the same risks.

Once the waterproof skin of his kayak was punctured, the kayaker was given little hope; a sealskin suit was not sufficient protection against the cold, black waters. If the hunter managed to drag himself onto an icefloe, it might be more than twenty minutes before relief came. Hypothermia might set in during the long journey home. So common were kayaking accidents, that death by drowning was considered to be the same as death by natural causes. Whenever the Inuit paddled off on a hunting expedition, their wives would gather on the hillsides each evening as they still do in Greenland, and gaze out to sea, waiting for them to return, just as the wives of miners wait today for news at the colliery after a pit disaster.

Another hazard was the mirror-like stillness of the water when there was no wind. The Inuk expecting to harpoon a suspicious seal might sit motionless in his kayak for hours, knowing that the slightest shift in position would frighten the seal away. He could move only his eyes. The glare of the sun was reflected in waters as still as a sheet of glass, inducing a semi-hypnotic state. Sometimes, a kayaker was unable to suppress his fear of this, and could no longer hunt, bringing humiliation on himself, and great hardship for his dependents.

The dangers on land and on the icefields were as great as those at sea. Despite their agility, hunters catching little auks or collecting eggs on the sea cliffs could slip, tumbling down the screes and rock faces to their deaths. Travel was equally hazardous. The Inuit were constantly on the move, either between settlements or on extended hunting expeditions. They were adventurous and restless, but the principal reason for their journeying was the wide distribution of their food source. Hunters might travel more than a hundred miles and not see a single seal. They needed the meat and fat of the walrus found on the fringes of the icefields, but were also obliged to journey far inland to find caribou skins for clothes.

As the Inuit never travelled south of the tree line, and their nearest neighbours, the American Indians, never moved north of it, there was virtually no barter between them. If the Inuit needed stone lamps and pots, it could take them several years driving their sleds and dog teams across the ice to find stone soft enough to carve. In the extreme temperatures of the polar winter, violent headaches and sudden lethargy were common complaints, reducing their will to struggle against the cold. Although the attacks were short-lived, Inuit would sometimes lie down in the dark and slowly freeze to death, unless help came quickly.

Falling into a crevasse, particularly when a snowfall blanketed a glacier, claimed the lives of many Inuit, although a few miraculously survived. One story frequently told is that of Usukutaq, a 27-year-old deaf semi-mute from Natsilivik, at the head of Inglefield Bay in north-western Greenland. In a hunting expedition at sea, he had already lost most of his family, including his parents. In 1926, the small community was snowbound. Poor summer hunting and the severity of the winter had prevented the hunters leaving their homes, and food stocks were negligible. When the weather cleared, Usukutaq knew it would be some time before the communal larders could be replenished, and decided to leave the settlement and cross the glacier to Uummannaq, now known as Thule, some 75 miles to the south.

The glacier, nearly 3,000 feet high, was deeply fissured. The ice groaned and creaked as it inched towards the coast where it calved icebergs more than a hundred feet high. Usukutaq, poverty-striken and hungry, told no one of his plan. In the murky light, he set off on foot with no food, and only a small knife. The going was rough, the ice slippery. Although he trod carefully, picking his way across the glacier proved very difficult. His clothes were thin and worn, offering little protection against −40°C., but he was determined not to return to the tiny settlement at Natsilivik, where he knew he was a burden. After a few hours, snow began to fall and soon everything around him was white and indistinguishable. Almost inevitably, he trod on a fragile bridge of frozen snow, which, collapsing under his weight, pitched him fifty feet down a crevasse.

Usukutaq might well have given up all hope. No one knew his whereabouts. His tracks were soon covered with snow. An Inuk, however, does not submit easily when death calls. Inuit orphans and the disabled were often particularly hardy because, according to custom, they were banished as children from the family igloo, and forced to sleep with the dogs in the entrance passage. The surviving outcasts were remarkably resilient, and often became valued members of the society which had spurned them. Indeed, arctic folklore is peppered with stories of orphans who fought courageously through an unhappy childhood and a life of solitude, eventually to brave great danger and become heroes rescuing others in peril.

Usukutaq, who was wedged firmly on his left side in the crevasse, calmly took stock of his situation. He could not reach his left arm. He was in agony from a searing pain across his neck and chest. Worse, he knew there was no question of a rescue party. In time, Usukutaq lapsed into a half-world between reality and hallucination. The long nights and equally dark days passed. No one came, and the semi-mute was unable to shout for help.

After great difficulty, Usukutaq managed to reach his small knife and cut pieces of ice from the walls of the crevasse, so that he could lick them to stave off thirst. The cold penetrated his worn sealskin trousers and caribou jacket. At one stage, the terrified Inuk thought he saw an enormous black dog with magical powers clawing through the ice. He claimed later never to have lost consciousness, although that seems unlikely. Hunger pains cramped his stomach. In order to stay alive he gnawed the sleeve of his jacket, ate his boots, their lining of dried grass and the lice which, as with most Inuit, infested his head.

On the tenth day, another hunter from Natsilivik traced the same route taken by Usukutaq. By now, food suplies in the village were almost finished, and the hunter knew that his only chance of survival would be to reach Uummannaq. Fortunately for Usukutaq, the hunter owned a dog team. On scenting Usukutaq's body, they sped towards the lip of the crevasse. Leaning over the edge, the hunter could hear nothing, but the dogs were insistent. Eventually, the hunter tossed a chunk of ice into the cleft, and from the depths of the crevasse, he heard a faint protest.

Lowering a skin noose, which Usukutaq managed to drag round his body, the hunter desperately tried to haul the unfortunate Usukutaq out of the crevasse. The first attempt failed, and Usukutaq fell once more, although this time with both hands free. Finally, the hunter managed to hoist the barely conscious Inuk to the top of the crevasse, and they set off urgently to the nearest settlement where, by chance, a Danish midwife was attending an Inuk birth. Usukutaq was placed at once in ice-cold water, rubbed down and given large doses of aspirin to alleviate the excruciating pain of re-circulating blood. He lived to a ripe old age but was unable to relate the story, except to the very few who could understand his inarticulate sounds and crude drawings in the snow. Usukutaq died in 1967, in a fire at a Home for the Aged.

For the Inuit, battling with the hostile environment was a way of life. Every day brought the threat of death and starvation. Only the fittest survived. The hunter no longer able to wield a harpoon, and provide his food and clothing, was a burden on the community, encumbered with the memories of his finest triumphs. For him, life was without value. His first love was for life itself, but if he was unable to participate in its most essential occupation, hunting, life was said to weigh heavier than death.

According to the Danish explorer, Peter Freuchen, who lived with the Polar Inuit at Thule for many years, an old Inuk, before he became too infirm, would call for a feast of prime *mattak* for his family and friends, in order that they might laugh and talk, and share once more the stories from times past. The sharing over, he would walk quietly with them to the shoreline or to the edge of the ice, and taking leave of his family and friends, he would ask his wife or his eldest son to help him into his kayak. This done, he would paddle proudly out to sea until he was quite certain that he was alone and unseen, and with a determined thrust of his paddle, capsize his kayak for the last time.

Not all Inuit chose to die in this way. Others either jumped, or asked to be pushed, over the edge of a cliff. In particularly savage winters when famine remained unrelieved, a family would sometimes agree to move on to another settlement in the hope that the Inuit there might share with them whatever meagre supplies were available. These journeys sometimes lasted for days, a few pitiful dogs dragging the family's scant belongings on a sledge, the starving parents and their sons and daughters walking beside the dogs. Only the family elders rode at the rear. No words were spoken. There were no farewells. The old people quietly eased themselves off the sledge, and waited in the snow for the end. This practice was continued until the end of World War Two.

In less harsh conditions when the pressures were not so intense, an old Inuk woman who could no longer chew skins, hold a needle or keep up with the dog teams because her legs were too painful would ask her eldest son to build an igloo in which she could spend her final hours. The rest of the family would implore her not to do this, because she would be so sorely missed, but eventually the eldest son would obey. The dying woman would take a last look round the family home, pick up the most dilapidated skin and a few personal belongings, and walk to her tomb. The member of the family assigned to the duty would close the entrance with a block of ice. When the igloo was sealed, the incarcerated woman was no longer considered to be alive, and was left in the cold for death to take her.

In some parts of the Arctic, an ailing woman would ask her son or daughter to kill her with a knife. Old men normally preferred to be hanged on a rope of walrus skin, which was considered to be an honourable end to life. Usually, this occurred during festivities when food was plentiful. The family and their friends assembled, told stories and jokes, and teased each other. Finally, the eldest son tied the rope to a narwhal tusk or whalebone at the apex of the tent and placed the noose round the old man's neck. With a cheerful farewell, the entire gathering then hauled the old fellow to his destiny.

Suicide, permitted only when the old were incurably sick and a burden on the rest of the community, was regarded as social euthanasia. Life for the Inuk was too precious to be regarded lightly. He killed only when absolutely necessary, and expected others to face up to their fate with courage. From time to time, elderly members of the family might consider themselves a nuisance, and try to hang themselves. If they were disturbed in the attempt, there would be a furious argument, especially if food was plentiful and the rest of the family did not regard them as a burden. More often than not, the old man agreed to the pleas of his family, and after peace had been restored, awaited an opportune moment to make a second attempt.

This propensity to suicide was not shared among other arctic peoples, such as the Sami, or Lapps, in Scandinavia, or the Soviet tribes, who lived closer to the boreal forests, and could benefit from the reindeer herds which provided them with a constant source of food. Nor were the taboos as strict as those among the Inuit, whose customs, songs and legends were meticulously recorded by Knud Rasmussen, a Greenlander who in 1921 embarked on the Fifth Thule Expedition, a four-year journey by dog sled from Greenland to Siberia. So bound by taboos were the Inuit, that life became almost intolerable. In times of hardship, a family might abandon a dying man or woman in order to avoid further suffering. This may seem callous, but such action was understandable. During five days of mourning, hunting was forbidden to all members of the family. In some tribes, close relatives were required to plug their nostrils. Kayaks, tools, skins and personal belongings were frequently placed next to the body to prevent their re-use, which would bring poor hunting and ill-fortune. Sledges were upended to show the spirits that the taboos had been obeyed. When the body was taken to its final resting place, usually a cairn of stones or a cave, only the next of kin were allowed to handle the corpse. They were required to wear hoods and mittens, subsequently thrown away, to avoid touching the dead person.

During the five-day period, no one was allowed to cross the path of those who had handled the corpse. Women were banned from sewing. Children were required to keep their heads and hands covered at all times, and were forbidden to speak or play, cut ice, or fetch water. If a child wanted a drink, water could be given only by an Inuk outside the immediate family. The Inuit believed that all animate and inanimate beings had a body, a name and a soul. After death, it was imperative to treat the body according to custom for fear of invoking the wrath of the spirits. The dead relative's name could not be mentioned again until a new child was born, and cried for the first time. Even today, Inuit are extremely reluctant to speak the name of the dead. It was necessary, after a relative had been enclosed in a death igloo, to release the soul of the dead person. A small hole was cut into the roof, left open for a specified length of time, then filled in again so that the spirit could not return.

The Inuit usually killed in order to survive. Nevertheless, Peter Freuchen, who accompanied Rasmussen on the Fifth Thule Expedition, records that in the Canadian Arctic, vendettas were common. Even warfare was not unknown. Conflict invariably followed a period of famine during which the Inuit had been forced to practise female infanticide. Knud Rasmussen discovered in 1921 that the Netchilik Inuit, who live near King William Island, had killed at birth approximately half the baby daughters born to the women with whom he spoke. The resultant shortage of women provoked a spate of abductions, fighting and murder. Strife between Inuit tribes might continue for several decades, perhaps understandably, for without a wife, no Inuit could hope to become a successful hunter.

Animals were slain only for food and to provide clothing. Unwritten law required that no living creature be put to death unnecessarily. In the Arctic, there was no room for waste. If extravagance and wastefulness were accepted, stocks might diminish with serious effects for the entire community. This was engrained in the mind of every Inuk from birth, and normally applied as much to the human community as to the animal kingdom.

The continual struggle for survival forced decent, family-oriented Inuit men and women to commit what in other parts of the world is considered the most heinous of all crimes, cannibalism. From Siberia to Greenland, the crushed skulls and split bones of victims bear witness to a catalogue of utter wretchedness and desperation. Arctic lore abounds with such tales: the old man who chopped up his grand-daughter, cooked the soup and ate the flesh in less than an hour . . . the wife almost too weak to move who devoured her dead husband, and split open his bones to remove the marrow . . . the woman who ate her own daughter. Some Inuit survived only to die within days of finding sustenance, the insatiable hunger that followed the first taste of food compelling them to eat until sated. Every warning unheeded, their starving bodies were unable to accept such bounty.

Starvation was accepted as a natural hazard in the Arctic, but it was a cruel master. If, during a period of intense hunger, a mother died in childbirth, while a family was on a protracted hunting expedition, the father would strangle the infant unless another woman could be found to act as a wet-nurse. If the father died, the mother was expected to carry out the deed. Weak and sickly children were always killed in times of hardship. Only one of every three girls was allowed to live. The others were put to death.

Occasionally, a mentally unstable or disabled child (like Usukutaq, who fell into the crevasse) was permitted to live, provided that it was not a burden on the family, but this was rare. The same applied to orphans, who were treated with equal contempt. With no parents, they were automatically a burden on the community. It was not that the Inuk was cruel, rather that individual strength was of supreme importance. Allowing the weak, the old and the helpless to die preserved the health and survival of the community as a whole, and this was infinitely more important than an Inuk's own life.

CHAPTER 5

The Egalitarian Society

Until the beginning of this century, Danish missionaries and traders in Greenland provided virtually the only source of serious information about the Inuit. Their letters and reports, written in Danish, spanned 150 years and eventually comprised hundreds of volumes, which were kept in archives in Copenhagen, unread by all but the most serious arctic scholars. Various whaling captains and explorers had also written accounts of their travels and encounters with Inuit in the north, but these were generally concentrated on their own exploits, rather than the complexities of Inuit society. There were a few exceptions, notably the American doctor Elisha Kent Kane, and the Norwegian Fritjiof Nansen, but it was not until 1927, when Rasmussen and Freuchen published the ethnographical studies undertaken during the Fifth Thule Expedition, that a clearer picture began to emerge of the way in which the Inuit lived.

The principal reason for their ability to survive was the strict egalitarian social order in which every effort was made to suppress individualism. As far as possible, the first person singular was suppressed in both speech and thought. An Inuk would seldom say 'I am leaving,' but 'Somebody here is going out for a walk.' The wife of a destitute hunter confronted with an empty larder would not ask 'What can I do?', but 'How can a poor woman cook when there is no food in the house?' If the hunter caught a seal, the catch would be shared with other, less successful hunters.

Life was based on the purest form of communism. The Inuk owned nothing, apart from a few skins and some personal tools such as his knife and his whip. Until recently, the concept of owning land or property never occurred to him. Housing, boats, hunting territories, game and food belonged to the group, which was all-powerful. A widow was permitted to inherit a few minor personal effects, but the dogs, sledges and kayaks of the deceased Inuk became the property of the group council, which usually passed them on to the dead man's sons and brothers.

This constant suppression of egoism ensured that every thought and deed of the competitive Inuk was directed towards the good of the community. The best hunter, navigator, boat or sledge builder was worthy of praise. The weak, the lazy and the dishonest were publicly criticised, held in contempt and ridiculed. Excellence was rewarded with a position of authority. Skilful hunters, who could provide regular supplies of meat, were elected to decide the community's affairs and its future.

The success of the group rested on the prowess of the hunters, and their inherent sense of justice, equality and solidarity. It was not enough that, after a hunting expedition, the catch should be divided among less fortunate hunters. Those who were successful were expected to share their portions with other members of the group, the widows and children, as well as the sick and aging who had not yet taken the decision to put an end to their lives. This gesture served to enhance the hunters' own authority. The hunter and the *angakok*, or shaman, were the group's natural leaders. Yet there were no village chiefs as such, and so great was the fear that individualism might erode the group's infra-structure that even shared power was delegated only for short periods, on a rotating basis.

After the meat had been distributed, each Inuk placed his portion on a rack at the top of a high stone tower where it would be safe from the constantly ravenous huskies. Here, the meat freeze-dried. Despite having been allocated to a specific Inuk, it remained common property as long as it remained on the storage racks. The meat could be taken down by anyone who climbed the tower, a practice which was not always viewed benevolently, although no one protested.

The distinction between sharing and stealing was sometimes obscure, yet thievery was uncommon. There was no need to lock houses. As each inhabitant knew what everybody else in the settlement owned, it was impossible to keep stolen goods without being detected. If an Inuk unnecessarily took more than his rightful share of meat, he would soon be ridiculed, and taunted as a worthless, improvident hunter. 'Is the hunting so poor that an Inuk cannot provide himself with so much as a seabird?' his neighbours would cry. 'How strange it is that a third harpoon has no meat.' The torrent of abuse could so devastate a greedy Inuk that he might be obliged to leave the village, knowing that his reputation would probably precede him, and make him unwelcome in settlements for many miles around. Few men could survive for long without the group, and in winter, such enforced travel could bring death from starvation.

Apart from fish, and a few roots and berries in the summer, meat was the only food available in the High Arctic. This diet was neither as monotonous nor unhealthy as one might imagine. Once the palate adjusts to the lack of vegetables and fruits, the various cuts of meat provide a variety of flavours. The hunters were particularly fond of the blood of seal pups. A typical meal began with warm, rich soup made from fresh blood. This was followed by large chunks of meat hacked from the carcass of a frozen seal or walrus, and chewed by the hunter until soft and edible, and then swallowed whole.

The sound of belches echoed round the igloo, but the host's wife would prepare and serve yet more food. If she chose caribou marrow, the men cracked the bones with their teeth and noisily sucked them clean. The Inuk woman would have boiled meat over a whale-oil lamp, and given this as a final course. The hunters, who were always conscious that each meal might be their last, invariably feasted until fully satiated, and then, having wiped the grease from their fingers and mouths with the wing of a seabird, would wash the meal down with a drink of melted snow, and collapse in sleep.

Later, somewhat refreshed, an engorged hunter would persuade his somnolent friends to continue the meal in his own igloo, offering as an inducement one of the most tempting of all dishes: *mattak* – preserved blubber packed in skin bags. Fermented meat was a choice dish for the Inuit, who delighted in its sweetness and were impervious to the pervasive stench of putrefied flesh. A favourite food was rotten guillemots and little auks. These were neither plucked nor gutted, but packed whole in fat, and left to decompose in a sealskin bag. In the summer warmth, the melting fat coalesced with the decaying meat. When the putrefaction process was complete, the birds were served as a delicacy. The Inuit also ate snacks of lice, which could be found in the hair and clothes of the majority of their fellows.

Excess meat from the summer hunt was stored in stone caches which provided a reserve source of food for the long winter months, when hunting activities came to a virtual standstill. The hunter who built these depots accepted that a passing wayfarer could feed himself and his dog team from the stock. The traveller's only obligation was to ensure that whatever meat remained was properly covered, so that it could not be plundered by foxes and bears. Similarly, if a hungry Inuk ate a fox caught in another man's traps, he was expected to return the skin to the owner. If the fox had frozen to death and could not be skinned, the traveller would reset the traps. Although ownership was alien to the Inuit society, it was not unusual for a village council to assert its exclusive right to all game caught on land close to the settlement. Once this claim had been established, hunters from other villages were obliged to seek permission before they could set traps in the area.

Many hunting expeditions took several weeks and it was customary for a traveller to enter an Inuit home, known to him or not, and join the family for a meal. Hospitality was never denied, however impoverished the hosts. The itinerant hunter was within his rights to stay for as long as he wished, but while he remained, the game he caught belonged to the common pot. So fearful were the Inuit of individualism that, in order to prevent attachment to a dwelling or a particular area, homes, and occasionally whole villages, were exchanged every few years.

Contrary to popular belief, the Inuit did not live in igloos. An *iglu*, from which the westernised word derives, was actually a sturdy, stormproof house built of stone and turf. The traditional domes of snowblocks were called *illuliaq*, and were used primarily by families travelling on long hunting expeditions. Despite the intricate design, the Inuit could build one of these in little more than an hour. Elijah Nutara, a hunter who still refers to himself as E.9912, the number given to him by the Canadians in the post-war years because, like most Inuit, he did not have a surname, demonstrated to me the ease with which this was done. With his long, broad-bladed knife, he hacked out large blocks of hard-packed snow, rather than ice which was too hard, and laid them in a circle roughly three metres across.

Elijah laid the wedge-shaped blocks in a spiral, so that each tier of snow leaned slightly inwards. When the walls were waist high, he cut the blocks smaller, and angled the wedges more acutely. As the dome began to take shape and the circles became narrower, he climbed inside to support the snow bricks until they reached the apex, which was about ten feet above ice level. Finally, he cut out a small hole at roughly chest height to allow excess heat from steaming bodies and moisture from cooking to escape before it rose to the top, melting the snow and causing the roof to sag.

In earlier times the rest of the family would pack loose snow into the cracks between the blocks to make the *illuliaq* windproof. When they had finished, the hunter hewed an arch-shaped hole in the wall and built an entrance tunnel, the length of which varied according to the weather, the time available and the Inuk's mood. The tunnel was just high enough to crawl through. It was designed not only to keep out the cold, but as a storage place and sleeping area for the dogs and orphans. When the family's temporary home was completed, the hunter attended to his equipment and unloaded the sledges, while his wife laid skins along a snow bench and in the well of their new home to make the *illuliaq* comfortable. The most effective insulation was achieved by placing one layer of skins with the fur facing downwards, and another with the fur closest to the body.

In summer, the inside of the *illuliaq* is unexpectedly light and spacious.

The snow blocks, comprised of air and crystals, admit a bluish-white daylight, giving the person inside the eerie impression of being suspended in a giant, upturned china bowl. When the weather threatens, it is a simple matter to block the ventilation hole, close the entrance and light a fire to raise the temperature so that the interior surface of the walls melts. The air hole can later be re-opened, allowing cold air back inside. Within minutes, the walls will be protected by a solid wall of ice, capable of withstanding the most violent storms.

Occasionally, the entire population of a village would travel in convoy across the ice. If the families were caught in a blizzard, several *illuliaq* would be built close together, and their entrance tunnels linked so that the occupants could visit each other without going outside. The heat generated by people and blubber lamps raised the interior temperature as high as 15°C., only six or seven degrees below today's centrally-heated home in the south. For the Inuit, who list warmth as one of their greatest pleasures, this was a time for relaxation during which they could strip off their heavy clothes for a few hours, and allow their bodies to breathe.

The permanent *iglu* was more solid and complex, usually built on a hillside overlooking the shoreline. The entrance tunnel was constructed with flat stones and was about five or six yards long. The first part of it was so low and narrow that a hunter on his hands and knees could just squeeze through. Half way along, the tunnel became higher and wider as it led down a slight incline to the front step of the main room. Here, however exhausted, the Inuk brushed his ice-encrusted clothes carefully. This was important. If the snow or ice crystals were allowed to melt, his clothes would become wet and heavy and might freeze.

Satisfactorily de-iced, the hunter was ready to crawl up the small step into the circular living quarters. The floor was laid with flat stones from the beach, but larger stones and rocks were used for the double walls, between which peat and turf had been packed as insulation. Immediately in front of the entrance, a long raised platform covered with skins extended the full length of the back wall, which was cut into the hillside. Here the family slept. A similar platform to the left of the entrance was reserved for guests.

Household utensils and lamps were stored along the right-hand wall. The single window, which was intended to allow light into the room rather than as a means of seeing outside, was made from the stretched gut of a seal or walrus. To the southerner, pampered with deodorants and sweet-smelling lotions, the atmosphere inside an *iglu* or *illuliaq* was never pleasant, an over-powering stench of dogs, sweat, urine and fetid meat. To the Inuk, even less than fifty years ago, this was part of his accustomed life. Dogs were as much a part of the family as children. Perspiration, particularly in winter, was the best means of cleansing his pores, the same principle as with a Finnish sauna. Urine was an instant source of warm water, which was used to ice the runners of the sledges and to seal the cracks of the *illuliaq* when there was no snow. A seal's carcass in the corner was a sign of plenty.

The family nucleus was crucial to the individual and to the group. According to the French anthropologist, Jean Malaurie, who in 1950–51 spent fourteen months with the Polar or Thule Inuit, in northwest Greenland, survival depended on strict rules against inter-marriage. In his book *The Last Kings of Thule*, probably the most exhaustive study of the Inuit since the Fifth Thule Expedition, he observed that at one time, an Inuk was prohibited from marrying a sixth cousin. Later, this was reduced to a third cousin and, in times of hardship, to a first cousin. A single man, or widower, would be forced to live either with his own family, or if he had no relatives, with another couple in order that his clothes could be dried and mended, and his boots softened.

As soon as he returned from hunting, he would hand over his catch to the family to pay for his keep. If a husband on a long hunting expedition with his family was killed, his wife and small children might starve to death, unless an unmarried hunter found and claimed her. In a few rare cases, to the consternation of the group, a widower who was unable to find another wife might sleep with his own daughter, driven by the knowledge that a man without a wife was ruined when he could not hunt successfully.

Necessity, rather than love, brought couples together, although each partner respected the other, and devotion often followed. Inuit men were always two or three times older than their brides. Boys had to learn to hunt and serve an apprenticeship of several years before they could marry. A shortage of girls, following a period in which female infanticide had been practised, could result in a hunter having to wait until he was well into his thirties before taking a bride. Girls, on the other hand, often married before they reached their teens. By then, they would be thoroughly versed in sexual matters. Their parents, and the guests in the house, made no attempt to be secretive. Indeed, parents encouraged small children to play together and explore each other's bodies, in a way that would horrify prudish societies in the modern world.

Apart from this open attitude to sex, children were brought up in much the same way as in any other country. They played tag, hide-and-seek and hopscotch, and their summer laughter echoed across the settlements. Young girls would cuddle dolls made from skins and fox furs, and furnish a miniature *iglu*, which was the equivalent of the western dolls' house. Girls were expected to help their mothers at an early age and learn the many household skills that would eventually be required of them. Time was short. Many would be married and pregnant by their thirteenth birthday.

Little boys would roll in the snow with the husky pups and play with whips and toy harpoons. Teenagers and young men played a raucous, anarchic ball game which was a cross between soccer and American football. The ball was fashioned from walrus skin and stuffed with feathers. There were no discernible rules and the game ended either with the disintegration of the ball or a serious, and sometimes fatal, accident. The pressure on boys was as great as that on girls. By the time they were eight years old, they were expected to be able to drive a dog team, navigate and forecast the weather, walk fifteen miles a day, throw a harpoon and, in more recent times, fire a rifle accurately. Boys hunted with their fathers, who taught by example. At fourteen, they would have caught their first seal and be considered grown men.

In view of their early adulthood, it was hardly surprising that parents failed to worry when adolescents did not come home on time. It was assumed that they were visiting the teenage 'love' *iglu*, which was to be found on the fringes of every village. Married couples were barred. This was a place in which young people from the age of eleven years were permitted to discover each other. Parties were held frequently. There would be a great deal of nose rubbing, cuddling and heavy petting. Kissing, in the western sense, was outlawed by common consent as disgusting. The Inuit kissed the tip of the nose, which they considered to be sensually important. The smaller and flatter an Inuk girl's nose, the more beautiful she was deemed to be. The proud owner of such a nose, and of round, chubby cheeks would be regarded as a village sensation.

By western standards, Inuit courtship was a brutal affair. Peter Freuchen describes in his *Book of the Eskimos* (pp. 314–25) how a hunter who took a liking to a girl did not necessarily bother to ask her to marry him, or discuss a marriage with her parents. In former times, he behaved more like the traditional caveman. Thrusting his way into her home and dragging her outside, he would throw her over his shoulder and carry her away. The girl, secretly pleased, but pretending to be outraged, impressed those around her with her apparent rage and scorn. Screaming and pounding his back with her fists and kicking her legs in the air, she would bite his hands and ears. This dramatic display of frustration and contempt would intensify as the other women emerged from their homes to watch the spectacle.

The hunter, disregarding the girl's rebelliousness, would dump her onto the sledge and drive off, shouting at his team to pull harder and faster. By now, the girl would have noted that the sledge was well provisioned, and hauled by an impressive number of fine, healthy dogs, but it would be several hours before she relaxed her show of temper. If spoken to, she refused to answer. When she had to jump off the sledge to help her new husband and his dog team to cross a crevasse, or an ice hummock, she criticised his ineptness.

In the evening, when the hunter built the *illuliaq*, his wife might at last settle down and begin to prepare a meal. She could carry on the angry pretence for several days or, by running away, demonstrate that the change in her life had not been for the better. The hunter usually waited with quiet amusement. When his wife returned, he listened to her muttered excuse that 'sometimes a poor woman must take a little air,' smiled wisely and remained silent.

With a few exceptions, a hunter who had taken a woman in this way continued to live with her for the rest of his life, although group custom periodically demanded that there should be a temporary exchange of wives. The purpose of this practice, which has been greatly misunderstood, was specifically to prevent a couple becoming too fond of each other, and to discourage mutual possessiveness. As important as the cohesive family unit was in Inuit society, it was imperative that it should not be allowed to take precedence over the unity of the group.

Wife trading was regarded as normal and healthy, dictated as often as not by circumstance. If a man's wife was sick, pregnant or too busy with small children to join him on a hunting trip, its success would be needlessly limited. The time he would normally have allocated to stalking the animals would have to be spent on such wifely chores as melting ice for drinking water, and cooking the evening meal. The hunter would not have enough time to dry his clothes, so he would need to pack a complete set of spare clothing and footwear. This used up valuable sledge space, which would be increasingly restricted by the weight of the heavy skins he caught. A wife normally stretched and scraped the hides, but without her, he would have to take them home frozen, and heavier. The obvious solution to the problem was to leave his wife at home with a neighbour, and take the neighbour's wife hunting.

Occasionally, after a period of famine, the *angakok*, or shaman, would order a temporary interchange of wives in the hopes of correcting the misfortune. If his initial permutations were not successful, he would repeatedly shuffle the couples round until the animals were again plentiful. A particularly successful hunt or the receipt of good news from another village might be celebrated in a similar way. Such decisions were not taken arbitrarily, but according to a strict code of conduct, and always by men. The onus was on them to move from one *iglu* to another. The women were expected to acquiesce without complaint, and usually did so.

Inuit legend records only one occasion when it was decreed that women, rather than men, should choose a different partner. The result was disastrous. Embarrassed by the burden unexpectedly placed on them, the women huddled together in a group in the centre of the village. Suddenly, a whale appeared offshore. The women apparently decided that if they were to make the decisions of men, they might as well hunt like men, and ran down to the beach. When the first harpoon was thrown, folklore explains, the whale took great offence at being injured by mere women, and surged out to sea. Thereafter, the hunting was so poor that the *angakok* decreed that for the rest of time, women must remain indoors during a whale hunt, a taboo which in parts of the Canadian Arctic is still observed.

From time to time, wife trading was practised for the sheer fun of it. In winter, a popular game was 'putting out the lights', when nude couples shuffled continually round the host's *iglu* until, at a given signal, they embraced the nearest person. When the lamps were re-lit, the guests rocked with laughter, and insisted that they had known all the time who it was that they were to face. Despite the sexual freedom and frivolity, the Inuit essentially remained an inhibited people. For all their boasting, the men were, and often still are, patently shy and sexually vulnerable.

In southern countries, the sexual traditions of the north have been misunderstood, and given rise to charges of immorality. Travellers to the Arctic have always been quick to criticise, condemn or attempt to change the Inuits' habits, or just as readily, to take advantage of them. Yet the Inuits' free sexual mores were governed by strict rules, and served a specific purpose within the community. 'Putting out the lights' was a means of preventing boredom, depression and possible violence during the long, dark polar winter.

Exchanging wives was intended not only to break down individual possessiveness, but to strengthen group ties. This was achieved naturally as a result of the many pregnancies which followed wife trading. The Inuit harboured the peculiar idea that conception was not possible during a casual relationship, although the number of subsequent births should have indicated otherwise. Babies born after an exchange of wives were always adopted by one of the parents. Each child was considered to be a blood relation of the other children born in similar circumstances. Although they were not allowed to marry each other, they were bound together by group law, which stipulated that they must honour and help each other for the rest of their lives.

Pregnancy was a more traumatic experience for a young Inuk girl than for women in other parts of the world because of the harsh environment and the arctic lifestyle. Timing was as vital for her as it was for the animals and the birds. It was important that a child's first vulnerable months should coincide with the mildest season, which meant that conception had to take place at the end of the summer. This was ideal because the Inuk's sex life tended to be seasonal, and at its height between June and August. But if births between March and May were ideal from this point of view, they were also months of intense activity and hard work, which had to be carried out at a time when, in any other country, a woman in the later stages of pregnancy would be taking a more relaxed attitude to life. This was when hunters embarked on long and arduous hunting trips across ice. If she accompanied her husband, the poor woman would be bumped and jolted for many hours a day as the dogs hauled the sledge over the uneven ice. Not surprisingly, miscarriages were frequent.

By contrast, giving birth was remarkably uncomplicated. The entire process often took less than three hours. From the breaking of the waters to the child's first cry, as little as thirty minutes elapsed. Malaurie tells how in the winter of 1910 a young woman giving birth squatted over a hole in the ground and supported herself on boxes at either side, so that when the time came she could allow the baby to drop into the hole, and herself cut the umbilical cord with a sliver of ice. If the birth was difficult, the husband looped a strip of skin round her abdomen, and sitting behind her with his feet on her back, pulled hard in order to press the baby out. Afterwards, the mother licked the child clean, wrapped it in warm furs, and gave it the first of thousands of meals from the breast. Inuit women did not wean their children for many years. It was common for a mother to continue to nurse a son until he was thirteen or fourteen years old, when he could drive a dog team with all the expertise of his father, and had probably caught his first seal.

CHAPTER 6

The Hunters' Best Friend

The Inuit's perpetual quest for food, and a desire for social contact with other settlements after the long winter, compelled them to travel for hundreds of miles across the arctic wastelands. Until recently, dog teams provided the only means of transport in the High Arctic. Without huskies, the culture of the hunting Inuit would have disappeared long ago. Today, the importance of dogs is diminishing, although in Greenland thousands of people are still dependent on them for long distance travel. It is indicative of their continuing significance to Greenlandic society that in some towns, the sledge team still takes precedence over motorised traffic.

Siberian huskies were originally bred from wolves, and trained for centuries as working dogs. Early breeders among the Russian Chukchi tribes concentrated on developing much smaller dogs than those in North America, capable of greater agility and speed. The Inuit needed larger, stronger animals, cross-bred so that their progeny inherited the courage and spirit of the mother, the strength and endurance of the father. Today's huskies are medium-sized and squarely built, with pointed noses, short ears, and a treacherous glint in their eyes. Their fur is coarse and compact, and much valued as clothing among the poorer Inuit families.

The dogs are predominantly grey, but some have black and white breasts, other are completely white, or tinged with red or yellow. Highly-strung and savage by nature, they still bear a close resemblance to the wolf. The Greenlanders, who consider it essential to maintain the strength and purity of the breed, do not permit ownership of pure-bred huskies below the Arctic Circle, where they could mix with lesser strains. Conversely, other working sledge dogs are forbidden north of the dividing line.

Dogs were the Inuk's status symbol, their health his greatest priority. Each hunter took pride in displaying his team to neighbours and travellers, who offered advice and discussed each dog, as a typical huddle of racing enthusiasts might weigh the merits of a thoroughbred.

Haunches were measured, teeth and eyes inspected. Well-fed dogs in peak condition reflected the hunter's prowess, bringing him praise and envy. Starving dogs with poor coats reflected his lack of hunting skills, or bad luck resulting from a failure to abide by group taboos.

Only the Inuk's son was of greater importance. However poor the hunting, the ravenous beasts were always the first to be fed. The family ate what was left. The Inuk's care and respect for the team was his expression of gratitude to the huskies for providing him with the means to acquire food. Apart from pulling the sleds, they helped the hunter to find game by following the trail of a polar bear, or by sniffing out a seal's blowhole.

Huskies spent nearly all their lives outdoors. Sleeping under shelter would inevitably have weakened them, making them useless for long journeys. The strong were separated from the weak at birth. Robust puppies, when held up by the scruff of their necks for inspection, arched their backs and struggled furiously. Weak puppies hung limply. These were thrown to the mother and the pack, and were devoured in seconds. The strongest litters, with thick, high-quality fur, were dropped in early spring. Soon after birth, the hunter ground down their sharp teeth with a stone or a file in order to prevent the puppies from chewing through their sealskin traces, not always successfully. Between eight months and a year, the pups were harnessed for the first time.

Each team was picketed separately, close to the hunter's home where the dogs lay curled up in the snow for most of the day. Their staple diet of seal meat or walrus skin was cut into small pieces to enable the dogs, which could no longer chew properly, to swallow them whole. They were seldom fed more than every second day in winter, or every third day in summer, for meat bolted in this way remained in the stomach undigested for a long time. Overfed huskies were unwilling to exercise. Faster and more alert when hungry, they were most effective when they were tense and lively before a journey. While the Inuk chopped their meat, the lead dog calmly watched the rest of the pack. Gaining his dominance only after many vicious fights, his title was repeatedly challenged. If in the end he lost a battle, his spirit was broken and he would probably die within months of his defeat.

The hunter respected the natural hierarchy of his team and fed the lead dog first. The other frantic huskies, eyes shot with fire, howled in anticipation and were jerked back by their chains or sealskin tethers each time they rushed at the food. The bliss of silence following the distribution of the meat lasted only for a few seconds, until the discordant chorus began again. Huskies do not bark like other dogs, but howl when they are contented. Apart from the creaking of the ice, this baying is the most arctic of sounds, one which can guarantee visitors many sleepless nights.

Before wood was introduced to the High Arctic in the early nineteenth century, the Inuit built their sledges with seal, whale or walrus bones, and caribou antlers. These ingenious vehicles from five to seven feet long, were two feet wide and no more than seven inches high, and were carved from countless pieces of ivory of various shapes and sizes, all of which fitted neatly into each other like the blocks of a Chinese puzzle. The pieces were lashed tightly together by strands of seal skin threaded through a series of small holes drilled into each block. Nails were unknown, and there were no proper tools. An Inuk patiently flattened, smoothed and finally cut the ivory with a stone. A single runner, which was less than an inch thick, and was square behind and rounded upwards at the front, could take several months to complete.

If it was necessary to travel across the sea ice, two stanchions were built at the rear of the sledge. These were made from walrus ribs which were secured to the runners, and from caribou antlers which were lashed across the top, partly to support the load, but also to enable the driver to control and steer the sledge. The building of a new sledge was the work of a lifetime; it was highly prized, one of the few items which the group allowed to be handed down from father to son, with each generation paying meticulous attention to the continuing restoration of the heirloom.

Where sufficient amounts of ivory were not available, the Inuit had to find other materials for building sledges. Several reindeer skins rolled tightly together and dipped into a hole in the ice of a lake proved an imaginative substitute for ivory. Thoroughly soaked and moulded into shape, the skins were left to freeze. These icy lengths formed the runners for the sledge. Smaller strips were treated in the same way to make the thwarts. Pieces of frozen walrus meat were sometimes used in place of reindeer skin, the large frozen salmon placed across the frame for the thwarts. The makeshift sledges were not particularly elegant but they served the purpose, and Inuit families travelled for long periods on conveyances of this kind. The advantage of such sledges, if starvation threatened, was that the Inuit could always eat them, one cross-piece at a time.

The dimensions of a sledge depended on the terrain. Where the ice was heavily rutted, particularly around Devon Island, Ellesmere and the north Greenland coast, a sledge had to be small so that the hunter could push and drag it easily over the pressure ridges. Inuit living further south, near Hudson Bay and the Foxe Basin, travelled mainly on land. Here, the flatlands were covered with layers of compact, frozen snow, and were free of obstacles, so the sledge was larger, perhaps eighteen feet long.

In the late spring and summer, with temperatures as high as $+5°C$. and the snow soft, the best material for the runners of a sledge was undoubtedly whalebone. But on the frozen snow of autumn and winter, mud was used. Collected during the summer months, it was rolled into balls which were stored until needed for a hunting trip. It was then brought indoors to thaw, shaped into crude runners several inches thick, and left to dry. Hours later, the Inuk planed the mud with his knife, repeatedly wiped it with a wet skin rag, and waited for each thin layer of water to freeze until the finished surface was even, and as smooth as glass.

When preparing to travel, the Inuk spread a seal skin across the thwarts of the sledge, securing it with thongs which were tied to the framework. After the introduction of wood and tools to the Arctic, he was able to take with him enough pine planks to replace the wooden cross-pieces which might be damaged on the journey, and an axe or a broad-bladed knife with which to hack steps for scaling the ice hummocks. He also carried meat for himself and the animals, spare mittens, boots and dried grass for insulation but no water, which would have been too heavy and would have frozen.

An essential item was a lamp for melting snow and ice. This small, stone dish was filled with blubber, preferably that of the seal, which burned more easily and brightly than that of walrus or whale. A twist of dried moss was inserted as a wick, and was ignited by striking a flint chip against a small piece of meteorite or with the help of a bow drill. Sea ice, which was salty, was used only for cooking. Snow, or blocks chopped from icebergs embedded in the icepack, provided the drinking water. As these originated on land, they contained what must be the purest water on earth, snowflakes which fell more than one hundred thousand years ago when there was no pollution, and were compressed and carried to the coast by glaciers.

Having loaded the sledge, the hunter secured its contents with a sealskin rope and covered them with a bear skin. If he needed to rest, or fell through thin ice, he could climb quickly on to it and wrap himself in its warmth. The significance of his preparations would not be lost on the huskies as they strained at their tethers, their impatient howling echoing across the settlement, to be taken up by every dog within earshot. Heedless of the commotion, the hunter would have tied a strong, skin rope approximately six feet long to the front of one of the two sledge runners, slipped the sealskin harness over the heads of each dog, and attached it to an eighteen-foot trace, at the end of which was a small ring of bone. The skin rope on the sledge was threaded through the rings and tied to the second runner with a slip knot for quick release in case the dogs scented a polar bear.

Harnessing the dogs could be tricky, particularly in the Canadian Arctic and Greenland where the dogs were hitched in fan formation. The Inuk had to hold each trace firmly. Once unchained, the excited dogs might disregard his commands, and dash off in all directions on the track of every scent which appealed to them. The hunter's only hope was to throw himself bodily across the traces and hang on until the huskies' exuberance died down, and he could regain control. A wise Inuk anchored his sledge to a stake before hitching it to his team. Ideally, this consisted of ten to twelve dogs, one of which was usually a female. By dominating her, the lead dog gained, and kept, his authority.

Pandemonium erupts during the last few minutes before departure. Finally released from their pickets, the dogs snarl and scrap with each other so that their traces invariably become tangled. The Inuk shouts and cracks his whip, cursing as he steps in to separate them. This done, he must at the same time slip the anchor rope and push the sledge a few yards before clutching the stanchions, and jumping onto the rear runners. The dogs bound forward, and with the lead dog in the middle, fan out, tearing their claws on the hard ice.

Each husky is capable of pulling about eighty pounds. In a day, under ideal conditions on a smooth ice, a team hauling 800 pounds can travel forty miles, but during bad weather and on rough ice, a team would normally cover only a quarter of that distance. Not even the bite of sea salt in their wounds deters them. The Inuk guides the sledge across the ice, and calms the galloping animals with soothing commands. When the team has settled down, after the first few hundred yards, he runs alongside the sledge until he can jump onto the seat of skins where, if the ice is smooth enough, he may sit hour after hour hunched up against the cold.

A loud voice and a long whip are all that are needed to drive a team. In Greenland, the command 'hurry' is the same as the signal to start: 'Aak-ka-ka-kaah! Aak-ka-ka-kaah!', or a short, barking 'Ah! Ah!'. In the islands of the Northwest Passage, however, the driver shouts a clipped 'Huut! Huut!' The order 'slow down', or 'halt', in Greenland is a long, drawn out 'Ayee! Ayee!', and a simple 'Woa!' in the Canadian Arctic. The Greenlander indicates an intended right turn by repeatedly shouting a high-pitched 'Illi-yilli-yilli', and a left turn with 'yoo-yoo-yoo-yoo'. On the other side of Baffin Bay, 'Woa-ek' and 'Aey-ek' are the relevant commands.

The commands to turn are frequently accompanied by a crack of the whip, aimed at the opposite side of the team from the desired direction. The 25-foot sealskin lash is tapered at the end, has a tendency to wrap itself round the body and can lacerate the face of the unskilled. Many young Inuit learning to handle a team have been blinded in this way, but a proficient driver can flick the lash with great accuracy, and time after time hit the same quarter of an inch of the dog's hide. Such skill is used sparingly. A good driver whips only when a husky misbehaves or, in earlier times, when he needed to fend off dogs that had caught the scent of his new bearskin trousers.

Occasionally, the hunter leaps off the sledge and runs alongside it for warmth, careful to avoid too much exertion. Perspiration can encase his body in ice, and cold air inhaled too quickly can freeze inside his lungs. His circulation restored, the Inuk sprints ahead of the sledge, and waits for it to draw level. This requires accurate judgement, particularly when travelling alone. Should his foot slip, he may see his dogs, the sledge and his provisions disappearing in a cloud of swirling snow hundreds of miles from home.

Riding a sledge over flat ice becomes dreamlike. The dogs pull steadily, their ears flat on their heads and their tails streaming behind them. The sound of their panting and the hiss of the sledge runners is mesmerising. There is a sense of complete isolation. It seems as if there are no other living creatures in the vast landscape. As the miles and the hours pass, it is easy to become lost in a stream of thoughts, and be lulled into a trance by the monotony of the journey, until the cold penetrates the clothing, or a change of direction is required.

The lack of dust particles in the atmosphere increases the visibility so that distances become distorted. Mountains that appear to be a few miles away may be more than a hundred miles distant. The scenery does not seem to change very much despite hours, or days, of hard driving. Huskies will haul a sledge until they drop dead, but driving them too hard is counter-productive as tired dogs take days to recover, and may not reach peak condition again for several months.

A journey across entirely level ice is rare. Although sea ice may seem flat, it is normally rippled with mounds of frozen snow and small pressure ridges which must be negotiated carefully, the driver pushing and pulling his sledge from side to side to avoid the obstacles. Driving a dog team is hard work. More than anything else, drivers and dogs detest powdery snow. The dogs sink in it up to their chests, and the hunter must somehow extricate the floundering animals, and keep his own strength. Nowadays, he can clamp on a pair of skis and make a track, but centuries ago, he had to flatten the snow by stamping a pathway with his feet. Ice hummocks twenty or thirty feet high are another hazard, and the driver must weigh the exertion required to drag his dogs over them against his own level of tiredness. If he becomes exhausted, he is likely to die with his animals.

Another hazard, especially in the late spring and early summer, is the ice cracking without warning, forcing the dogs to swim across an open lead, towing the sledge after them. On land, it was important for traditional hunters always to be alert for stones poking through the snow. Damage to the mud runners of the old-style sledges had to be repaired immediately. The smallest chip caused a drastic reduction in speed. The most efficient repair was to press frozen walrus meat, free of fat and chewed until malleable, into the crack like putty. As it took valuable time to light a stove and melt snow to provide water for the ice layers of the runners, the Inuk urinated on them, carefully allowing each application to freeze before adding another, until the finished surface was smooth again.

The experienced traveller keeps a close eye on the weather. At the first sign of an approaching blizzard he quickly builds an *illuliaq*, or pitches his tent before the wind strengthens. A tent should always be sited on sea ice, well away from icebergs and from the coast, where the wind might bring falls of ice and rock. For protection against the storm, a snow wall to the windward side, approximately three-quarters of the height of the tent and made strong enough to support drifting snow, gives additional insulation against the cold, and prevents the wind from tugging the flaps of the tent.

Having unloaded the sledge and stowed the contents safe from the wind and the dogs, it is important to stow the rifle under the caribou skins covering the ground, close to the side of the tent where the metalwork can be kept cold. This avoids condensation which, once the temperature rises inside, would otherwise settle on the metal. Failure to observe this simple rule could mean that in an emergency, within seconds of leaving the tent, the condensation would freeze, rendering useless the trigger mechanism of the rifle.

Outside, the dogs, secured to an iron stake or a piece of ice, jostle for position in the snow, each struggling for the warmest place at the centre of a knotted heap. Having quietened down, their muzzles tucked under their tails, they huddle together until covered with snow. Here, they sleep, if necessary for several days, until the storm blows itself out.

Inside the tent, the principal difficulty today is to keep the hairs shed by caribou skins out of meals, or cups of tea and coffee. Generations ago, a stormbound Inuk would survive on seal or walrus meat, and blubber. He would melt a piece of ice chopped from an iceberg when thirsty, and scoop a small hole in the sea ice underneath his caribou skins. Lighting his blubber lamp, he would place it next to the block of ice at the edge of the hole, so that the pure water dripped into it. By the time the hole was filled, the water was polluted with soot from the lamp. This, however, was unlikely to deter an Inuk, down on his hands and knees, drinking noisily.

The wind abating and the sledge reloaded, the hunter relieved himself either on the tent site, or inside the *illuliaq*. When he had finished, he released the picketed dogs to clean up. Huskies have an insatiable fondness for human excrement, which was useful for clearing a camp site, but which could create problems for the solitary traveller confined to a small area by rough ice. The cold does not encourage a sledge driver to waste time while performing the requirements of nature. A pack of dogs fighting viciously at his heels in order to wolf down a warm meal made speed imperative.

Under clearing skies, the driver would resume his journey, having slowed his dogs to a steady trot. Sitting on top of the sledge with his chin on his chest and his legs tucked under him, the Inuk would sink into a reverie, his thoughts probably revolving around the storm of the past few days, and on *Sila*, the great force which he believed resided in all things, and which governed the lives of all Inuit.

Sub-consciously, he might touch the strand of carved animals hanging round his neck, perhaps seeking re-assurance from the tiny, ivory amulets which enabled him to be on good terms with the spiritual powers. He believed that *Sila* spoke not with words, but through storms and blizzards and heaving seas, or, when all was well, through the presence of game, and the sun shining on the ice. If a hunter lived in accordance with the taboos, and had not abused life, the omnipotent *Sila* was said to return to the infinite nothingness. It was when an Inuk was alone on the ice with only his dogs for company, that he felt closest to Him.

CHAPTER 7

Amulets and Angakoks

During spring and summer, when they applied themselves to the practicalities of community life, the generally superstitious and fearful Inuit appeared to be content and cheerful. Yet perpetual sunshine can be wearying, white-outs and summer fog can deprive the senses and induce disorientation. Beneath their carefree appearance, the Inuit in winter often harboured a host of secret terrors. Before the missionaries and traders brought Christianity and a more modern way of life, their thoughts focused gloomily on hunger, sickness and a world of spirits. The Inuit told Fritjiof Nansen that they believed that every object, animate and inanimate, had a soul, its *inua*. Everything was alive: stones, sledges, harpoons, the creaking ice, the waves in the sea and the air they breathed. Even hunger, pain, sleep, love and laughter were thought to be possessed.

Such beliefs, ridiculed by most people today, were natural for small groups of primitive people living in a vast and isolated world, which was in constant motion from rock falls, heaving seas and creaking ice. Thousands of years ago, when the early Inuit first saw glaciers giving birth to icebergs, they must have been awestruck, convinced that the process was the activity of live creatures.

Nansen surmised that when a primitive Inuk dreamed he was out hunting, and awoke to discover that he had not moved, he could not help but believe that his body was inhabited by an *inua*, a word which originally signified 'living being', and from which he took his name. The Inuk must have reasoned that if glaciers could produce offspring like Inuit women, they must also be governed by *inua*, and if that were true, the same must surely apply to the animals and birds, the rivers which spawned the fish, the mountains and headlands which produced rocks, and everything seen and unseen, or experienced. In some communities, people and animals were thought to contain several *inua*, one for each bone in the body.

Some Inuit believed that animals, inanimate objects and the earth itself were inhabited by the souls of the dead. In parts of the Arctic, the Northern Lights were stillborn children at play. The Kamchatkans of

Siberia believed that animals and insects were reborn in the underworld. A giant polar bear sucking water through its huge nostrils at the bottom of the sea was thought to be the cause of whirlpools. After death, human spirits could travel to special half-worlds between the earth and sky, or beneath the earth and sea. The upper region was blessed with sunshine, an abundance of wildlife, and the time in which to sing. The lower half was colder and darker, very like the earth with snow, ice and terrible storms. These spirit worlds were the equivalent of Heaven and Hell, although there is no evidence to suggest that an Inuk's behaviour in life had any bearing on the ultimate selection.

The supreme Deity was *Sila*, the vital force which created and permeated all things and, like the Chinese *Tao*, was inexhaustible and intangible. The wrath of *Sila*, expressed through blizzards and storms, had to be avoided at all cost, although the Inuit were equally anxious to appease the numerous other mythological figures and spirits which influenced their lives. There was Sedna, the sea goddess who provided animals for hunting; Narssuk, the giant child who lived in space and, presumably with the help of *Sila*, was said to control the weather; and the Moon Man, who determined the tides and, when angered by Inuit ignoring their taboos, eclipsed the moon. The imaginations of most Inuit in the Far North were filled with such a variety of supernatural creatures that it seems miraculous they were able to keep their sanity. A few spirits were helpful, warning kayakers of the dangers ahead, or helping hunters to kill a whale or walrus, but most of them were to be feared.

Sickness and death were the work of *ilisiituk*, who secretly dabbled in magic. Much hated, these evil old men and women brewed potions from plants and insects, and human flesh and bones, like wizards and witches in the Middle Ages. They were soul robbers who took possession of hunters, turning them against their families and persuading them to reject the community for a life in the mountains, where the victims, known as *qivitok*, became half-savage. Rumour and exaggerated fear gave these unfortunates an unwarranted reputation. Some were rumoured to be thirty feet high, and able to leap from one mountain to another, hunting without weapons.

The *ilisiituk* were particularly adept at preparing sorcerers' monsters, or *tupilek*, small animals employed to inflict injury or death on the *ilisiituk*'s enemies. This was done secretly. A variety of bones and skins were collected, wrapped in a skin bag with seal meat caught by the intended victim, and a piece taken from his clothing. The *ilisiitok*, wearing his anorak back to front with the hood over his face, sat on the banks of a river or fjord, chanting magic formulae and waving charms over the bag to bring the *tupilak* to life. When it had emerged and grown to full size, the grotesque creature slipped into the water, disguised itself as a seal or walrus, and swam close to the enemy against whom it had been despatched. As soon as the hunter came within harpoon range, the *tupilak* struck. Usually the Inuk was doomed. If he managed to escape, and the monster failed in its task, the *tupilak* would return to kill its creator.

With so many spirits and supernatural creatures abroad, it was important to observe the manifold taboos and rules of life evolved from the experience and wisdom of previous generations. Conscious of the sensibilities of the earth, which was a living thing, the Inuit tried to avoid placing the skins of dead animals directly on the ground in case their spirits passed into the soil. The death of animals was mourned, and words which might be offensive to their souls, such as 'harpoon' or 'knife', were avoided. Inuit who did not show respect for the animals they killed, or incurred the displeasure of the deities, could bring storms, poor hunting and sickness to a village. At such times, many Inuit died from starvation, leaving the survivors confused and uncertain. It was in response to their need for guidance that the *angakok* emerged to assume an influential and powerful position as spiritual counsellor, doctor and policeman in the community.

An *angakok*, usually male, was the equivalent of the American Indian medicine man, the African witch doctor, or the spiritualist's medium in the west. He claimed to be clairvoyant, conversant with spirits, and capable of outstanding feats of mental agility. On southern Baffin Island, Inuit legend describes how the first *angakok* experienced his astral body flying through the roof, able to see the souls of his companions. On the Melville Peninsula, he was an Inuk who dived into the sea to persuade the Sea Mother, Sedna, to provide enough game to end a famine. Other Inuit believed the first *angakut* were spirits who descended from the sky, looking for unborn children whose bodies they could inhabit, and from which they could practise their shamanic knowlege.

The *angakok*'s principal tasks were to communicate with the relevant deities and spirits, to ensure beneficial weather and hunting, and to instruct the Inuit in the complexities of group taboos, making sure that they abided by them. He was also their doctor and, as such, was required to do battle with the evil spirits responsible for causing sickness. Minor illnesses were blown, sucked and thumped out of the body, or brushed away with bird feathers. Burns were treated with an application of blood and fat, or phlegm. Wounds were cleansed with urine, boils were lanced, broken bones were set and severely frostbitten limbs were amputated.

In the case of internal illness, the patient was exhorted publicly to confess to a breach of the taboos. Such transgressions were believed to attach themselves to the soul, weighing it down with sickness and ultimately causing death. Confession was usually the only cure needed, but in extreme cases the *angakok* might assign new taboos as a precaution. When he examined a patient, his verdict was awaited with dread. If he decided that he could not, or would not, help the sick person, there was no alternative for the unfortunate Inuk but to return home and die.

Magic was frequently used to effect cures. One popular legend tells how a boy's eyesight was restored after his local *angakok* employed loons to carry him to a lake, where they repeatedly dipped him in the water. Arctic loons, or black-throated divers, were closely associated with shamanism. Their feathers adorned the shaman's costume and their skulls, decorated with artificial eyes, were used as ceremonial artifacts. Siberian *angakut* used the birds as familiars, to help them to embark on long journeys to the spirit world. If an Inuk was sick because his soul had been stolen by spirits or an evil shaman, it was the *angakok*'s responsibility to find, recover and restore it to its rightful owner.

Such journeys could be undertaken only after considerable preparation. The ability to induce a trance was essential. An *angakok* would fast, and deny himself water until he began to hallucinate, or retreat to an isolated spot on the outskirts of the settlement to meditate. To concentrate his mind, he rubbed a stone in a circle on the ground for hours at a time, like an assistant to a master of Japanese brush painting preparing an ink block on a stone trough.

In winter, when the Inuit lived in their stone and turf houses, he would use another tactic and hold a seance similar to those organised in western communities today. With the windows and entrances covered, and the lamps extinguished, the *angakok* sat in the centre of the gathering, singing and chanting. The participants, hushed and fearful, listened as his voice, keeping time to the beat of a skin drum, ranged from groans and moans to a high-pitched whining and hysterical shrieking. Often a practised ventriloquist, his performance included rustling and whistling, sounds purporting to be voices from the underworld. In this way, the *angakok* convinced his audience that he was battling with the offending spirits.

If bad weather prevented hunting and the settlement faced starvation, drastic measures were needed. The *angakok* was then required to travel through space to appease the Moon Man, or descend to the depths of the oceans to pacify Sedna, a goddess common to all Inuit legend from Siberia to Greenland. Among the Inuit of western Canada, this was achieved by building an *illuliaq* on the sea ice, and through a hole carved in the floor, the shaman and his audience sang to her. Her anger quelled, Sedna would explain which taboos had been broken. The *angakok*, acting as mediator, exhorted confessions from the onlookers until the goddess was satisfied, and relenting, replenished the supply of game.

In the eastern Arctic and Greenland, the process was not so simple. In most parts of the Arctic, communication with Sedna was difficult and dangerous. Variously known as *Nerrivik, Neqiviq,* and *Arnarkuagssoq,* she was the most powerful of all influences on the Inuit, with the single exception of *Sila.* From all accounts, she was an irascible woman, and with good reason. Inuit mythology, clearly embellished in recent times, tells how Sedna married a seagull whose eyesight was so poor that he was obliged to wear glasses. When his wife saw him without them for the first time, she was appalled by his hideous eyes, and sobbed throughout the night. At dawn, when her husband was out hunting, she fled in a skin boat with her father, and sailed far out to sea. The seagull, finding his wife gone, was so angered that he sought out the boat and attacked the occupants. The frightened father, trying to save his own skin, threw his daughter over the side, and when she clung to the gunwales, chopped off her hands so that she disappeared into the depths.

Encouraged by *angakut* who had a vested interest in sustaining and nurturing superstition, the Inuit believed that the secret sins of those who did not confess sank to the bottom of the sea, and became entangled in Sedna's hair where they turned into lice. These impurities, and the irritation caused by them, attracted the fish and mammals away from the coasts, depriving the hunters of their game. The solution for such a crisis was for the *angakok* to descend to the sea bed and, by combing Sedna's hair, soothe her ill-temper.

Perhaps the most difficult of all his duties, this could not be done without the help of ministering spirits known as *tornat.* Most *angakut* owned several of these familiars, using them variously as counsellors, assistants or avengers. They were despatched to their tasks in much the same way, and for similar reasons, as the *tupilek* sent forth by those who practised black magic.

The journey to the sea bed was long and dangerous. The shaman and his *tornak* first passed through the underworld, where they battled with the spirits of former enemies, negotiating crevasses and running the gauntlet of angry, biting seals. A vicious dog guarded Sedna's home, the entrance to which narrowed until it was no wider than the blade of a knife. At this point, the *angakok* was obliged to cross an abyss to reach the house where the irritable old woman sat, flailing arms as big as whales' tailfins in an attempt to rid herself of the lice. If he was not agile enough to avoid her, a single blow would end his mission. Sedna did not always welcome visitors, and it was often necessary for the *angakok* and his *tornak* to hold her down while they combed her. That done, and the lice eaten, Sedna grew quiet and in gratitude returned the animals again to the hunting grounds.

Despite the difficulties of his profession, the advantages of being an *angakok* were considerable. His ability to foretell the future and restore the balance of life gave him a position of authority, influence and power. He was respected and feared, and was said to be immortal. In Inuit terms, he was also a rich man. Although he was not reimbursed for services to the community at large, he could charge more or less what he liked when administering spiritual or medical advice to individual Inuk. A broad-bladed knife or harpoon was usually payment enough for a minor illness but, in more serious cases, he might demand a number of dogs or a tent, a kayak or a whalebone sledge.

If there was a chance that the patient might die, he could insist on receiving his fee in advance, and as the life of the sick Inuk was in the balance, there was no alternative but to pay. Inuit mythology does not explain what the *angakok* did with his growing collection of material goods, but in some cases payment was made with services. Remuneration for assisting at a birth might be the favours of the mother on recovery. The solution to the problems of a childless couple was never questioned. Many women regarded it as an honour to lie with an *angakok*, and their husbands allegedly welcomed and paid for it, especially if the association was fruitful.

There was no shortage of applicants for the position of *angakok*, but the chosen neophyte was expected to serve a testing apprenticeship of as much as ten years. This was to be undertaken secretly, and involved spending long periods in solitude, during which the novice learned how to induce a trance and find the spirits which, once touched, would become his helpers. He was required to slip into a state of meditation so deep that he would die of fright, and return back to life again. Other ordeals included battling with a polar bear and being eaten by a walrus, after which he was expected to repair his broken body, and return to the settlement in one piece. His probationary period served, the apprentice publicly proclaimed his attainment and entered into practice as a junior partner to the established community *angakok*.

Although solitude was necessary for many of his activities, the *angakok*'s efforts to change the weather, cure the sick and fight evil spirits, or visit Sedna and the Moon Man, were always performed in front of an audience. He also officiated at various ceremonies, especially in Alaska where milder weather left the Inuit less concerned about survival. Elaborate rituals and dances, at which the participants wore distinctive costumes, were held throughout the year. Masks to hide their identity from the spirits were made from skin and bone, or when it was available, wood. Seals' teeth were fitted in the mouth of the mask. Eyebrows and moustaches were made with dog fur, and beards with feathers. Along the outside edge, a string of exquisitely carved ivory charms was attached to prevent spirits entering the eyes, ears, mouth and nostrils. Mittens, which reached to the shoulders, were adorned with jade and pieces of white quartz, or the beaks of birds.

These amulets were worn as a protection against evil spirits and soul robbers, and could also be made from odd pieces of hair, skin and fingernails, or tiny animal carvings of ivory and bone. They were normally worn next to the skin, but women wanting strong sons sometimes carried them in the topknots of their hair. Men, hoping for safe travel and good hunting, wore them on belts and armbands, or packed them in skin pouches hanging round their necks. Others were placed in the roof of their homes, on sleeping benches, or in their kayaks. Especially beneficial were the eyes and beaks, claws and feathers of birds. Strings of ravens' feet were hung round the necks of newborn children as a preventative against hunger. The foot of a raven, a bird held in high esteem because it could find food in the most inaccessible places, was considered the most potent. Wood, which had no feelings, was thought to ensure a rich and painless life. Courage could be gained from the skin of a polar bear's upper jaw. The skull of a fox imparted cunning. Girls anxious for an easy pregnancy carried the eggs of a snow bunting in their clothing. Many amulets were handmade, and a miniature pair of *kamiks*, for example, was said to protect the wearer from drowning.

With so many accoutrements dangling from their costumes, the dancing Inuit produced a rattling sound as they writhed and gyrated to the beat of the ceremonial drum. This was the only musical instrument in the whole of the Far North. Its large circular frame, more than two feet across, was made from the ribs of a seal or walrus, although from the nineteenth century, wood was used. The skin for the drum was taken from the throat of a walrus or the stomach lining of a whale, caribou or dog. The drummer, holding the instrument in one hand by a small handle attached to the frame, stood with his legs apart, knees slightly bent, swaying from side to side as he beat the rim, rather than the skin of the drum, with a short stick of bone. As the rhythm took hold, he allowed his head to vacillate in an exaggerated fashion until he fell into a trance.

At this point, another Inuk would rise from the audience and stand directly in front of him, singing a few simple notes. There were no words: just a pulsating 'Aya-ya-a ... aya-a ...' sung in quarter and half tones along half an octave. Soon, the onlookers would be captivated by the mood and monotony of the music, and join in with a refrain. As the beat grew more insistent, the singer's voice rose to a piercing scream, at which point the drummer intervened, singing his own phrases. The two men continued to sing alternately, so that the performance became a duel, rather than a duet. Sweating profusely, they continued until they were physically and emotionally drained, and other musical combatants took over, singing throughout the night and well into the next day.

Another contest involved throat singing. This captivating use of the glottis and vocal chords was a technique which affected the modulation of the voice, and was practised mainly by women. Singing was the Inuits' great joy. When hunting was productive, songs from one voice or another echoed continually across the settlements. So important was their singing that song contests and drum dances eventually evolved into a unique judicial process for settling disputes.

Ever fearful of ridicule, the litigants took turns in singing satirical verses which lampooned the misdemeanours and failings of their opponents. The skills of the hunter or parts of his anatomy were derided. Each taunted the other. This musical banter, accompanied by outrageous over-acting, brought success to the contestant who raised the loudest laughs. For the loser, however, the experience could be so painful that the shame of defeat forced many an Inuk into exile.

Inuit songs and poems were brief and did not rhyme or scan, yet were as simplistic and direct as the Haiku poetry of Japan. The following examples demonstrate a similar preoccupation with nature.

> The mighty weather
> storms through my soul,
> and I tremble.

> Bleached bones!
> Wind-dried skeleton
> crumbling in the wind!

Inuit art is stark. In all their work, the refinement and concentration of ideas reflects a life in which there is time only for essentials. Yet their environment, the constant battle against starvation and an existence based on fear has produced a rich culture. From the dawn of time, the ability to sculpt and carve was as necessary as eating and sleeping. Tools, lamps and pots had to be hewn from bone, ivory and stone. The desire for amulets led to a spate of miniature carvings representing the surrounding wildlife. Close study of the habits of animals and birds, observed against the immense arctic landscape which so isolates non-white objects that they stand out in sharp detail, enhanced the Inuit powers of observation and understanding, and gave poignancy to their sculpture, poetry and painting. The Inuit captured not only the form, but the essence of their subjects, showing brilliantly the arrogance of a polar bear, the fear of a seal, the evil of a *tupilak*, or the humour of a drum dancer.

The Inuit's intimate relationship with Nature continued almost undisturbed until the mid-eighteenth century, when they were first exposed to the culture of white men from the south. A few communities, notably the Polar Inuit of Thule, in northwest Greenland, remained isolated until the beginning of this century, and one group, in Angmagssalik in East Greenland, had virtually no contact with the rest of the world until World War Two. Yet in these relatively few short years, foreign influence has eroded and undermined the old hunting culture.

In Alaska and Canada, it is now the foreign tourists who wear the furs. The Inuit have adopted down-filled parkas. Apart from Greenland, where it is still an important means of transport, the dog team has become a rarity. Today, young Inuit with mirrored sunglasses race noisily across the ice on Ski-doos purchased with the help of social welfare payments. Others spray the walls of empty wooden frame houses with graffiti. Poverty and despair are dividing families, leaving the Inuit confused and bitter.

The *angakok* is dead, replaced by doctors, nurses and the spiritual surrogates of white bishops in the South, whose own way of life has engulfed the Inuit, and left them dependent on the very industrial mono-culture which threatens to destroy them. Its relentless advance has turned them into second-class citizens in an emerging, largely unknown and under-developed world – a Fourth World, in which other nations have shown little interest apart from the exploitation of its people and its resources.

PART TWO

The Marauders

CHAPTER 8

Whalers and Whisky

The erosion of the Inuit hunting culture began with the arrival of the European whalers. These rough seafarers were intent exclusively on plundering the seas and exploiting the local inhabitants, whom they treated with contempt. Money was their only interest. Lured into arctic waters by the promise of handsome profits, they spent months working round the clock in miserable conditions, their lives frequently in danger.

In the European markets, their cargoes were awaited eagerly. The strong and flexible bone plates which enabled the whale to filter its food from the sea were used for the corsets of fashionable women, for the ribs of umbrellas and in the manufacture of furniture. On the tables of the aristocracy whale tongues were considered a delicacy. The price of whale oil, which was used to fuel street lamps, was so high that the income from two or three whales was enough to pay for a new ship.

Vessels from Holland and Britain, Germany, Scandinavia and North America came to Baffin Bay and Lancaster Sound as if to a seaborne gold rush. The Inuit, who had lived in complete isolation for 5,000 years, were completely unprepared for such an invasion. In their innocence, they welcomed the newcomers, and were deeply hurt when the whaling crews abused their traditional arctic hospitality, cheating them shamelessly and sowing the seeds of mischief which would bedevil their lives until the present day.

Lars Dalager, a Danish trader in Godthab, reported to his government in 1756 that English whalers had stolen from one settlement in northwest Greenland the Inuits' entire supply of whaling products, and that in another village, Dutch whalers had not only taken the blubber and whalebone from five whales, but also attempted to kidnap an Inuk. The whalers were frequently drunk and violent, sometimes frightening the Inuit away from their settlements. Svend Sandgreen, a Danish trader from Godhavn, wrote that 'the vice of drunkenness has unfortunately become rife,' and in 1775 reported that Dutch whalers had 'snatched' a whale that had been harpooned by the Inuit. When the Greenlanders paddled out in their *umiaks* in an attempt to retrieve it, Sandgreen wrote, the Dutch ship tried to run them down.[1]

The Basques, who probably began whaling in the eleventh century, were the first to arrive in arctic waters. According to Basque tradition, they were led there by the baleen and sperm whales, which during the thirteenth century abandoned the Bay of Biscay. The Basques, armed only with hand-held harpoons and lances, hunted the whales from small, open boats, and it is possible that the whales left following a depletion of their stock. By now, the compass had passed into common use, enabling the Basques to follow the whales across the North Atlantic. Moreover, a harpoon shaped like a crossbow made it possible to catch the whales directly from the decks of the larger ships needed for the voyage. By 1372, the whalers were reputed to have reached Newfoundland, where Basque names are still in evidence. The Basques continued to follow the whales northwards, into Davis Strait and Hudson Bay, and for 200 years they hunted them without competition. In 1576, aware of their success, the English Muscovy Company sought and was granted a monopoly to kill whales, but with a singular lack of business acumen took no action for nearly forty years. Not until the navigator Henry Hudson reported seeing schools of whales off Spitsbergen, where he had been searching for a northeast passage to Asia, did the company begin to exploit whale resources in the Arctic Ocean. Despite hiring experienced Basque crews, the fortunes of the early English expeditions were limited. This was partly due to the presence of the Dutch, who viewed the English intrusion into their whaling grounds with hostility, a rivalry tantamount to open warfare which persisted until the late seventeenth century.

With more experience than the British, the Dutch enjoyed a dominant position, establishing a shore-based processing plant at Smeerenburg, on northwest Spitsbergen. The factory enabled the whalers to continue hunting while the men ashore boiled the blubber and stored the oil in casks ready for shipment home. A huge increase in personnel was needed for the efficient running of the plant, which was soon surrounded by a small town, known as Blubber Town. At the height of the season, apart from the British, German, Danish and Norwegian contingents, 300 Dutch ships and 18,000 men were employed by the Smeerenburg industry. At times, 450 ships were engaged in hunting and processing whales. The continual daylight of the arctic summer allowed men to work shifts day and night, and the outcome was inevitable. Eventually, the whale stocks dwindled, and were finally depleted to 'commercial' extinction.

New whaling grounds had to be found. The Basques, who had previously fished off Iceland and Greenland, pointed the whalers in the direction of Davis Strait and Baffin Bay. But once more, the Dutch in 1719 were the first to arrive, followed six years later by the British, whose fortunes had hitherto been mixed, with the result that the merchants were slow to invest money in a trade which, despite the potential profits, appeared to be languishing.

To stimulate the industry, parliament passed The Bounty Act of 1749, entitling merchants to receive £1.0s.0d. a ton for every British ship of more than 200 tons fitted out specifically for whaling. This offer was subsequently doubled, and with the demand for oil and bone increasing, the number of vessels sailing to the Arctic grew steadily: nearly fifty in 1753, more than eighty three years later. By the turn of the century, approximately 140 British ships and 6,000 men were plying arctic waters; with the ships of other nations, the whaling fleet off the coast of Greenland every summer amounted to several hundred vessels, and more than 10,000 men.

Their prey was the bowhead, or Greenland whale, seventy feet long, and weighing sixty tons. Migrating north through Baffin Bay and the Bering Straits in the spring, this cumbersome creature could yield twenty tons of oil. It was a prime source of food, fuel and light for the Inuit west of the Mackenzie Delta and in Alaska, where a whaling cult evolved round the hunt. To this day, festivals are held to honour the mammal. Then, as now, there was no wastage; the flesh was stored in the permafrost, the carcass stripped of the materials which enabled the Inuit to survive. European whalers took only the blubber and whalebone, or baleen, discarding the remainder into blood-filled seas.

To offset the expenses of a voyage, a ship's crew needed to catch at least three medium-sized whales, yielding forty to fifty tons of oil. On many occasions, they returned home with 150 tons, enough to finance possible losses for years ahead. The smallest whale was worth more than £100; a large one could fetch £1,500, but a sailor's average monthly wage was only £3.0s.0d., or £67.0s.0d. (about $100) at today's values. The Master received £8.0s.0d., the Mate £5.0s.0d. and the Second Mate £3.15s.0d. To bolster enthusiasm for the task ahead, the ship's complement, of about fifty men, was paid a percentage on the cargo. The spektioneer, or chief harpooner, for example, received an additional 10s.6d. for every ton of whalebone, and 7s.9d. per ton of oil in addition to his monthly salary of £2.15s.0d. A sliding scale reduced this for the ordinary seaman, who was paid a wage of £1.10s.0d a month, 1s.6d. per ton of oil, and 2s.0d. per ton of baleen.

When the three-masted sailing ships were replaced by coal-fired vessels, the owners' costs rose dramatically and a cargo of at least eighty tons was required to make a voyage profitable. Despite the higher margin, the introduction of steam, and subsequently the explosive harpoon, enabled ships to travel further and faster, tracking down and catching the whales more efficiently. Conditions on board were appalling. The decks, which leaked like sieves, were coated with blubber grease, an unctuous substance which pervaded every corner of the ship. If the voyage was successful, coal was sometimes shovelled out of the bunkers and piled on deck ready for use as required, while the increasing mounds of blubber and baleen were stored below. Indescribably filthy, the decks were strewn with sawdust to prevent the men slipping in the glutinous mess, which clung to the soles of their boots and was continually being trampled below decks.

The risk of fire was considerable, but cooking was permitted day and night, and the galley fires were not once dampened during the six month voyage. For men who might be away from the ship for as long as 24 hours after a whale was sighted, with no food or sleep until they returned, it was important that they should have the opportunity of cooking a hot meal throughout the day and the night. Before leaving harbour, each man was given a ration of food, which he kept in his sea chest. It was supplemented by whatever game he could catch during the voyage, although for obvious reasons, whale meat was unpopular.

Commander Albert Hastings Markham, who sailed with the Dundee whaler *Arctic* in 1873, records how food stocks were replenished with the meat of seal and little auks. The latter were so numerous that 45 of them were killed at one discharge from a gun, and 33 more from a second shot. In all, nearly 1,500 birds were brought down, including finches, eider duck, loons, dovekeys, petrels, terns and a gyrfalcon. Additionally, the crew killed nineteen narwhals, twenty seals and twelve polar bears, one of which was kept alive and presented to Clifton Zoological Gardens. Commander Markham, whose attitude to wildlife left much to be desired, recorded how one bear had been shot.

> On rounding the berg, we observed Master Bruin ... a ball from my little rifle, however, stopped his career, passing through his skull and killing him instantaneously. The fact of his being clothed in his winter coat makes his skin more valuable than it otherwise would be ... We are now fully prepared and anxious to wage war with the huge monsters of the deep.[2]

As the ships rounded Cape Farewell, the southernmost tip of Greenland, and sailed up the west coast into Davis Strait, the boats were hauled up from below and hoisted alongside the ship. Whaling ships carried seven or eight catchers, each with a designated crew of six or seven men, who at this juncture of the voyage stowed the harpoons and coiled the ropes in readiness for the hunt. The operation, known as 'spanning on', was carried out with great care, as a knotted rope could cost the men their lives. The harpoons were made of soft Swedish steel, which was less brittle than the British product, and not so likely to snap when the stricken whale turned and dived, with the possibility of losing the ship's owners more than £1,000.

Unsuspecting, the whales played off the Greenland coast, waiting for the ice to break up so that they could reach their breeding grounds further north. In time, the whalers would follow them all the way to Melville Bay and Lancaster Sound. As soon as a ship approached the vicinity of the whales, the engines were stopped. Posting a continual watch from the crow's nest, the captain guided the ship round icebergs and through the pack ice, which was in constant motion. When a whale was sighted the boats put out immediately, their every move watched anxiously from the decks of the mother ship.

The crews always endeavoured to approach their quarry from behind, in the area where its acute hearing and eyesight were least effective. When the harpooner was successful, cries of 'A fall! A fall!' echoed for miles over the water. Chaos ensued. As the whale dived, the coiled rope, of best untarred hemp, snaked out at high speed over a bollard in the bows, whining and smoking from the friction. Frantically, the harpooner doused it with water to prevent fire from snapping it.

Simultaneously, a jack was hoisted to signal that the boat was 'fast'. On the parent ship, seamen dashed about half-dressed and bleary-eyed as orders were shouted to lower more boats. Their crews rowed furiously to assist the 'fast' boat as the whale headed for the firm ice. By now, the wounded creature could have run out more than a mile of line. This was a worrying time for the captain. Expensive line might be lost, and the crews in the 'loose' boats pursuing the whale through the swirling pack ice could be crushed between floes 25 feet thick and weighing several tons. Many men saved themselves by jumping out of the boats and hauling them onto a floe before resuming the chase. A whale struck by a second harpoon while surfacing for air might be spurred into renewed action, and it was not uncommon for a bowhead to tow two or three boats along at five or six knots, a welcome rest for the exhausted oarsmen, but a terrifying experience should the boat be halted by a head-on collision with ice.

When the disabled whale could no longer resist, the 'loose' boats encircled it and the crews repeatedly plunged their lances deep into its body. Unable to withstand such an attack, the whale finally rolled onto its back and died, to the cheers of its tormentors. Drenched with blood, the men cut holes in the fins, which were lashed together to prevent the catch snagging on underwater obstructions as its bulk was towed back to the ship. Once alongside, tackle from the fore and main rigging was attached to the tailfin and the whale's jaw, while the fins were secured to the upper deck. That done, the flensing process could begin.

Armed with blubber spades, half a dozen men leapt onto the whale, wearing crampons to prevent them slipping, and proceeded to cut out long strips of fat. These were hoisted on deck and hacked into chunks approximately two feet square so that they could be stowed temporarily below decks. Finally, the whalebone was extracted and the remains of the whale were discarded into an opaque and viscous sea, crimson for a quarter of a mile around. Later, in a process known as 'making off', the blubber would be cut into smaller pieces and separated from the whale skin. The *mattak* was thrown overboard, rich pickings for the seabirds swarming round the ship.

The perils of whaling were so great that, however lucrative the trade, the men more than earned their wages. Many of them paid with their lives. Boats were tossed high into the air with a single blow of the whale's tailfin, toppling its crew into the icy water. Those who were not killed instantly would attempt to swim to an icefloe, but so great was the cold that the strength of all but the hardiest men failed. The majority slipped away to their fate.

Numerous vessels found themselves irretrievably trapped after trying to force a passage through the ice by alternately steaming ahead and astern, while the men dashed from side to side to roll the ship and crush the ice alongside. As the pressure built up, great masses of ice were pushed over, often engulfing the vessel. In the years when gales from the south packed the ice into Melville Bay, as many as twenty ships were lost in this way, and hundreds of men perished. When the order to abandon ship was given, some members of the crew, fearful of what might be in store for them, made immediately for the casks of brandy, rum and whisky, a decision which further imperilled their lives.

Notwithstanding the risks, the European whaling ships returned year after year to amass fortunes for their owners. In 1873, the crew of the *Arctic* caught 28 whales between May and August, returning to Dundee with an unprecedented 265 tons of whale oil and 14 tons of baleen, a cargo worth £19,000, or approximately £425,000 at today's values. At the peak of the whaling bonanza, with several hundred ships in the area, the whalers were depleting stocks in Davis Strait and Baffin Bay at the rate of 2,000 to 3,000 whales a season.

American merchants were equally determined to capitalise on European demand, and to market whale products to a growing American nation. By the mid-nineteenth century, the American whaling fleet numbered more than 700 ships, but these concentrated on catching sperm whales off Nantucket and Long Island. Some ships rounded Cape Horn to catch Californian grey whales in the Pacific. It was in pursuit of these that, in 1848, the captain of an American barque first sighted bowhead whales in Bering Strait, a discovery which was to have a devastating impact on the Alaskan Inuit.

For the next fifty years, hundreds of ships left San Francisco harbour for the whaling grounds in the Arctic Ocean. In the winter of 1871, 34 American ships were lost in the ice, but to the whalers this was no deterrent. Larger ships displacing 400 tons were built, their hulls reinforced with double planking. These were the first factory ships in the Arctic, equipped with try-works, or huge brick ovens, which enabled the men to reduce the blubber to oil during the voyage. With an estimated 15,000 bowheads in arctic waters, there was plenty for everyone, including the Russians and the Japanese. Some American captains, anxious to capture as many whales as possible, extended the hunting season to the limit and found their retreat cut off by the ice. With the help of the Inuit, they survived the winter tolerably well, and in time, a two-year voyage to the Arctic became common practice.

A favourite place for wintering was the natural harbour on Herschel Island, close to the Mackenzie Delta. Here, the first contacts were established with the Inuit. The whalers were ill-equipped for the arctic cold and were anxious to trade, but the wary inhabitants had little use for coffee and tobacco. When the Americans offered them needles, knives and blubber spades, which would make their lives easier, the Inuit showed greater interest. In return, they exchanged meat, seal skin and the pelts of musk rat, an aquatic rodent with fur similar to that of the beaver. Trade soon flourished. In subsequent years, appreciating the value of the furs, the whalers packed as many trade goods as the ships could carry. The merchandise was bartered for enormous quantities of furs, which were sold at high prices in San Francisco and New England.

With several hundred Americans on Herschel, the island soon became the Klondike of whaling. Drunkenness and lawlessness were rife. The whalers showed the Inuit how to use tobacco, gave them whisky, and taught them to distil spirits from molasses and potatoes, which they traded for slippers and tobacco pouches of seal skin. Grievously unable to cope with the effects of drink, hundreds of Inuit, many of whom had acquired firearms from the Americans, died as a result of violence and alcohol-induced illness.

The whalers, deprived of female company for many months, capital-ised on traditional Inuit customs, corrupting the women and treating their menfolk with disdain. Soon, venereal diseases were rampant. Sickness ravaged the Inuit population still further. The whalers, lacking vitamins and dehydrated by the dry atmosphere and an excess of whisky, succumbed to a variety of illnesses which they passed on to the Inuit.

Having no resistance to the white man's diseases, eighty per cent of the indigenous population were struck down by epidemics of measles and mumps, influenza and tuberculosis, all of which in those days could be fatal. In 1910, when whaling in the Bering, Chukchi and Beaufort Seas was no longer deemed to be a commercial venture, the Americans steamed south, never to return. In the space of twenty years, the Inuit of the Mackenzie Delta region, who had survived for 5,000 years, were nearly extinct. Of the original 2,000 inhabitants, only forty survived.

In the eastern Arctic, contact with the European whalers left a similar legacy. Settlements in northwest Greenland were all but wiped out by influenza. Many Inuit died, and the few survivors lost their hair. Children were terrified of the whalers, who descended on the communities in large gangs, frequently forcing the villagers to take refuge in the hills. Nevertheless, there were a few advantages from the whaling era. For a race which for thousands of years had hunted whale and walrus with little more than harpoons and spears tipped with stone and ivory, metal became readily available. New tools and consumer goods made their lives easier. Guns improved hunting methods, but the disadvantages far outweighed the benefits. When the whalers in the eastern Arctic finally departed, the Inuit had become heavy smokers, their lifestyle had changed radically, and the bowhead whale was virtually extinct.

The whalers did not restrict their slaughter to whales alone: sea cows, or walrus, were also considered fair game. These ponderous creatures can weigh more than a ton, and were valued for their ivory tusks, hides and oil. The skin of a bull could be an inch thick, so tough that as the best material for shields and armour, and later, for bicycle seats, it became the most expensive of all the hides in use. The viscid oil was a valuable sealing agent for ships' planking, the ivory, perfect for toilet accessories for women.

The English Muscovy Company was again at the forefront of the slaughter. In less than a decade after the discovery of a herd of about 20,000 walrus near Bear Island, 150 miles south of Spitsbergen, Muscovy hunters had killed so many of them that there were no longer enough left to warrant the expense of another voyage. Across the Atlantic, French and New England hunters systematically butchered tens of thousands of walrus, ultimately annihilating the species between Nova Scotia and Cape Cod. When European ships first sailed into the Gulf of St Lawrence, there were more than 250,000 walrus. In two centuries, the herds had been virtually exterminated.

With the walrus populations in the warmer, southern seas all but extinct, the French hunters headed for arctic waters. Here, they combined with the Europeans and Americans who, having killed off virtually every whale of commercial value, were themselves showing a mercenary interest in the walrus. The British exterminated a herd on Franz Josef Land, east of Spitsbergen. The discarded bones of thousands more littered the rocky coast of Greenland. Between 1868 and 1873, European whalers in the eastern Arctic were slaying an average 60,000 sea cows a year. Simultaneously, American whalers massacred an estimated 200,000 to 300,000 walrus in the Bering Strait and Beaufort Sea. By the time the slaughter was finished, they had accounted for approximately four *million* walrus.

The carnage left Inuit hunters, who had been deprived of whales and were increasingly dependent on walrus for food and fuel, facing starvation. Many more died, and others lived their lives in misery. In Greenland, the Inuit economy had become based almost exclusively on seal-hunting, which produced far less oil. The need to economise, and the desire for greater security as a protection against drunken whalers, led them to build larger, communal houses in smaller, scattered settlements. This was a significant change, and it did not augur well for their future.

Eventually, international legislation was introduced to protect the sea cow. Yet its ivory is still coveted, and on the illegal international markets fetches as much as £450,000 ($675,000) a ton. How much is sold can be judged by an official diplomatic protest lodged with the United States by the Soviet Union, which objected to the number of decapitated walrus washed up on the Siberian coast.

The butchery in the north caused little concern to the merchants of the south. Always ready to pander to the demands of fashion, they directed their ships to the colonies of hooded and harp seals off Newfoundland. In the latter part of the nineteenth century, the French, the Newfoundlanders and the whalers battered to death for their fur more than twenty million seals. Few men made fortunes: thousands died, victims of the ice.

During the 1930s, the Norwegians first wrote off their own colonies of harp and hooded seals, then joined the Newfoundland hunt. Only World War Two saved the species from extinction. Reproducing more quickly than whales and walrus, their numbers rose during the war years to three million, but when peace came the hunt resumed. Millions more seals were killed, until concerned animal welfare groups, and later governments, intervened, and by forcing through an import ban on seal products, reduced the hunt to a minimum.

With northern seas no longer a viable commercial proposition, the whalers turned southwards to the Antarctic. There, they renewed the quest for whale oil with vigour, utilising as many as twenty factory ships and 250 catchers. In the 1958 season, nearly 2,400 humpback whales, and about 20,000 blue, fin, and sei whales were harpooned for three million barrels of oil. After that, the catch again declined, and when the survival of these whales was endangered, the whaling industry was finally brought under strict control.

With only 600 to 1,800 bowheads apparently remaining in the Arctic, the International Whaling Commission, which had been founded by 22 member states in 1946, proposed in 1977 the imposition of a total ban on hunting bowheads. The concept of a zero catch came as a shock to the Alaskan Inuit, who had pursued the bowheads for subsistence, never for profit. In the same year, with little experience of the political arena, the outraged hunters made representations to the Commission, and denounced the ban as a needless intrusion.

Led by Ebem Hopson, the mayor of the Alaskan whaling town, Barrow, the hunters claimed at a special meeting in December, 1977, that the Commission's figures seriously under-estimated the bowhead population. They argued that if they were not permitted to hunt bowheads, the basis of community life would be destroyed for 100,000 people living in small villages along the arctic coasts of Alaska, Canada, and Greenland. Reluctantly, the Commission acquiesced. A small catch was re-instated: twelve bowheads landed, or eighteen struck.

Disappointed but not defeated, the Inuit returned home and appealed to American marine biologists to conduct a new, independent study on their behalf. Counting the whales as they migrated, the scientists eventually established the bowhead population at 2,264, nearly twice the Commission's previous estimate. Armed with the new statistics, Hopson and his fellow hunters flew to London, and demanded that subsistence whaling should be treated separately from commercial operations, in which whalers from countries like Japan and the Soviet Union killed thousands of whales of all species. The Inuits' efforts were rewarded with a small increase in the quota – from twelve to fourteen bowheads landed, or from eighteen to twenty struck.

The new quota was still a long way from satisfying the needs of the Inuit. In the following year, 1979, they again flew to London, this time taking with them an *umiak*. Hauling it into the Café Royal, the hunters climbed on board, and thrusting hand-held harpoons into imaginary bowheads, demonstrated their hunting techniques and explained how teams of four to six men establish a camp on the edge of the firm ice, where they wait until a bowhead swims close enough to be harpooned. When the whale dives, the hunters launch *umiaks* one-third its size, spreading out in a wide circle until the whale surfaces two or three miles away. Here, inflated bladders are attached, slowing the whale's progress so that it can be lanced for the kill. Afterwards, the carcass is cut up and divided among the crew, as it was in ancient times, the first harpoon taking his share, followed by the second, third and fourth harpoons.

Subsequently, the meat is shared with other villagers, and elaborate festivals are held to honour the whale. For the Inuit, whaling remains an important source of meat. Two-thirds of the carcass is edible, and none is wasted; what they do not eat themselves is fed to the dogs. The baleen is used for carvings, which are sold through local stores and provide the only form of cash income. Above all, whaling is a source of pride, a way of showing the rest of the world that they are still 'Real People'.

'It was all very exciting,' the Secretary of the Whaling Commission, Ray Gamble, said. But the Inuits' initial foray into politics was only partially sucessful.

By 1984, the quota for all the Inuit of Alaska was raised to 43 bowheads during the following two-year period, with no more then 27 whales to be killed in any one year. The hunters were far from content, not because they were being made to suffer for the greed of the white men, but because they still hunted in much the same way as they did a thousand years ago.

Although the introduction of the Commission's quota system was designed to conserve stocks and develop the industry in an orderly fashion, the new rules were soon the subject of controversy, and the extent to which they were being honoured was brought into question. In November, 1984, the Japanese Whaling Association revealed that eighty per cent of the Japanese eat whale meat and seventy per cent opposed the Commission's rulings. In the same month, the environmental group, Greenpeace, photographed Japanese whalers hunting sperm whales in defiance of an international ban which had already been breached by the Soviet Union and Brazil.

In July, another conservation group, the Environmental Investigation Agency, released a report accusing eight countries, led by the Japanese, of the 'systematic organisation of pirate whaling operations, and drastically increasing the threat of extinction to many whale species'. This was in defiance of rules passed by the International Whaling Commission in 1982 to protect certain species and phase out commercial whaling, banning it completely by 1986. Japan, the Soviet Union and Norway did not agree to the ban, flouted conservation quotas, and killed hundreds of protected sperm whales in the Pacific every year. Chile, Korea and Portugal also killed protected species. Spain admitted that it had operated a pirate whaling operation. Iceland indicated that it planned to kill protected whales and Greenland was found to be exporting whale meat illegally.

Nevertheless, at the end of the Whaling Commission's annual meeting in Bournemouth, in July, 1985, Greenpeace announced that the number of whales killed annually by the major whaling nations had fallen from 16,000 in 1980 to 6,000 in 1985, and that all major whaling nations would end whaling within a few years. The Soviet Union said it would halt its whaling industry in 1987; Japan made a similar commitment with 1988 as the target date.

In the meantime, the Commission gave protected status to the sperm whales hunted by Japan, and minke whales sought by Norway and Korea. With no authority to impose penalties, the Commission relies on the goodwill, and honesty, of the member nations. As the meeting ended, Greenpeace and the World Wildlife Fund both warned that several nations, led by Iceland, were planning to skirt the commercial ban by claiming that they were catching whales only for 'research', although they fully intended to sell the meat.

Additionally, the Whaling Commission pledged to keep tighter controls on aboriginal subsistence whaling. Inuit in west Greenland were forbidden to kill humpback whales, the most endangered species still being exploited. A quota of only ten fin whales was established for the same area. At the same time, the maximum annual catch of minke whales off west Greenland was reduced from 300 to 130. Finally, the Commission decreed that the Alaskan Inuit would be permitted to catch no more than 26 bowhead whales in the Bering Sea in any one year.

CHAPTER 9

Polar Exploiters

While the Inuit suffered at the hands of the whalers, the contemptuous treatment meted out by the polar explorers left them bewildered and demoralised. Yet the Inuit continued to offer their traditional hospitality, although their welcoming smiles were increasingly tempered by anxiety. This concern was understandable, given that some of the men who named the channels, bays and headlands of the Arctic were liars, cheats and thieves. The Inuit would have been even more bemused had they known that the pioneers would be greeted as heroes on their return home, for the accomplishments of some of these undoubtedly brave men were not always as praiseworthy as they appeared.

Driven by the prospect of fame and fortune, the first arctic explorers sought a northern sea route to India and China, then known as Cathay. After the Venetian traveller Marco Polo returned in the mid-thirteenth century with glowing accounts of the riches and splendour of the East, ships of the republics of Venice and Genoa were bringing back silks, spices, gold and jewellery for the European market, affluence and power to their rulers. Anxious for a share of this lucrative commerce, the English merchants were distressed to find that their ships were denied access to the East by the Spanish and Portuguese.

Exploring the eastern coast of South America, Spanish captains had discovered the Magellan Straits, and through them the Pacific, and by sailing northwest eventually reached Cathay. Similarly, the Portuguese, who had long been trading along the west African coast, rounded the Cape of Good Hope and headed across the Indian Ocean towards the East Indies. Each country rigorously monopolised its own route, and regarded the ships of other nations as piratical. With the southern routes closed to them, the English had no option but to look northwards, firstly to the northeast and later, with greater persistence, for a passage to the northwest.

English mariners had already heard of Greenland, where a small colony of Vikings had settled, and of Newfoundland, to which some of the Norsemen had sailed. Believing that the way to Asia must lie north of the route between them, the fifteenth-century navigator Sebastian Cabot wrote:

> There increaseth in my heart a great flame of desire to attempt some notable thing ... I began therefore to sail toward the north-west, but after certaine days, I found that the land ranne toward the north, which was to me a great displeasure. Nevertheless, sailing along by the coast [of Labrador] to see if I could find any gulf that turned, I found the land still continued to the 56th degree under our pole. And seeing that there the coast turned to the east, despairing to find the passage, I turned back again, and sailed downe by the coast to that part of this firm lande which is nowe called Florida, where my victuals failing, I departed from thence and returned into England, where I found great tumults among the people, and preparations for warres in Scotland.[3]

At this juncture, Sebastian left the English and Scots to their own devices, and temporarily entered into the service of the King of Spain. His navigation was either not as perfect as he supposed, or he was guilty of deception. The coast does not turn east at 56 degrees but continues directly northwards until it reaches the southern entrance to Hudson Strait. Had Cabot been more persevering and continued his voyage northwards, he would have been acclaimed a hero. As it was, his principal achievement was to fuel the enthusiasm of other merchants and mariners. In 1527, Master Robert Thorne, of Bristol, exhorted Henry VIII 'with very weighty and substantial reasons to set forth a discovery even to the North Pole!' Despite Thorne's zeal, and his two ships being manned 'by divers cunning men', the expedition ended in disaster when one vessel sank as it rounded the southern tip of Greenland.

It was another eight years before the explorers came into contact with the inhabitants of North America. This was during an ill-fated undertaking organised by one Master Hore of London, a gentleman reputed to be 'of goodly stature and great courage, and given to the studie of cosmographie'. Whatever his attributes, Master Hore was no judge of men, and by all accounts, an inefficient planner. After receiving the King's blessing for the voyage, he persuaded thirty gentlemen from the Inns of Court and of Chancery to accompany him on the expedition. In view of the known dangers, this was a peculiar choice, all the more remarkable because the legal gentlemen were hopelessly outnumbered by a singularly unpleasant crew. Indeed, 'the whole number that went in the two tall ships, were about six score persons ... which were all mustered in warlike manner at Gravesend.'

On reaching the Newfoundland coast, the ships *Trinitie* and *Minion* were approached by a boat paddled either by Indians or by the most southerly coastal Inuit, the descendants of the old Dorset culture. The English crews wasted no time launching boats 'to meet and take the savages'. This was subsequently deemed impolitic, especially as the natives immediately turned about, landed and disappeared.

The pursuers rushed into an encampment nearby, discovered the side of a bear roasting on a spit, and ravenous after being on short rations, ate the lot. Had they conciliated the 'savages', one commentator observed later, they need have suffered no inconvenience from hunger. As it was, after their meal, the men set off to find the inhabitants, but soon lost their way. With no food, they were quickly reduced to scavenging herbs and roots, their plight eventually becoming intolerable. Contemporary records tell how

> the relief of herbs being to little purpose, one fellow killed his mate while he stooped to take up a roote for his reliefe, and cutting out pieces of his body whom he had murthered, broyled the same on the coles, and greedily devoured him.[4]

On learning of the cannibalism, the ship's officers, who believed that the missing men had been killed either by the 'savages' or wild animals, now failed to act. The ships' stores were spent, so the crews agreed among themselves to cast lots as to who should be the next to die. No sooner had this decision been taken than a French ship appeared 'well furnished with vittaile, and such was the policy of the English, that they became masters of the same, and changing ships and vittailing them they set sayle to come to England.'[5] The fate of the French crew is not recorded.

Successive voyages gradually pushed the boundaries of known waters further north. Martin Frobisher, a hard-bitten sea captain of little education and dubious reputation, discovered the southern coast of Baffin Island and gave his name to Frobisher Bay. He was the first navigator to distinguish himself in the quest for a northwest passage, at least in the eyes of a gullible English public fooled by what must have been one of the greatest confidence tricks of that time. For years, Frobisher had sailed the African coast, cramming slaves into the holds of his ship, and accumulating a private fortune. He returned to England after narrowly escaping being hanged, drawn and quartered as a pirate.

Undeterred, he pompously expressed the opinion that the discovery of a northwest passage 'was the only thing of the world that was left yet undone, whereby a notable mind might be made famous and fortunate.'

Inexplicably, Frobisher managed to obtain the support of Dudley, Earl of Warwick, and fitted out a squadron of three small sailing ships, one of which was little more than a rowing boat with a small sail and a three-man crew. The combined displacement of the vessels was only 75 tons. As the flotilla sailed past Greenwich, Queen Elizabeth I reportedly leaned out of a window and waved them farewell.

The voyage progressed without incident until the ships ran into a storm off southern Greenland, where the smallest ship sank. The captain of the second ship immediately turned for home. Frobisher, enraged, was obliged to quash an attempted mutiny on his own ship, *Gabriel*, before sailing on. By July, he had crossed the Atlantic. After sighting the Labrador coast, he turned northwards until he found himself in a torrent of ice and in danger of sinking. Although he could not have known it, Frobisher was close to Resolution Island at the mouth of Hudson Strait. Here, every July, in an area as big as the entire land mass of France, Spain and Portugal, the winter ice of Hudson Bay is carried on treacherous currents through the straits into the open sea.

Pushing northwards as best he could, Frobisher rounded Resolution Island and sailed into an inlet, grandiosely calling it Frobisher Bay. Here, he saw 'a number of small things floating in the sea afarre off ... porpoises or seals or some kind of strange fish'. They turned out to be Inuit hunters in their kayaks. One of them, intrigued by a small bell which Frobisher dangled over the side of the ship, was persuaded to go on board, and was given a knife in return for piloting the ship along the inlet to the Inuit settlement. Frobisher arranged for the Inuk, who had presumably left his kayak with his companions, to be ferried home in a boat accompanied by five seamen. Despite strict orders not to go ashore, the men quickly disappeared and were never seen again.

Frobisher claimed to have been deeply afflicted by their loss. In his reports, he maintained that the five men had been captured by 'savages', but this would have been completely out of character for the Inuit, who continued to visit the ship. Frobisher must have known that the men, probably some of the unsuccessful mutineers, had deserted. Nevertheless, he waited for five days, firing guns and sounding trumpets to attract their attention. Receiving no response, he again rang his bell to entice a kayaker to the ship's side, pretending to offer it as a gift. As the Inuk moved to receive it, Frobisher 'caught the man fast and plucked him with maine force, boat and all, into his barke out of the sea.' With this 'strange infidel, whose like was never seen, read, or heard of before', he set sail for England.

On arrival, Frobisher was commended for his 'great and notable attempt, specially for the great hope he brought of the passage to

Cathaia'. As the navigator basked in glory, the Inuk captive was forced to display his hunting skills for the amusement of London Society. His reputation soon spread to Greenwich, where Queen Elizabeth entreated him to harpoon the royal swans. Sadly, the Inuk's fame was shortlived; unused to the damp climate, he soon died of a common cold, although some accounts suggest that the cause might have been English cooking.

On his return, Frobisher had produced a piece of rock which he had found on Lower Savage Island, at the mouth of Frobisher Bay. After analysis, the rock was shown to contain traces of gold. Intensely excited, the London merchants quickly commissioned another voyage, directing Frobisher to concentrate on finding as much ore as he could, rather than 'searching any further discovery of the [Northwest] passage'. Eventually, he set sail with three larger ships, landed on Lower Savage, and mined 200 tons of the supposed gold ore.

As he supervised the loading of it, Frobisher saw a group of Inuit, and tried to capture one of them, but missed his footing on the slippery ground. The Inuk, seizing a chance too good to miss, hastily shot an arrow at his attacker and struck the captain astern. At this, a former Cornish wrestler among the crew gave chase, and 'shewed his companion such a Cornish trick, that he made his sides ake for a month after; and so being stayed he was taken away.' What happened to the hunter remains a mystery.

In London, smelting proved the ore to be no better than graphite, but Frobisher, still keen to be the first to find the Northwest Passage, managed to produce some gold dust, persuaded the merchants that it had been refined from the ore, and convinced them that it would be in their interests to finance a third voyage. The ruse was successful. In 1578, he sailed down the Thames again, this time with fifteen ships. His mission was not only to bring back more gold, but to colonise the region.

On the way, one of the ships carrying supplies and a wooden hut vital to the success of the colony conveniently hit an iceberg and sank. All hands were saved, and Frobisher, who probably had no intention of establishing a colony, continued his exploratory voyage, sailing deeper into what is now Hudson Strait. He almost discovered the Bay (ahead of Hudson), but once more was forced back by the chaotic ice. Defeated, he returned to the mine at Lower Savage Island and loaded 1,300 tons of ore, knowing it to be worthless. Aware that his days of arctic exploration were over, Frobisher, who had been well paid for his services, shamelessly announced on his return to London that he had successfully passed through the Northwest Passage into the Pacific Ocean.

There is a curious sequel to the story. Three centuries later, when the American explorer Charles Francis Hall landed on the coast of Baffin

Island, the Inuit gave a detailed account of Frobisher's visit and the kid-napping, as well as the fate of the five missing seamen. Thoroughly dis-contented with life on the fo'c'sle of a ship run by a former slaving captain, they had opted for a life with the Inuit rather than risk their lives sailing in increasingly dangerous waters under a man who, in their view, was a tyrant. Years later, suffering from homesickness, they had built a small boat, and ignoring the advice of the Inuit, set sail for England and were never seen again.

Not all the navigators seeking the Northwest Passage were as ill-suited for the quest as Frobisher. John Davis, a shrewd, indomitable mariner from Devon, was a notable exception. One of the few early explorers to acknowledge the skills of the Inuit, he shook their hands and made many friends. When Inuit kayakers surrounded his ship, he asked musicians in his crew to play the hornpipe, and the sailors to dance, 'making tokens of friendship'. This goodwill was reciprocated. On later voyages, hundreds of Inuit who remembered him paddled to the ship bearing seal and caribou skins, white hares, and 'samon and cod, dry caplin, with other fish, and partrig, fesant, gulls, sea-birdes and other kinds of fleshe'.

Sailing to a latitude of 75° N., Davis gave his name to the straits between Greenland and Labrador, and discovered the potential there for cod fishing and whaling. Highly regarded, he was recognised as having been of immense service to British commerce. He more than anyone would have been horrified by the behaviour of the whalers and his fellow explorers.

The arctic map was continually being re-drawn as the navigators extended the limits of known waters. Henry Hudson forced a way through Hudson Strait and found a huge inland sea beyond. In 1615, Captain Robert Bylot sailed into Baffin Bay, but because of his allegedly rebellious tendencies, the honour was given to his lieutenant, William Baffin. The two men went on to discover Smith Sound and, later, more importantly, Lancaster Sound, the entrance to the Northwest Passage.

At home, news of these voyages fuelled the expectations of merchants and politicians, who were convinced that trade links with Cathay would soon be established. In the excitement, parliament in 1817 sanctioned inducements to the arctic explorers; £1,000 for reaching 83° N., £5,000 pounds for 89° N. The navigator who reached the Pacific Ocean was to be paid £20,000, a sum which today would be worth more than half a million pounds, or three quarters of a million dollars.

The writings of some of these explorers show their mental approach to the Inuit. Commander Albert Markham, who sailed with the whalers and in 1875 took part in the biggest and best equipped exploratory expedition of the time, under Captain (later Admiral) Nares, left the reader in no doubt as to his sentiments:

> The settlement itself consists of some half-dozen wooden houses, a church, and a few native dwellings of primitive construction, which might be more appropriately termed hovels ... The dwelling places of the natives are most pleasing when viewed from the outside, and the greater the distance off the better. They are built chiefly of stone and turf...
>
> If sufficiently brave to encounter the offensive stench which pervades everything, as to risk a visit to the interior, one passes through a long narrow entrance, having almost to crawl upon hands and feet, emerging into a small room, not unlike the cabins on board very small and ill-found merchant ships ... The state of the interior may be better imagined than described, as the Eskimaux are notorious for being particularly dirty and filthy in their habits; in addition to which, the rotten and stinking pieces of seal and other animals that are left strewed about must largely contribute to the offensive stench that pervades their habitations.[6]

In contrast to John Davis, who marvelled at the elegance of kayaks and the hunting skills of the Inuit, Markham saw men who, 'with their general wild and excessively dirty appearance, were more like some amphibious animals than human beings.' He was equally disparaging about a dance to which he had been invited:

> The women are by no means comely, the prettiest part being certainly their costume ... what with the closeness of the apartment and the perfume exhaled by the dancers, we were not sorry to leave the ballroom and reach the open air. They seem a good-tempered merry set of people, though decidedly deficient in the virtue of gratitude; taking things as a matter of course that may be given to them, and asking for things, no matter of what value, that take their fancy. The idea of giving anything in exchange is, with them, quite a visionary one.[7]

The explorers failed to understand the reason for the Inuit's apparent thievery; that in a communal society it was customary to take what one wanted, and that having no wood, iron, steel or tin cans of their own, they valued such items highly. Pilfering frequently drove the explorers to distraction. In Greenland, the American navy physician Kane was as renowned for whipping Inuit caught stealing as for his discovery of the

basin north of Smith Sound, which separates northwest Greenland from
Ellesmere Island. Kane appears to have been a thoroughly unscrupulous
leader, always ready to capitalise on the Inuits' fear of the unknown.
Claiming to be a powerful white *angakok*, he ordered his Inuit guides to
find fresh supplies, or be tormented for the rest of their lives by evil
spirits.

Though brave, Kane was a bully, and as unpopular with many of his
companions as with the Inuit. Yet the conduct of some of his colleagues
was no less contemptible. When three members of Kane's expedition
defected, they slipped opiates into the drinking water of the Inuit who
tried to help them. Stripping the sleeping hunters of their clothes and
boots, the rebels stole their dogs and left them to die. On waking, the
Inuit found enough blankets for makeshift clothes and boots, and in
desperation followed the tracks of the Americans, whom they eventually
rejoined. The explorers ignored their pleas for help, forcing them at
gunpoint to take them back to Kane's winter headquarters where,
incredibly, they were greeted like lost brothers.

A lesser known explorer, James Hall, behaved so atrociously towards
the Inuit that when he returned on a later voyage, he was mortally
wounded by an Inuk 'who, with his dart, strook him a deadly wound upon
the right side, which our surgeon did think did pierce his liver.'[8]

This was exceptional behaviour and the Inuk would almost certainly
have been admonished by his own people. The Inuit regarded white men
who beat other human beings with contempt. In their own society, such
treatment was reserved for the dogs, and then only when absolutely
necessary, the maltreatment of animals demonstrating an Inuk's lack of
authority, rather than an affirmation of it.

Unable to comprehend the white man's attitude, the Inuit nursed their
hurt pride and discussed the possible reasons for it. Peter Freuchen tells
the delightful story[9] of an Inuk hunter who was cheated by the captain of
a visiting ship. The Inuk, Ukujag, was one of the Inuit to accompany
Robert E. Peary, the American who, in 1909, claimed to be the first man
to reach the North Pole. He had been hunting in Melville Bay and shot a
polar bear which, for the rest of his life, he remembered as being the
largest and most beautifully pelted bear he had ever seen. He skinned it
with the claws and nose intact, and contacted the ship.

Ukujag expected a special reward for his skin, but when the captain
asked him what he wanted for it, he began the bargaining process
modestly, according to Inuit custom, and said that he needed some
cartridges for his gun. At this, the captain promptly took the bear skin,
gave the hunter fourteen rounds of ammunition, and disappeared into his
cabin. Much later, Ukujag told the story as proof of the ignorance of

some of the white men. 'Just think of this man being master of a big ship and not knowing that such a fine bearskin was worth much more than fourteen cartridges!' And everybody laughed at the foolishness of the white man.

Peary probably exploited, terrorised and relied on the Inuit more than any other polar explorer. During each of his seven expeditions to northwest Greenland, he employed large numbers of Inuit hunters as guides, paying them with the basic requirements for a modern life: weapons, wood, tools, canvas, coffee, tobacco, white man's food and clothing. Once the Inuit had grown dependent on these new luxuries, he bartered with them shamelessly for more than twenty years, taking home shiploads of blue and white fox furs, and ivory, the 'white gold' of the North. Demand for these goods in America was insatiable, the prices extortionate. Peary was reputed to have made a profit of more than a million dollars at a time when the Inuit were on the verge of starvation. Needless to say, they saw none of the profits. As soon as his ship was filled with goods, Peary returned to New York, knowing that he would not be back for many years, and that the Inuits' supplies could not last.

Arrogant and selfish, Peary had little regard for the Inuit problems. Children and adults feared his ill-temper. Hunters wore amulets to protect themselves from his violence. After an argument with one group of families who worked for him, he reduced their rations so drastically that they nearly died from starvation. If an Inuk worked well, Peary allowed him to hunt walrus from the deck of his ship, but insisted that the tusks be left on board. Jean Malaurie recalls how, in 1967, an Inuk who accompanied Peary on his North Pole expedition was still so afraid of him sixty years later that he peered outside his house to make sure the explorer's spirit was not listening. The Inuk, who referred to him as 'the great tormentor', is quoted as saying:

People were afraid of him ... really afraid ... like I am this evening. His big ship ... it made a big impression on us. He was a great leader. You always had the feeling that if you didn't do what he wanted, he would condemn you to death ... I was very young, but I will never forget how he treated the Inuit.

It was in Uummannaq [Thule], in July 1908, and this voyage was to be his last. His big ship arrives in the bay. He is hardly visible from the shore, but he shouts; 'Kissa Tikeri-Unga! – I'm arriving, for a fact!'

The Inuit go aboard. Peary has a barrel of biscuits brought up on deck. The two or three hunters who have gone out to the ship in their kayaks bend over the barrel and begin to eat with both hands.

Later the barrel is taken ashore, and the contents thrown on the beach. Men, women and children hurl themselves on the biscuits like dogs, which amuses Peary a lot. My heart still turns cold to think of it. That scene tells very well how he considered this people – my people – who were, for all of that, devoted to him.[10]

The Inuit's loyalty did not prevent Peary from stealing their only source of iron, four meteorites embedded in a glacier near Cape York, in Melville Bay. For thousands of years, hunters had chipped small flakes of metal from them for the tips of their harpoons. In 1897, Peary shipped the largest meteorite, weighing nearly fifty tons, to New York, where he sold it to the Museum of Natural History.

A few years later, the three remaining meteorites were removed to the United States and Denmark. The explorer also sailed home with six Inuit, intending to exhibit them during a tour of America. When four of them died, Peary, always an opportunist, returned to the museum and persuaded the curators to buy the skeletons. On returning to Greenland, he neither gave nor offered the Inuit payment for the meteorite, nor compensated the bereaved families, who, deprived of their breadwinners, had been left impoverished.

Not only was Peary a thief, there is strong evidence to suggest that he lied when he claimed to be the first man to reach the North Pole. Peary's story was that he had reached 90° N. on April 6th, 1909, with his manservant, Matt Henson, and four Inuit guides. The remaining members of the expedition had been sent south five days previously to enable him to make his final dash for the Pole. He claimed to have spent thirty hours there making observations and records, and wrote on a postcard to his wife in Australia:[11]

> 90 North Latitude, April 7th.
>
> My dear Jo,
>
> I have won out at last. Have been here a day. I start for home and you in an hour. Love to the 'kidsies'.
>
> Bert.

Shortly after writing the card, in the early afternoon of April 7th, Peary and his team left the 'Pole', arriving at Cape Columbia on Ellesmere Island on the 23rd, sixteen days later. He wrote then:

> My lifework is accomplished. The thing which it was intended from the beginning that I should do, the thing which I believed could

be done, and that I could do, I have done. I have got the North Pole out of my system after twenty-three years of effort, hard work, disappointments, hardships, privations, more or less suffering, and some risks. I have won the last great geographical prize, the North Pole, for the credit of the United States. This work is the finish, the cap and climax of nearly four hundred years of effort, loss of life, and expenditure of fortunes by the civilized nations of the world, and it has been accomplished in a way that is thoroughly American. I am content.[12]

Careful analysis of Peary's records provides convincing evidence that he did *not* reach the Pole. Navigational aids at that time were not sophisticated enough to establish 90° N. with sufficient accuracy, the margin of error being approximately a hundred miles. His claim to have travelled more than forty miles a day *as the crow flies* is untenable. The route to the Pole does not lie overland, but across an ice cap continually drifting *southwards* across the Arctic Ocean. He would have had to make extensive detours to avoid channels of open water, known as leads, and negotiated barriers of jumbled ice forty feet high and ten miles wide. Skirting these obstacles would have entailed taking a zigzag route, travelling at least eighty miles a day.

Compared with the progress of other men, Peary's claim, as set out in his report of the expedition, stretches credibility, and is fully discussed by Dennis Rawlins in his 1973 study *Peary at the Pole: Fact or Fiction*. Other explorers regard Peary's contention that he travelled more than forty miles a day with scepticism. The greatest of all polar explorers, Fritjiof Nansen, averaged less than twenty-five miles a day over a period of twenty days. The British explorer, Wally Herbert, whose 3,720-mile expedition from Alaska to Spitsbergen via the North Pole was the longest sledge journey ever made, recorded a personal best of twenty-six miles in a day, in perfect conditions.

A team of four Americans and two Canadians led by Will Steger reached the Pole with dog teams in May, 1986, after a journey of 56 days. The Norwegians, Ragnar Thorseth and Trygve Berge, drove to the Pole on snowmobiles in April, 1982, taking 57 days. Both men are adamant that it would have been impossible for Peary, who was using dogs, to cover the distance in a mere 37 days. Furthermore, Peary's sledge teams consisted of seven or eight dogs, as opposed to ten or twelve favoured on long journeys by the Inuit. He had five sledges and 38 dogs and, despite the obstacles, claimed to have made the return journey of nearly 500 miles to Ellesmere Island in 17 days, approximately thirty miles a day.

Peary was well aware that this was to be his last expedition to the

North. After visiting the Arctic for nearly a quarter of a century, he was finally faced with the realisation that his lifelong ambition to reach the Pole might be thwarted. In the circumstances, cynics may wonder why Peary chose his manservant to accompany him during the final stages of the journey, when Captain Robert Bartlett, the navigator whom he recognised as the most valuable member of the expedition, could have authenticated his evidence and given him powerful support in the dispute which followed his homecoming.

The Chairman of a United States Navy sub-committee set up to investigate the claim let it be known that he viewed Commander Peary's evidence as far from convincing. Despite their misgivings, however, the committee members accepted Commander Peary's word as an officer by four votes to three. The National Geographical Society's sub-committee were unanimous in reaching the same decision. Today, Peary's name still appears on maps and in atlases as the first man to stand on top of the world. The Inuit regard his performance as so remarkable that whenever the issue is raised, they chuckle with amusement.

Inundated with medals, university doctorates and honorary member-ships, Peary was assured a coveted place in history. It was blemished only by his attempts to discredit his arch-rival, Dr Frederick Cook, who claimed that *he* had reached the Pole nearly a year earlier than Peary. It has been established that Cook left the north coast of Ellesmere Island on April 23rd, 1908, returning on April 18th the following year, twelve days after Peary was supposed to have reached his goal. To that extent, Cook was well ahead. If his story was true, he *must* have arrived at the Pole first.

Peary, furious, ridiculed the claim on the grounds that Cook had no evidence to support it, a surprisingly hypocritical standpoint in view of the weakness of his own proof. Cook quietly insisted that what he said was true, but the American press had one hero and did not need another; Cook was denounced as a charlatan. The issue remains contentious. Some of the Inuit who had worked with Cook were convinced that he really had been to 90° N. Others were adamant that he had hardly travelled out of sight of land.

There the matter rested until 1934, when Edward Shackleton led an Oxford University Expedition to Ellesmere Island. Here they were joined by a Sergeant Stallworthy, of the Royal Canadian Mounted Police, who, three years earlier, had hired an Inuk hunter, Itukusaq, to help him to find a missing German explorer. During the search, Itukusaq had pointed to a spot where, he said, Dr Cook had taken the photographs which he later claimed to have taken at the North Pole. It was at 82° N., within sight of Ellesmere Island.

The tendency of some polar explorers to exaggerate their achievements is common enough in the Arctic. Yet the accomplishments of men like Cook and Peary did not need embellishment. Few man can cope with the solitude of the immense landscape, or the dangers of freezing temperatures, blizzards, white-outs and cracking ice.

Whatever doubts may be harboured about the rivals, their courage and determination cannot be denied. Cook's fourteen-month journey round Ellesmere Island was one of the longest ever undertaken. Peary, despite the amputation of all but one of his frostbitten toes, struggled further north than any other man of his time. That in itself was all the more remarkable when one considers that, unlike explorers today, he had no radio contact and could not be re-supplied by pilots landing their Twin Otter aircraft on the ice. Nor could he be picked up in an emergency and flown back to the centrally-heated comforts of a modern base camp, to watch a videotaped recording of his exploits on television. Today, the few adventurers who battle their way to the Pole cannot but be thankful, as they gaze out of the windows of the aircraft which takes them back to Resolute Bay in a mere fourteen hours. In the old days, the return journey was as long and arduous as the outward struggle.

All too often, as the explorers reaped the rewards of heroism, real or imagined, the Inuit who made their exploits possible were forgotten. When Peary returned to New York for the last time, he left behind two sons, neither of whom ever heard from him again. Nor did the son of Matt Henson, the manservant who saved Peary's life on at least two occasions, but who received no help from the great man when he was unable to find satisfactory employment after his return to New York. Peary wrote of 'his' Inuit:

> They had served us well. They had, at times, tried our tempers and taxed our patience; but after all they had been faithful and efficient.
>
> Moreover, it must not be forgotten that I had known every member of the tribe for nearly a quarter of a century, until I had come to regard them with a kindly and personal interest, which any man must feel with regard to members of any inferior race who had been accustomed to respect and depend upon him during the greater part of his adult life.
>
> We left them all supplied with the simple necessities of Arctic life better than they had ever been before, while those who had participated in the sledge journey ... were really so enriched by our gifts that they were assumed the importance and standing of Arctic millionaires.[13]

These words were penned even as the Danish government, which had colonised Greenland, was purchasing supplies and chartering a ship to sail to Peary's old base at Thule to help to ease the miserable plight of the Inuit he had left behind.

CHAPTER 10

Trappers and Traders

Peary's departure from Thule, in the far north of Greenland, left the Inuit not only short of food and ammunition, but unable to satisfy their craving for coffee and cigarettes, a predicament which was alleviated only when Knud Rasmussen established a small trading post at the settlement. Rasmussen, himself a Greenlander, used his profits from the store to finance numerous exploratory expeditions. The most notable of these was the Fifth Thule Expedition, the sledge journey from Greenland to Siberia, in the course of which he assembled a comprehensive collection of Inuit songs and legends, and for the first time established the integrated nature of Inuit culture.

One of the few explorers to care deeply about the Inuit, Rasmussen persuaded them to exchange fox skins for the few trade goods he had managed to purchase with private capital. He explained that the skins were much more valuable than they had previously been told by Peary and the early whalers, and that although the exchange would be unfair for the first year, he could, if they trusted him, sell the skins for a handsome profit in Denmark, and with the income pay them a fair price the following year. The deal would enable him to offset his own costs and bring back a greater variety of merchandise, which they could then buy with their earnings. In this way, Rasmussen explained, the Inuit would receive regular supplies of whatever they needed each year.

The idea was an instant success. In the first year, Rasmussen and his fellow explorer, Peter Freuchen, sold skins worth £30,000 to £40,000, a figure which doubled in the next five years. Each hunter received a small income and was able to buy oatmeal, biscuits, margarine, coffee, tea, tinned milk, sugar and tobacco as well as weapons, ammunition, tools and essential items such as nails and matches. In addition, wood, textiles, gas and coal were available whenever they were needed. The Rasmussen store was the Inuits' first experience of a cash economy, and for a people who until that time did not know how to count, it was a revolution, plunging an Ice-age people into the modern world.

Rasmussen's store flourished for a quarter of a century, but eventually it was taken over by the Royal Greenland Trading Company, a monopoly which had been set up by the Danish government in 1776 as a means of establishing colonies in southern and western Greenland. Isolated for most of the year, each colony was an enclave, controlled by a Danish official. The only means of communication was by kayak, dog team or the annual supply ship. Travel was so difficult that it was not until 1921, 145 years later, that the Danes were able to impose their rule on Thule.

Although the purpose of colonisation was to monopolise the profits from the domestic whaling trade and the sale of skins, the Danes did not consciously set out to exploit the Inuit. Indeed, they were deeply concerned about their treatment by Dutch and English whalers, who stole their whaling products, often leaving settlements short of fuel for the winter. Yet, whenever the Dutch and English ships appeared, the Inuit rushed to the shore to meet them, fearful of the consequences but unable to control their need for the alcohol which they knew would be made readily available to them. The Dutch amused themselves by getting the Inuit drunk on Dutch genever; the English exchanged gin and brandy for the down of the eider duck, which was used for pillows and quilts. One Danish official wrote despairingly:

> The unfortunate distilled spirits of the ships lure everything from our Greenlanders, even the furs off their bodies ... Brandy is the chief source of ruin in the settlement.[14]

Indeed, it was not uncommon for an Inuk, awakening from a drunken stupor the next morning, to find himself on the deck of a whaler bound for Holland, where he was sold to a travelling showman and exhibited at fairgrounds across Europe. Kidnapping became increasingly common, and many families deprived of a hunter were left to starve.

Alcohol was not the only problem; most Inuit adults had also become addicted to tobacco, which was taken as snuff. Observing this, the Danes were quick to realise the potential for profit. Lars Dalager, a Danish functionary in the capital, Godthab, forecast that tobacco would be good business, and noted cynically that its addictive powers could be used to make the Inuit work harder.

> I have already seen them take the clothes off their backs to pay for tobacco. Instead of a Greenlander buying shirts, stockings, caps or pewter and copper utensils, which are all goods he can well do without, he can buy tobacco, snuff-boxes and handkerchiefs, and he is thus always obliged to be more industrious if he cannot do without the latter and yet wants some of the former.[15]

Dalager's prophecy was correct: whole communities became addicted. Heavy smokers traded so many skins that there were not enough to clothe the children, or to cover kayaks. In the capital alone, consumption rose from 63 pounds in 1755 to 362 pounds in 1770. When the Danes tried to raise the price, one Inuk broke into a warehouse and stole 14 pounds of tobacco, the first crime of its kind ever to occur in Greenland.

Although the introduction of alcohol and tobacco caused irreparable damage to Inuit society, the impact of the flintlock musket, which the Dutch and English made equally available, was devastating, and changed the whole course of the country's future. One immediate result was that as soon as the ice broke up in the spring, the Inuit living in Disko Bay packed their muskets and ammunition, and moved south to the fjords near the capital where they could shoot reindeer.

These animals could be killed with less effort than that required to catch seals, and they provided more meat. The disadvantages were the rapid depletion of the reindeer herds, and, owing to the neglect of seal hunting, a consequent shortage the following winter of skins, and blubber for the lamps. Nor did the Inuit have enough skins with which to trade. This caused considerable concern among the Danes, who had already expressed alarm at the number of accidents caused by poorly maintained guns, and the fatalities resulting from arguments between Dutch traders and armed, usually drunken, Inuit.

Despite their mercenary attitude, the Danes were genuinely anxious to protect the Inuit from violence, plunder and exploitation by foreigners. Halting the arms trade would clearly be beneficial for everyone, but it could be achieved only by prohibiting Dutch commerce. Accordingly, in 1782, the Danish government declared Greenland a closed country to all but authorised members of the Royal Greenland Trading Company, a restriction which continued for more than 150 years, until World War Two.

So rigorous were the new rules that even Danish citizens were not allowed entry without special permission. The edict amounted to little more than an official protection racket: security for the Inuit in return for a trade monopoly and absolute power. The Inuit were given no choice in the matter: the decision was taken unilaterally. Community leadership slipped from their hands into those of the Danes, who explained that as so many officials had been sent to ensure their safety, it was only fair that they should contribute towards the cost. In other words, the Danish King wanted to impose taxation.

In order to guarantee continued supplies of skins, the Royal Greenland Trading Company instructed its employees to maintain and protect the Inuit way of life. Brandy was banned except for medical purposes.

Restrictions were placed on the sale of flintlocks. Danish labour was imported to work at the whaling stations, and to carry out what were deemed to be 'non-native' jobs, so that the Inuit hunters could devote their time to hunting foxes and seals. The Danes always paid the Inuit a fair price, and for the first time, the hunters were relatively affluent. Prosperity, however, led to a surge in the population, straining the country's resources to the limit.

At the same time, the Norwegian Fritjiof Nansen completed his journey across the polar ice cap in *Fram*, discovering huge seal colonies off the Greenland coast. Within months, the Norwegians, hearing of this, and having destroyed their own seal stocks, were taking pups from the coast by the thousand. As a result, the seals moved further north, while the Inuit, their hunting grounds barren, were reduced to starvation. Their plight was so wretched that the Danes were obliged to distribute emergency rations, the country's first social welfare. Intensely ashamed, the Inuit were confused by the swift turn of events. The basis of their hunting culture had disappeared. They relied on the Danes for their food and clothing, and for the first time found themselves second-class citizens in their own country, a status which has continued until the present day.

The Inuit in Canada fared no better. Inroads into their way of life began with the arrival in Hudson Bay of two Frenchmen, Médard Chouart, Sieur des Groseilliers, and his brother-in-law, Pierre Esprit Radisson. These enterprising adventurers soon realised that by establishing French colonies along the bay's coastline they could guarantee a monopoly of the trade in beaver fur, which was rapidly becoming fashionable among the European nobility. Proposing this to the French government, Groseilliers was ridiculed as a foolish visionary, but learning of his rejection, the English Minister at Paris wrote him a letter of introduction to Prince Rupert. In London, the Frenchman was given a flattering reception, a ship, and instructions to form a settlement in Hudson Bay and to find the Northwest Passage to China.

In this, Groseilliers was unsuccessful, but having sailed to 75°N., he established a trading station, which he called Fort Charles, on the west coast of the bay. A year later, on May 2, 1670, he obtained a charter from King Charles II in which he and eighteen other gentlemen and merchants were incorporated under the name of 'Governor and Company of Adventurers of England Tradeing into Hudson's Bay', later to be known as the Hudson's Bay Company, or simply 'The Bay'. The royal charter was granted on the explicit condition that the search for the Northwest Passage be maintained. It gave the directors the exclusive right to exploit all land adjoining Hudson Bay as far west as the Pacific Ocean, a legal privilege which lasted until 1867, although its directors enjoyed an effective monopoly on all commerce in the Northwest Territories until 1964, when the Canadian government established its own trading posts.

The Adventurers, wearing top hats and frock coats, established numerous forts in the bay, to which they enticed the Indians, who bartered valuable beaver furs for rifles, ammunition, alcohol and other inexpensive commodities. In their enthusiasm for instant profit, the traders neglected their obligation to seek a route to Asia, forgetting that failure to exert themselves in the name of geographic discovery carried the risk of forfeiting their legal claim to the territories.

Finally remembering this, and intrigued by Indian reports of a copper mine and 'yellow metal' in the Barren Lands northwest of Hudson Bay, the Adventurers decided to mount an exploratory expedition, selecting a servant of the company, Samuel Hearne, to find the large river on the banks of which the mine was said to exist. Hearne, thought to be well qualified for the task, travelled across the Barren Lands until the weather deteriorated, his Indian guide deserted him and his provisions were exhausted. He returned after five weeks, defeated and barely alive. Refusing to admit failure, a year later, in December, 1770, the Adventurers ordered the unfortunate Hearne to set out again. After travelling across the tundra for six months, he finally reached the Coppermine River on the edge of the tree line, but failed to note down his position or the route he had taken. No sooner had he arrived than his Indian guides discovered a group of Inuit sleeping in tents nearby, and prepared to attack. At one o'clock in the morning the Indians '... rushed forth from the ambuscade and fell on the poor unsuspecting creatures, unperceived till close at the very eave of their tents, when they soon began the bloody massacre, while I,' wrote Hearne unashamedly, 'stood neuter in the rear.'[16]

Constant feuding between the Indians and Inuit placed the Hudson's Bay men in a delicate position. Wishing to trade with both groups, they persuaded Inuit from the northern part of the bay to visit the trading posts further south, but when they did so, the Indians disappeared. As the beaver supplied by the Indians was of far greater value than the occasional seal skins and walrus tusks offered by the Inuit, the company had no alternative but to confine trade temporarily to the Indians.

The attitude of the English traders towards the Inuit was from the beginning one of mistrust. Making no attempt to understand their customs, they regarded them as sly, treacherous, fraudulent, revengeful and cruel, at the same time recognising their amicable and good-humoured nature. If the opportunity presented itself, the captains of company ships were instructed to trade, but were warned to be on their guard, and on no account to allow the Inuit on board.

This suspicion was sometimes justified, as the first company employees trying to penetrate the interior of Labrador discovered. After meeting a group of Inuit near the Little Whale River, on the east coast of Hudson Bay, they felt there was sufficient goodwill to warrant taking two of them back to the main outpost at Richmond. Here, in a spirit of obvious friendliness, security was relaxed. Eventually, the men left the camp in the charge of an apprentice. When they returned, they found that the store had been looted, and guns stolen. There was no trace of the Inuit or the boy. A few days later, another band of Inuit appeared outside the post, shouting 'Chimo, Chimo', a word meaning 'Hello, are you friendly?' Three of the group were lured inside the post, and seized. Using sign language, they were told that two of them would be held captive until the third returned with the apprentice. The hostages appeared to be unmoved, but in the middle of the night they seized some rifles, and not knowing how to use them, tried to club their way to freedom. In the ensuing fight, both were shot. Soon afterwards, the Hudson's Bay men discovered the body of the apprentice within 200 yards of the post, which was subsequently abandoned. It was many years before Company agents again attempted to trade in the interior of Labrador.

Trading stations were usually established close to a river, or inlet, in the bleakest and most exposed locations imaginable. The post at Churchill was constructed on a windswept point where sixty Danes, previously forced to winter there, had died of exposure and starvation. There was no wood. Water was scarce. The company's first Governor-in-Chief of the Bay, James Knight, observed:

> It was the Difficultest piece of Work as ere was done in this Country, [which is] so bare that it affords neither fish nor flesh. I never see such a Miserable Place in all my life ... Them natives to the Norward are Savage and brutelike and will drink blood and eat raw flesh and fish, and loves it as well as some does Strong Drink.[17]

The early Hudson's Bay traders were chosen as much for their fitness and mental stability as for their business sense. Assigned to manage a new outpost, a young employee was taken in the company sloop to the appointed site, set ashore with enough wood, tools and nails to build himself a small house, and given a stock of commodities with which to trade. He was then left to fend for himself until the ship returned the following year.

With only a few transient Inuit for company, the loneliness drove many men to drink. Employees were allowed to buy English brandy from the stores, but to prevent immoderate drinking, the Company stipulated that no more than one quart of brandy, which tasted more like rough gin, could be purchased at a time, with a maximum limit of six gallons a year. The company's policy towards drinking was perhaps best reflected in the price: 5s.0d. a gallon, which made a full gallon of brandy available for the price of two *Books of Common Prayer*.

For the Inuit, whose social customs allowed them to take what they needed, whenever it suited them, trading was a new concept. With patience, the Hudson's Bay traders won their confidence and taught them the rules. Andrew Graham, a naturalist and employee of the Hudson's Bay Company, noted that the Inuit brought whale oil, baleen, and the skins of seals, wolves, and polar bears to the store. 'In return', Graham wrote, 'they receive from us wrought iron-work, such as harpoons, lances etc., also beads, looking-glass etc. And we are very kind to them giving them many presents, which conduct is not only commendable in the Company, but has ingratiated us into their good opinion ... So fond are these poor people of iron-work, that they lick it with their tongues before they put it by; indeed, I have seen them so transported with pleasure as to fall into dreadful convulsions.'[18]

Not all Hudson's Bay agents were so enthusiastic. Nicol Finlayson, a Scot, observed that trade with the 'eskimaux' consisted only of a few deer skins, sealskin thongs, ten gallons of oil and a few deer tongues.

We might have purchased a quantity of meat from them [he wrote] but from the dirty manner in which it is butchered in the first instance and afterwards kept, it is fit only for an Eskimaux stomach. The bowels with their contents, liver, lungs, blood etc. are all sewed up in large bundles with the meat, which soon becomes tainted and offensive; in addition they roll them in the sand and dirt, sit upon them etc., etc. .... Every useful article in the store was displayed to their view and every encouragement held out to induce them to hunt fur animals ... The manner of dressing and preparing the skins was also explained to them.[19]

Although trade in the Far North was increasing, the Hudson's Bay pioneers remained suspicious of the Inuit, and exercised caution. For decades, store managers were not permited to trade firearms with them. This put the Inuit at a distinct disadvantage when they were attacked by their traditional enemies, the Indians, who frequently raided their settlements, forcing them to flee and leave behind vital tools and utensils. In 1756, at least forty Inuit were massacred on the east coast of Hudson Bay. Inevitably, Inuit demands that they be given guns for their trade goods grew more persistent. Eventually, the Hudson's Bay agents capitulated, and by 1790 many Inuit were trained marksmen.

As in Greenland, the spread of firearms changed Inuit hunting patterns. Greater numbers of caribou were slaughtered during the spring migration, and musk oxen in winter. Arctic hares, foxes, ptarmigan and eider were taken more easily. Fish hooks and twine for making nets were also available from the trading station, and as with the rifle, initially helped the Inuit to catch more game than at any time previously. Yet these benefits were short-lived. Although the preparation of hides and dummies during previous caribou hunts was time-consuming, and spears and bows and arrows had a limited range, this method of hunting was silent and did not disrupt the migration routes of caribou from the forests to the Barren Lands. The rifle drove the fearful animals far from the settlements, making hunting more difficult, and sometimes impossible. As a result, famine was frequent, and, as the scattered human bones on archaeological sites testify, entire villages succumbed to starvation and cannibalism.

As the traders urged the Inuit to become trappers of the blue and white foxes, traditional weapons were gradually replaced by rifles, knives and steel fox traps. The Hudson's Bay agents gave little thought to the consequences of such encouragement. They introduced a system of credit which enabled the Inuit to draw the food, traps, nets and weapons necessary for a hunting trip, not realising that they were undermining the cornerstone of the Inuit's social structure.

For as long as anyone could remember, the Inuit had hunted caribou in the summer, and seal in winter and spring. In the Canadian north, the seal hunt was a communal occasion, during which families built inter-linked snow houses, *illuliaq*, to make the winter nights more tolerable. Unfortunately, this social gathering coincided with the brief period when the fur of the white fox was in its prime, and many Inuit consequently abandoned the hunt, heading off in different directions to lay and check trap lines hundreds of miles long. As a result, families were left without skins for clothes, boots and tents, or winter seal meat, surviving on food purchased on credit from the trading post. If the intention of the Hudson's Bay agents had been to make the Inuit totally dependent, they could hardly have succeeded more brilliantly.

Nevertheless, the Hudson's Bay traders generally treated the Inuit fairly, providing them with more than adequate supplies for their trapping expeditions, although the abundance of credit goods often overwhelmed the hunters. For centuries, when food was plentiful, they had been accustomed to gorging themselves, and feasting with their friends and neighbours. As the Inuk trapper needed only what he could carry on his sledge, the temptation to boast about his apparent affluence was too great. Extravagance was a means of proving his prowess as a hunter and trapper, so with little thought for the future, food that should have been saved for the winter was shared in spontaneous bouts of gluttony. This need for ostentatious celebration exists even today. In *The Last Kings of Thule*, Jean Malaurie describes how, after a particularly good month's fox hunting, Ululik, an Inuk from Thule, decided to hold a birthday party for his five-year-old son:

> The women were saying that Ululik might acquire a boat, but other people thought he would buy lumber for a new house. I arrived at his home around four o'clock. I stopped on the threshold, dumb-founded; before me I saw the most wonderful igloo an Eskimo Peter Pan could have imagined in his wildest dreams. The walls were studded with multicoloured candles; the ceiling was hung with coloured streamers. In the middle of the room, pans of milk gave off a fragrant steam that mingled with the steam from a kettle of coffee; heaps of seal meat and narwhal skin, *mattak*, and buns were heaped in one corner; chocolate and tobacco everywhere.
>
> Alone on the platform bed sat Aqqaluk, Ululik's son, as if on a throne. He was wearing party clothes, and seemed both stunned and enchanted. As if he were a stallion at a fair, someone had put a red ribbon around his neck. Saliva drooled over his lips; his beautiful white anorak was already spotted with chocolate. What did it matter! The presents – a knife, cloth, ivory teeth, soap, a cup, a whip – were already piled on the floor at his feet. When Ululik saw me walk in, he came over and took me by the arm, saying: 'You see, in Ululik's house coffee, milk, and everything else run like rivers!' People had come from thirty miles around; my host was blissful; his round face was creased with satisfaction. He strutted up and down, shook people's hands, and bustling about, played the Important Person to his heart's content. He was now ruined for a whole month, but never had he been more sincerely happy.[20]

Hearing of the Hudson's Bay Company's success, unscrupulous merchants headed for the Barren Lands to capitalise on the new market. These free traders were intent only on making a quick profit, exchanging rifles for an exorbitant number of fox skins, well aware that once they moved on, the Inuit would be unable to find ammunition for their guns.

The greed and callousness of the free traders knew no bounds. Demonstrating how kerosene stoves could transform a harsh life in the North to one of comfort, they neglected to tell the Inuit that they would not be returning, that the nearest fuel was hundreds of miles away, and that the stoves would therefore be useless. For all its faults, the Hudson's Bay Company was reliable, and able to supply the Inuit regularly, placing their orders for despatch on the next ship north if goods were not available in the store.

As the company expanded its operations further inland, there was a sharp increase in the number of beaver and fox skins brought to the trading posts. Eventually, beaver skins became a form of currency with standard rates of exchange; one beaver skin was equivalent to two fox skins, six musquash or 2,000 goose quills. These purchased a pound of tobacco, a mirror, twelve needles, ten fish hooks or three knives. A gallon of English brandy, or 'waters strong', cost four beavers, whereas seven skins were needed for a pistol, and fourteen for a rifle.

At Churchill, records from 1771 showed that in the preceding seven years, the Indians bartered nearly 100,000 beaver skins. Many of these went for alcohol, which became a constant problem, fuelling inter-tribal wars and feuds with the Inuit. The Indians killed so many beaver that stocks were depleted, forcing them to move further west. In 1789, a Scottish employee, Alexander Mackenzie, paddling his canoe through the network of lakes, rivers and streams to the northwest, discovered the second largest river in North America. In time, it would become a major trading route to the arctic coast, opening up the Northwest Territories more quickly than any other region in Canada.

Despite this rapid expansion, the Hudson's Bay Company did not penetrate the arctic islands north of the mainland until the beginning of this century, when the whaling industry collapsed. Many whalers stayed on to become trappers and, gradually, modern commodities became commonplace. There were pockets of isolated Inuit who still believed that they were the only people on earth, but most were by now equipped with white man's tools, eating imported food and wearing manufactured clothing. Earlier suspicions of the Inuit had long since evaporated. On arrival at a trading post after a long journey with their families and dog teams, the Inuit were usually invited to stay for a couple of days, as guests of the company, while they traded goods and news of other settlements.

Although the Hudson's Bay Company radically changed the Inuit way of life, adverse effects were matched by benefits. Life was easier. Steel knives reduced to an hour the days formerly taken to flense seals and walrus with flint and bone tools, enabling the Inuit to return to the hunt immediately, and catch enough food for a month. Matches liberated them from the chore of rubbing sticks together to make fire. Metal pans reduced to minutes the hours needed to cook meals in stone pots. Families moved from their cold, damp *iglu* of stone and turf into the heated, wooden shacks equipped with linoleum, tables, chairs, sofas, iron beds and alarm clocks.

Yet time weighed heavily, for the price of this relative luxury was boredom and continual debt. When fashions in Europe and North America changed, and long-haired fur such as fox was no longer required, the Inuit, together with the Indians and Metis, or half-breeds, were left destitute. As in Greenland, fierce pride succumbed to shame as they grew dependent on the government for social security payments. The Hudson's Bay Company boasted arrogantly that its initials meant 'Here Before Christ', but it showed little moral responsibility towards the Inuit. Suffering from famine as recently as 1963, some of them were forcibly removed from their villages on Baffin Island to communities in the arctic islands, where the hunting was said to be more productive.

The manager of a Hudson's Bay trading post no longer travels by dog sled, or lives in a wooden hut with a stove and a few rickety chairs. He sits in a centrally heated office, wearing a business suit, next to a secretary tapping a word processor. 'The Bay' has grown into one of Canada's biggest commercial groups, owning 21 shopping centres, an interest of between ten per cent and fifty per cent in 28 others, as well as their assets in oil and mining companies.

Each arctic store is packed with heavy clothing, boots, tools and nails, but now an Inuk wife can also buy cotton dresses, stiletto-heeled shoes, leather handbags and cheap jewellery. Fresh vegetables, lettuce, tomatoes, apples and oranges are flown in two or three times a week. Assembly-kit furniture, plastic toys for the children and souvenirs for tourists jostle for space with a selection of camping equipment, vacuum cleaners, microwave ovens, typewriters, stereo radios, colour televisions and video recorders. Copies of soft porn magazines like *Playboy, Club* and *Mayfair* are on prominent display among the birthday cards and paperback novels. Each store has a fascinating array of 'southern' products, and is a focal point of community life, where Inuit with time on their hands meet to gossip. For the majority, the only money they have to spend is their unemployment benefit.

CHAPTER 11

The Missionaries

The bulging shelves of 'The Bay' and the Arctic Co-operative stores represented all that was desirable about the white man's life in the South, and underlined the deficiencies of the Inuits' living standards. An Inuk possessing the most worthless commodity was envied because his purchase was a status symbol, raising his standing in the community. A cheap alarm clock was meaningless in the arctic environment, but it was fun and focused attention on its owner; a new rifle guaranteed superiority over fellow Inuit still hunting with harpoons; the latest model of an outboard motor or snowmobile impressed friends and neighbours, who gathered round to appraise its finer points as they had once discussed the merits of a dog team. That the coveted item had been purchased with a social security hand-out was of little account.

In the cash economy, the old customs were suddenly inappropriate. It was more important to keep up with the arctic equivalent of the Jones's; to show that the Inuit, too, could possess the same trappings as the *qallunaat*, the white man. Unwittingly, the whalers, explorers and traders had initiated a process which was to alienate the Inuit from their own traditions, a quite unforeseen consequence of their presence. The deliberate and systematic attempt to destroy the Inuit culture was perpetrated by a fourth group: the men who sailed north in the name of God.

Nowhere was the subjugation of northern peoples as ruthless, or achieved more quickly than in Greenland. The first missionaries arrived there in 1721, expecting to provide spiritual direction to descendants of the original Viking settlers. Nothing had been heard of these early colonists for more than 300 years, and it was feared that with no priests to instruct them, they had reverted to paganism.

The first Vikings had arrived in the summer of 984 AD from Iceland, a volcanic island whose limited pastures were no longer enough to support the growing number of Viking farmers emigrating from Norway. After a dispute over the ownership of farmland, a local Icelandic chieftain, Eirik the Red, was outlawed for murder. Setting sail with his supporters in 25 open-decked merchant ships, or *knarr*, Eirik headed towards an inverted mirage which reflected the pack ice and hostile mountains of the east Greenland coast. It was as far west as any man had sailed, the edge of the known world.

Only fourteen vessels reached their destination; the others either sank, or turned back. Unable to penetrate the icepack, Eirik followed the coast south, finally sailing into the southern fjords, which he named 'Green' land. Much later, this led to accusations of false representation, but deceit was not Eirik's intention. He merely wished to attract as many new settlers as possible, and in summer, the hills flanking the fjords beneath Greenland's inland icecap are indeed as green as any in Iceland, or Eirik's homeland, Norway.

The Vikings eked out a meagre existence until, after a series of misfortunes, they perished about 500 years later. Climatic fluctuations bringing colder weather were partly to blame. A mini-glaciation period brought the Inuit further south and into conflict with the Norsemen, who contemptuously referred to them as *skraelingar*, the wretched ones. At the same time, vast quantities of ice from the polar seas drifted on the East Greenland current as far south as Cape Farewell, blocking entry to the fjords in the south. This was disastrous. *Knarr* bringing vital supplies from the colonial rulers of Scandinavia were unable to penetrate the icepack and reach the settlements.

Trade soon became unprofitable and the Scandinavian kings, who had begun to forge commercial links with the Hanseatic League in Europe, lost interest in their remote colony. The Greenlanders, who no longer possessed their own *knarr*, or enough wood to make them, were isolated. Cold and ice decimated their sparse crops and livestock. By the early fifteenth century, the remaining Vikings were in a pitiful state. The last ship sailed from the colony in 1408, leaving behind a tiny population riddled with scurvy and tuberculosis. Inbreeding led to stunted growth and deformities. Disease, weather, Basque pirates and possibly the plague picked them off one by one. There were no survivors.

None of this was known in Scandinavia, although three centuries later the lack of information about the Norse colonists was a source of worry to a Danish theologian, Hans Egede, who had read about 'wild people and men' living in the south and west of Greenland. Aware that the Vikings had been converted to Christianity, Egede was convinced that, if these were the Norse descendants, it was the solemn duty of the Church to establish a mission as quickly as possible, an idea which was given a cool reception by the autocratic Lutheran bishops of the state-controlled Danish-Norwegian Church.

Not to be defeated, Egede persisted, petitioning the King and trying unsuccessfully to solicit money from merchants. Believing that gold could be created from base metals, he studied chemistry and dreamed of creating his own financial backing for the mission by means of alchemy. Hans Egede persevered for eleven years, and in 1721 finally mounted the combined trading, whaling and missionary expedition that was to change the course of Greenland's future.

Disappointed at finding no trace of the Norsemen, Egede decided to spread the Gospel among the Inuit. This was a mammoth task, virtually equivalent to civilising those who, in his ignorance, he regarded as barbarians. With appalling living conditions and an acute shortage of merchandise and materials, he frequently despaired, overwhelmed by a sense of responsibility for his family and the other members of the expedition. His first difficulty was communication with the 'pagans' whose ways he so despised. He drew pictures of the Devil and punched the nearest Inuk in the face to show that Satan was to be feared, a tactic which succeeded only in frightening the superstitious Inuit. Groping for words, Egede tried to teach eternal damnation, but in the absence of an Inuktitut vocabulary to illustrate the concepts of Christianity, the Inuit were unable to grasp what he was trying to tell them, and in any case, were far more concerned with hunting. Intensely frustrated, Egede concluded that, as the Inuit were unaware of God, they were no better than 'dumb animals' whose entire way of life was the work of the Devil.

The Inuit could see by Egede's attitude that he was a *qallunaat* leader. His cassock and clerical ruff set him apart from other men, and although his thunderous sermons were incomprehensible to them, it was obvious that he wielded authority. To the Inuit, Christian services such as baptism and communion were clearly rituals designed to assuage the spirits. The Bible was thought to be a magical device used for protection against hunger and disease. The missionary was undeniably a powerful *angakok* to be feared.

Determined to surmount the language barrier, Egede ignored the wishes of Inuit parents and compelled their children to visit his home to teach him Inuktitut. This uncharitable practice earned him a place in the very Inuit tradition he was trying so hard to displace, here described succinctly in the following song.

> There has come a strange man
> Over the Great Sea from the West,
> Who steals boys,
> And gives them thick soup
> With skin upon it [porridge],
> And dried earth [ship's biscuits] from his own land.[21]

One indication of the ill-feeling caused by Egede's zeal emerges from the comment of a boy's mother, who, when asked if she would allow her son to stay with him in return for a present, suppressed her fear and replied that her children were not articles of commerce. Despite the setbacks, Egede composed a glossary of nearly 300 words, many of them inaccurate, but sufficient to help him to explain some of the basic Christian concepts. Few missionaries learned more than a few words of Inuktitut, and most were obliged to preach through an interpreter.

When the scriptures eventually came to be translated, the theological difficulties were sometimes greater than those caused by the language. The missionaries found it difficult to explain why the *qallunaat* had killed Christ, a man who could perform miracles and bring the dead back to life, and who, in Inuit eyes, was clearly the most powerful *angakok* the world had ever known. There was the dilemma of whether to include certain biblical stories in translations. Accounts setting out the murder of Abel, the rape of Dinah, the treachery of Jacob, the polygamy of the patriarchs, the sinfulness of Sodom and the wickedness of Simeon and Levi were hardly likely to persuade unbelieving Inuit to accept Christianity without question. In teaching the catechisms, it was necessary to explain the punishment for European sins such as gaming and profiteering, which were not committed in Greenland. Yet to tamper with God's word was arrogant, and to change the strict Lutheran interpretations, to which the orthodox Danish Church was wholly committed, was dangerously unwise.

Compromise was sometimes necessary. When Hans Egede tried to teach the Lord's Prayer, the Inuit asked: 'What is this daily bread that is so important that you must ask the *qallunaat* God for it every day?' Egede responded with the amended translation 'Give us this day that which tastes good,' but the Inuit were still not satisfied. 'Are there no seals in your heaven?' they asked. Eventually, Hans Egede capitulated, changing the translation to 'Give us this day the seal meat we need.'

In order to impose Christianity on the Inuit, it was imperative to destroy the authority of the *angakok*, whom the missionaries regarded as a natural enemy of God. Well aware that he was a linchpin of Inuit society, they reasoned that if they could unmask him as an absurd eccentric, his role as teacher, doctor, adjudicator and spiritual adviser would be undermined. The structure of Inuit community life would collapse, and in the confusion, the Inuit would be forced to turn to them for help and guidance. Egede began his campaign by ridiculing Inuit myths and taboos, and by insisting that the hunters and their families renounce their amulets. He assured them that as faith in the Lord guaranteed eternal life, such charms were without significance or worth. Many hunters accepted his promise. Others continued to wear their amulets secretly. If discovered, they risked a severe beating from the ill-tempered missionary. Egede himself recorded his reaction to an Inuk who refused to obey him:

> I had to give him a few blows across the back, for nothing can make them see reason except beating and punishment, which I have to practise occasionally, having found that this worked.[22]

Intimidation and violence were as much a part of the missionaries' disposition as ritual and prayer. Ranting incessantly, they were apparently not concerned that their exhortations were nearly incomprehensible to the Inuit. Nor did they worry unduly if their potential converts were perturbed by the constant beatings. Determined to stamp out all superstitious practices, Egede was not averse to threatening individuals with their lives. His son, Niels, was equally forceful in his attempts to convert the 'heathen' Inuk to the benefits of Christian charity. Describing his approach, he wrote:

> I gave him to understand that if he would not let himself be persuaded by fair means, but despised the word of God, he should receive the same treatment from me as other *angakoks* and liars had received, namely a thrashing.[23]

Such action appears to have been common, rather than isolated. On another occasion, he admitted:

> When I had tried all I could by means of persuasion and exhortation, without avail, I had recourse to my usual method, flogged him soundly and turned him out of the house.[24]

Having insisted on the abolition of amulets, the Lutherans seized every opportunity to challenge the power of the 'witch doctors'. One *angakok*, unwise enough to observe that it would be an easy matter for the Inuit to rid themselves of the foreigners, was taken prisoner, put in irons for three days and given a beating which, Egede claimed, 'he accepted, being thankful that his life was spared.' Blackmail and thuggery eventually subdued the Inuit, and the imposition of the missionaries' will became less dependent on violence, but relied on ridicule and intellectual superiority instead.

When one *angakok* asserted that he had flown to the *qallunaat* Heaven, where the pillars were crumbling, Egede's other son, Poul, demanded that he provide tangible proof. Unable to do so, the *angakok* was derided as a humbug. Others were shown to be hopelessly ineffective when the missionaries forecast, with far greater accuracy, the date of the sun's return after the winter darkness. This relentless campaign had the desired effect. The Inuit soon began to laugh openly at the hocus-pocus of the *angakok*, who in desperation cast spells and urged *tupilek* and other spirits to kill his enemies. These efforts were counter-productive, merely adding to his humiliation when the missionaries survived unharmed.

Despite the relentless verbal and physical attacks on the *angakut*, the missionaries made slow progress. Their efforts were just beginning to show signs of success, with an increase in the number of converts, when disaster struck. The Danish king, impatient with the scanty results of Egede's first twelve years, sent three German Herrhuter, or Moravian missionaries, to help him with the task of converting and colonising Greenland.

No sooner had they arrived than Egede quarrelled with them on fundamental theological matters. The Moravians retaliated by setting up a rival mission. This was a serious development, overshadowed only by an outbreak of smallpox a few weeks later. Within six months, nearly 900 people had succumbed to the epidemic, including most of Egede's converts and his wife, who had been nursing the sick. Panicking, the Inuit, who no longer had faith in the abilities of the *angakok* to deal with the problem, fled from their settlements to the capital, seeking protection from the unknown illness. They were dismayed to find that the missionaries, who had guaranteed them eternal life, were equally helpless.

The partial centralisation of the Inuit population was little consolation to Hans Egede, although he had complained for years that the perpetual wanderings of the Inuit hunters made it all but impossible to preach Christianity. He had advocated the use of force to prevent their travelling, but here he fell into direct conflict with the traders, who shared responsibility for the colonisation of Greenland, and were anxious that the hunters remain scattered in remote settlements, close to the hunting grounds and the game that provided their profits. So intense was the dispute, that fights between the missionaries and traders became commonplace. The Lutherans also came to blows with the Moravians, whose revivalist methods they despised, not least because of their evident success.

In contrast to the gaiety of the Moravian gatherings, at which Inuit songs were accompanied by violins, zithers, French horns and flutes, the orthodox Lutheran services, with their translated hymns sung in the slow, slurring manner still prevalent today, were found dull and boring. The Moravians wore white surplices; the Lutherans black cassocks and ruffs.

The Inuit regarded the Moravian services as popular entertainment, in every way preferable to those at the Royal Mission.

Depressed by his inability to compete, Hans Egede so protracted his hell-fire sermons that the Inuit sometimes interrupted him, demanding to know how much longer he intended to go on. When he measured the time on his arm, the Inuit returned to their seats, pointedly moving their fingers down their own arms as a reminder. Hans Egede was determined to give the Inuit a fundamental religious knowledge prior to baptism. The Moravians appeared to be interested solely in boosting the membership of their mission. So lacking in theological instruction were the Moravian catechists that, according to Nansen, one of them baptised not only the parishioners, but also their husky puppies.

The Moravians insisted that baptised Inuit should live in, or as close as possible, to the mission hall. This soon led to over-crowding, but was essential for what the Moravians euphemistically called 'church discipline'. Believing in the principles of group therapy, the Moravians divided the congregation into 'choirs', ostensibly to assist spiritual development, but actually to prevent defections. There was another, more insidious reason for herding the Inuit into small groups; it enabled the Moravians to establish a spy system, and pry into every aspect of the private lives and behaviour of their converts. The penalty for transgressing the rules was exclusion from communion, a fate as shameful as losing a drum dance.

Despite the apparent cheerfulness of their services, the Moravians cast the Inuit into greater depths of misery than any other foreign intruders. Their policy was to divide and rule. Inuit who had not been baptised were ordered to leave the mission hall immediately after the sermon. Friendship between the baptised and the unbaptised was firmly discouraged. Cohabitation between the two groups was tantamount to a mortal sin, and brought instant criticism and punishment.

Baptised Inuit were isolated from the rest of their families in much the same way as the followers of the Rev. Sun Myung Moon today. When a baptised hunter died, his widow and children would make their way to the mission, aware that the Moravians offered presents of food to potential converts. The grieving, and starving, Inuit soon learned to feign interest in the *qallunaat* God, hanging their heads and rolling their eyes in false humility, and allowing themselves to be drawn into the Church against their better judgement.

Christian teaching served only to confuse the Inuit.

Hans Egede's son, Poul, who was also a missionary, described in his reports[25] in 1741 how the Inuit, on learning of the Garden of Eden, were unable to understand why Adam and Eve would want to waste time talking to a serpent. They asked why, if God was omnipotent, He had allowed them to eat the 'big berry', knowing it to be a crime so great that the entire human race would be condemned as a result. One Inuk girl, who had been told that her deceased parents were burning in Hell because they had not known God, expressed disbelief that any God could be so cruel, when surely He must have known of their ignorance.

If Christianity was so important, she asked, why had God not told the Inuit about it previously, so that her parents could have gone to Heaven? When the girl quoted the missionary's own words, 'Blessed are the poor in spirit, for theirs is the kingdom of heaven,' and demanded to know why, if that was true, her parents had been sent to Hell, the missionary responded that it was the 'Will of God', and gave her a severe beating. Nor could the Inuit understand why the poor in spirit, who were a burden on the community, should be permitted to go to Heaven.

The image of Heaven was a difficult one for the Inuit to comprehend. Visions of white-robed angels gliding through immaculate gardens, and singing psalms in marble palaces decorated with silver and gold, were meaningless to a people who had never heard of such things, and were interested only in the availability of seals and fish. If Heaven was truly such a wonderful place, they asked, why was it wrong to help a sick Inuk to reach it? Old people had always taken their leave of society by paddling out to sea, jumping off a cliff, falling off a sledge or hanging themselves when life weighed heavier than death. Why should the souls of those who helped them be damned for evermore? Surely this was a charitable act? And why was there so much marble, silver and gold in Heaven when the missionaries themselves had said that God would not forgive the rich, that it was easier for a seal to pass through the eye of a bone needle than for a rich man to enter the Kingdom of Heaven?

The Inuits' doubts were understandable. In their egalitarian society, riches were shared and theft did not exist. Yet when a hungry Inuk was seen taking a piece of seal meat from a neightbour's doorstep, as custom dictated was his right, the missionaries denounced him as a thief and threatened him with the wrath of God. Having experienced the wrath of Hans Egede, this was a less difficult concept for the Inuit to envisage. On hearing from the missionaries of the effects of an earthquake in Portugal, one group of hunters and their families were so terrified that they fled from their settlement 'to another quite as unsafe'.

An insight into the mental turmoil into which the missionaries had thrown the Inuit is evident in a letter written by Pauia Groenlaender, an Inuk who had been baptised by Hans Egede. Writing in 1756 to Egede's son, Poul, who had returned to Copenhagen, he explained how the Inuit, given sufficient food and enough skins to keep them warm, were a contented people, whereas he was not sure what to think of the Christians:

> They leave their own beautiful land, and suffer much hardship in this country, which is to them so rough and disagreeable, simply for the sake of making us good people; but have you seen so much evil in our nation? Their teachers instruct us how we are to escape the Devil, whom we never knew; and yet the roystering sailors pray with the greatest earnestness that the devil may take them ... This year in particular I have heard so much of the Christians, that if I had not, in the course of long familiarity with them, known many good and worthy men among them ... I could have wished that we had never set eyes upon them lest they should corrupt our people ...
>
> Your people know that there is a God, the creator and upholder of all things, that after this life they will either be happy or miserable, according as they shall have conducted themselves here, and yet they live as if they were under orders to be wicked, and it was to their honour and advantage to sin. My countrymen on the other hand, know nothing either of a God or a devil, believe neither in punishment nor in reward after this life; and yet they live decently, treat each other kindly, and share with each other peaceably when they have food to share ... We are indeed contented with our lot. Fish and flesh are our sole food. Our drink is ice cold water; it quenches the thirst and does not steal away the understanding or the natural strength like that maddening drink of which your people are so fond ...
>
> Murder is very seldom heard of among us. It does not happen unless someone is suspected or accused of being a magician and of having killed someone by his witchcraft, in which case he is killed without remorse by those whose duty it is, who think they have just as good right as the executioner in your country to take the lives of malefactors; but they make no boast of it, and do not give thanks to God for it like the great lords in your country, when they have killed all the people of another land. It surely cannot be to the good God of whom you teach us, who has forbidden us to shed blood, that they give thanks and praises; it must be to another who loves slaughter and destruction. I wonder if it is not to the *tornasuk*, (the Devil)? Yet that cannot be either; for it would be flying in the face of the good God to give any honour to Satan. I hope you will explain this to me at your convenience.[26]

Further confusion arose when the missionaries introduced 'Sundays' into arctic life. Until then, the Inuit year was marked only by the seasons and the milestones in their lives, and those of their children. In order to observe the sabbath, it was imperative to divide the year into weeks, so calendars were created: blocks of wood, each with seven holes into which children could fit a wooden peg. The notion of a day of rest every seventh day was completely alien to the Inuit, who ate when they were hungry and slept when they were tired. What would happen, they asked, if, after a period of blizzards and poor hunting, the first fair weather fell on a Sunday, and the seals were sunning themselves on the ice? Was hunting in such circumstances an infringement of God's Law? And, if so, what was the point of praying to Him every day to 'Give us this day the seal meat we need'?

Notwithstanding their inability to answer such questions satisfactorily, the influence of the missionaries became so powerful that their religious zeal gradually smothered the artistic creativity of the Inuit. Like a fire starved of oxygen, their art was denied inspiration, and was eventually extinguished along the entire west coast of Greenland. Songs and poetry were banned, and soon forgotten. The only music permitted was the singing of hymns and lullabies. Dancing, and watching others dance, was punishable by excommunication. All forms of enjoyment were discouraged.

Every aspect of Inuit art was forbidden. Women were no longer allowed to tattoo their faces, hands or bodies. Cultic figures and masks were seen as a threat to Christianity, and destroyed. Every Inuit ceremony was outlawed, including the drum dance. Ignorant of its legal benefits, and making no effort to discover the true purpose of the contest, the missionaries regarded it as a pagan tradition, and therefore immoral, although a minority disagreed with its proscription. One Danish clergyman, Henric Christopher Glahn, admitted that he saw nothing sinful in beating a drum, 'nor that the refrain of a song ... should be more blameable than the melody of a psalm.' He was overruled. The pursuit of religious learning became the Inuits' sole diversion from the hardships of arctic life.

The Inuit could not understand why the missionaries should find dancing and sexual passion sinful, especially as these were the only recreations which made them happy, but by now, they were oppressed by a tyranny from which there was no escape. When the Moravians learned, presumably by prying, that Inuit women wore only foxskin briefs in their homes, their sense of propriety was outraged. From their pulpits, they publicly admonished the women, not realising that nakedness, in the intense heat generated in the stone and turf houses, allowed them to perspire freely and keep their bodies clean. After teaching the Inuit the importance of decency and bodily shame, many hunters were too embarrassed to approach their wives, especially when living in cramped conditions with other members of their families. The missionaries were also affronted by the occasional necessity for exchanging wives when husbands embarked on a long hunting trip, or in the interests of group survival when a wife was unable to bear children.

Polygamy, which in Inuit tradition seldom allowed more than two wives, soon led to conflict and insoluble ethical problems. Hunters seeking baptism were horrified when the missionaries insisted that one of their wives should be abandoned. Yet neither the Moravians nor the clergymen of the Royal Danish Mission were able to provide satisfactory answers to the hunter who wanted to know which one of his wives should be cast off, if both had borne his children. When it was pointed out that women discarded in this way would suffer inevitable hardship, and perhaps starvation, the missionaries ruled once again that such was the 'will of God'. Nor were they able to suggest who should look after the children.

The idea of forsaking healthy offspring was incomprehensible to the Inuit, whose customs, moral or otherwise, had maintained group numbers and enabled them to survive for 5,000 years. Adultery and premarital sex were of little significance, and unmarried mothers were free of social stigma. In their contempt for the 'heathen', the missionaries vehemently denounced such practices, although this did not prevent them taking Inuit wives, or conducting clandestine affairs. Christian ideals and sexual morality seem to have been reserved exclusively for the Inuit; few, if any attempts were made to restrain the activities of the whalers and traders, who, like some clergymen, were quick to take advantage of what they regarded as the 'loose morals' of Inuit women. Nor did the piety of the missionaries preclude them from trading in arms. When Nicol Finlayson, a Scot employed by the Hudson's Bay Company at Ford Chimo, in Labrador, discovered that the Moravians were able to sell their rifles less expensively, he asked his London headquarters to order 'cheaper guns for the Eskimaux', and suggested the second-hand flintlocks from York might serve the purpose.

Tradition had never required Inuit women to conceal illicit relationships, and conscious of the new-found modesty of their menfolk, they gloried in sexual encounters with Europeans, often preferring the most uncouth deckhand to a successful hunter. This social and sexual intercourse soon led to such a large admixture of the blood that the pure-bred Inuit along the west Greenland coast became almost extinct. Baptised Inuit women wishing to marry Danish officials usually renounced their former way of life, leaving the Inuit men to nurse their inferiority complexes. Half-caste children were brought up according to

European customs, and were untrained in the arts of hunting and survival. The hunters grew so concerned that they threatened to defy the wishes of the missionaries, and seek wives among those who had not been baptised.

At this, the Royal Greenland Trading Company established a set of conditions for mixed marriages. The consent of the prospective bride's parents was obligatory. The groom committed himself to remain in the country permanently, and bring the children up 'in both the mission and the company'. He had to accept that their half-caste children would never be permitted to visit Denmark, even for the purposes of education. Marriage services were valid only if they were conducted by clergymen, not Inuit catechists. In some isolated settlements, this meant that couples had to wait as long as two years for their wedding, and it was not uncommon for a bride to be confirmed and married, and her first child christened, on the same day.

Isolation may have been hard, but it was necessary. The influx of baptised Inuit to the Moravian mission in the capital, Godthab, soon became an intolerable strain on the food source, so much so that supporters of Hans Egede's Royal Mission, whose own success in hunting was jeopardised, referred to them as 'blubber grabbers'. Eventually, despite tenacious resistance, the Moravians were forced to disperse by government order.

Only in a handful of remote east coast settlements did the Inuit culture survive. Here, it was not until 1921 that the last Inuit were baptised. Their ceremonies, songs and masks were retained in secret for several years more, but as in the rest of the Arctic, gradually fell into disuse. The Inuit culture, which had taken thousands of years to evolve and spread to these ice-bound hamlets, was dead. With scant knowledge of the Arctic or its people, the missionaries had attacked, and ultimately eradicated, Inuit customs simply because they did not conform to their own Christian views. Legends preserved orally through countless generations were discarded, to be replaced with European folk tales. Inuit songs were forcibly displaced by hymn singing. Poetry was crippled.

The missionaries preached righteousness, propriety and salvation, establishing missions which divided the Inuit into Protestants and Catholics. In the scramble for souls, they built rival hospitals and schools where one was adequate. Pupils attending the churchmen's lessons usually emerged devout catechists, but were educated to little more than primary school level. Deprived of practical parental guidance owing to their attendance at the mission classes, they were left seriously lacking in the skills of survival.

Had it not been for the ethnologists who appeared after the Second

World War, much of the Inuit culture in Greenland would have been lost, but by earnestly prodding the Inuits' memories, the songs and legends of the past were re-captured. The ethnologists collected the few remaining masks and displayed them in the museums of Europe. They inspired the Inuit to resume their carvings, and to sell the weird *tupilek* and other cultic figures to the traders. Today, the little bone carvings are marketed in the tourist shops, and one cannot help wondering whether their creators still harbour a certain fear, and respect, for the spirits of their past. In 1894, Fritjiof Nansen posed a question which is as relevant now as it was then:

> Can an Eskimo who is nominally a Christian, but who cannot support his family, is in ill-health and is sinking into deeper and deeper misery, be held much more enviable than a heathen who lives in 'spiritual darkness', but *can* support his family, *is* robust in body, and thoroughly contented with life?[27]

Such questions were not the true concern of the missionaries, who regarded on their terms the imposition of Christianity and moral rectitude essential for the salvation of the world. The Arctic was merely another region to be challenged, and conquered. Like the whalers, traders and polar explorers, the men of the Church were the vanguard of a force which not only introduced new ideas and customs, but paved the way for the *qallunaat* who were intent on exploitation, and able to mobilise the full weight of the industrial mono-culture against Inuit everywhere.

CHAPTER 12

Into the Space Age

From Australia to the Americas, the image of the classic Eskimo is still that of Nanook of the North, the indomitable hunter clad in a sealskin anorak and polar-bear pants, his harpoon poised for the kill, his son playing happily with the husky puppies on the ice outside the family igloo. In the Arctic today, this vision is as ludicrous as that of Caesar, his toga flowing behind him, a bunch of grapes in one hand and a silver chalice in the other, striding through a traffic jam in Rome.

Yet it is a sobering thought that, in Canada and Greenland, anyone over the age of thirty will almost certainly have been born in a sealskin tent, a snowhouse or an *iglu* of turf and stone. During the brief post-war years, the whale-oil lamp has given way to electric light and the microwave oven, the bone needle to the sewing machine, the year-long sledge trip to the direct-dial telephone. Sledges are no longer created from walrus meat, whale bone and salmon, but made from processed timber flown in from the south. The thwarts and stanchions are fastened with nylon cord from the Co-op, rather than twine of seal gut. Mud is no longer used, runners are carved from plastic sheeting, or made from steel strips polished with emery paper.

In Alaska, Inuit watch the whale hunt through binoculars and use walkie-talkies to communicate with the *umiak* captains. Afterwards, they may congregate in the 'Drop-In' bar for a coke and a hamburger, or caribou-burger, perhaps feeding a handful of dimes into a fruit machine while younger Inuit peer into the screens of electronic games which permit them to drive racing cars, fly supersonic fighter aircraft, and repel Space Invaders, Aliens and Asteroid Attackers.

Today's 'Eskimo' has developed a political awareness, and become an Inuk. His sealskin anorak is more likely to be an American army surplus parka, his pants a pair of jeans or quilted trousers. The rifle has displaced his harpoon, the motor boat his kayak, and a snowmobile his dog team. Rather than tumbling with young sledge dogs, Inuit children ride bicycles across the ice or play on the balcony of an apartment block. Or they may be found in an abandoned, pre-fabricated wooden house daubed with graffiti, the modern version of the teenage *iglu*.

The transformation from Stone Age to Space Age began during World War Two. In Alaska and Greenland, roads, airfields and naval bases were constructed, but in Canada, the daily life of Nanook of the North remained much the same in the 1950s as it had been 4,000 years ago. In 1953, the year of Queen Elizabeth II's coronation in Westminster Abbey, some of her Inuit subjects in Canada were dying of starvation. Few Canadians, ninety per cent of whom lived within a hundred miles of the American border, were aware of the problem.

Eventually, the Canadian administration showed an interest in the potential of its northern territories. Bureaucrats, teachers and nurses headed northwards to the settlements, conscious of their government's newly-expressed intention to give the Inuit the same opportunities, rights and responsibilities as other Canadians. Ships sailed to Inuit communities laden with insulated prefabricated houses, complete with central heating and plumbing for hot and cold water. On arrival, electric cables were attached, and telephones installed. No one thought to ask whether the houses from the south were suited to arctic life.

Inuit parents were told that it was in their best interests to send their children to boarding schools. The children were given Cornflakes, sausage, bacon and eggs for breakfast, and were taught French and English, but forbidden to speak Inuktitut. On returning home, they found the traditional diet of seal meat too rich for them, and many had forgotten how to communicate with their families.

Education served only to make Inuit teenagers disillusioned with their traditional life. Few students graduated to high school. Now, throughout the north, young unemployed Inuit hang around the focal point of their communities, wearing mirrored sunglasses, basketball sneakers and Indian headbands, or baseball caps decorated with patches proclaiming the names of arctic townships and American automobile manufacturers. Furs and polar-bear pants are rarely seen. It is the white nurses and teachers who wear the sealskin *kamiks*, whose parka hoods are trimmed with the fur of arctic fox. Inuit women wear lipstick, paint their finger nails, wear cheap cotton print dresses, and bright orange and yellow rubber boots. The men wear plastic boots lined with thick felt socks, American jeans and quilted nylon anoraks, or in summer, denim and leather jackets edged with studs.

Although little of the old life remains, every effort is made to keep the traditional Nanook image alive, but no one seems willing to face the reality of today's Arctic. The official emblem of Canada's Northwest Territories, found on flags, crests, letter headings, and vehicle number plates, is the polar bear. Postcards illustrate the old way of life, rarely the new. Magazine editors and television producers are generally more excited by pictures of icebergs and hunters in kayaks, or the 'Eskimo' Olympics and the Alaskan dog race, than scenes of the modern Arctic. Advertising men photograph fashion models posing in expensive furs among the ice hummocks, or on a dog sledge, unaware that there are probably fewer than a score of dog teams left in the entire Canadian Arctic. Pond Inlet has only two of them. There are only two in Canada's most northerly community, Grise Fiord, on Ellesmere Island. They are rarely used for hunting, but are available to tourists and would-be adventurers for $100 an hour.

A more accurate image of the Arctic is of man-made ice islands, oil rigs and huge tracked vehicles lumbering across the ice. Giant C-130 Hercules aircraft ferry drilling rigs, fuel, tracks, machinery, and supplies for oil camps, mines, 'The Bay' and the Co-op. When there is enough space, the odd passenger hitches a lift. Boeing jetliners from Edmonton and Montreal land on gravel runways, and sometimes on the ice itself. The front half of the aircraft is reserved for freight, the pallets neatly packed with the commodities needed to support the southern way of life. Some aircraft are so heavily loaded that passengers are frequently asked to occupy the rear seats only, thereby distributing the load factor and assisting take-off. In the shabby airport lounges, oilmen, engineers, scientists, politicians, administrators and tourists mingle with Inuit families, who regard each flight arrival as a social occasion.

Aircraft are to the Arctic what buses and commuter trains are to suburbia in the south: without them, and with the lack of roads, life in the north would cease to function. The 'bush' pilot must fill the multiple roles of taxi, bus and truck driver, as well as ambulanceman, delivery man, mailman and messenger. The arctic taxi is the de Havilland Twin Otter, a STOL (Short Take-Off and Landing) aircraft which can carry twenty passengers and seemingly endless piles of freight, from barrels of fuel to snowmobiles and dog teams. When Larry Audlaluk, from Resolute Bay on Cornwallis Island, hired his dog team to a Japanese film crew, the dogs and sledges were transported between Resolute and Grise Fiord by Twin Otter, ordinarily a month's journey, yet completed by plane in one-and-a-half hours. Sudden changes in the weather can mean lengthy delays and unscheduled stops, giving rise to the pilots' most popular saying: 'Hurry up and wait'.

Flying at 10,000 ft is the only way to appreciate the vastness of the Arctic. As far as the eye can see, in every direction, there is nothing but ice and uninhabited islands. For the uninitiated, it can be an unnerving experience. Notices tacked on the bulkhead of the Twin Otter's ferociously hot cabin advise the passenger where to find the survival equipment, and how to use the Emergency Locator Transmitter, an automatic transponder which transmits a radio signal, and acts as a beacon for search and rescue aircraft. When the Twin Otter is fitted with hydraulic skis instead of wheels, it can land on ice so rough that a crash seems inevitable. Yet there are remarkably few accidents, and the pilots have the confidence of men who know that if they get into trouble, another aircraft will probably have located them, and landed beside them, by the time they have retrieved their portable stove from the hold, and boiled enough ice for their first cup of coffee.

The sounds of the wind and the creaking ice, of village activity and Inuit songs is broken by the hum of generators, air conditioners and the waspish, high pitched whine of the snowmobile. Known as a Ski-doo in Canada, Greenland and Lapland, and as a Snow-go in Alaska and Yukon, it resembles a 250cc motor-scooter, with skis instead of a front wheel, and a tracked rubber belt replacing the rear wheel. Often of Japanese manufacture, snowmobiles are driven endlessly, aimlessly and frequently without silencers by Inuit of all ages. More than any other transport, snowmobiles have been responsible for shattering the arctic peace and are destroying the ancient art of living on the ice. Since they were introduced little more than a decade ago, few youngsters have bothered to learn how to drive a dog team, and fewer still know how to build an *illuliaq*.

Where once the Inuk hunter sat motionless for hours waiting to snare a seal, he now drives noisily across the ice, pushing his Yamaha or Nordic up to thirty miles an hour, racing from one blowhole to another, taking potshots at basking seals with a high-velocity rifle. For every seal taken in the Canadian Arctic, at least two more are wounded and escape. Caribou have been over-hunted because the snowmobile enables the hunter to drive within easy range of them. Yet its value is questionable.

Unlike a dog team, it cannot provide warmth or food in an emergency. On long journeys, the uninterrupted noise from the engine can cause deafness. Breakdowns have cost many lives. Now, the wise Inuk travels with a companion, or makes sure that he has plenty of fuel and enough spare parts for every eventuality, although this can add substantially to the cost of his journey. Priced at $6,000, the snowmobile can be used only during the brief summer weeks, and rarely lasts more than two winters. On the edge of every arctic township, there is now a snowmobile graveyard, a tangled heap of discarded machines, dumped because extreme temperatures split the vinyl seat coverings, and winter snowdrifts ruin the engines and metalwork.

Not only is the life expectancy of machinery far less than in the south, it is much more expensive to run. Power points must be installed on the outside of every building to warm the batteries and engines of vehicles overnight. Batteries go flat within minutes from the cold and in the daytime, engines are left idling for hours to avoid starting problems. Some owners prefer not to switch the engines off for the whole of the winter, an expensive habit because the cost of fuel and electricity is exorbitant. Fuel supplies for the year are shipped in each summer and stored in tanks on the edge of the towns. Shipping costs are borne by the consumer. In Resolute Bay, the power station is capable of generating 4,000 kilowatts of electricity, but averages between 800 kw and 1,000 kw, for which civilians are charged 37 cents a kilowatt, five times as much as in Montreal. Snowploughs and council trucks used for delivering water and collecting garbage must be kept in heated garages. Not to do so is to invite trouble.

Resolute Bay, formerly a joint Canadian-American weather station, was established in 1953 when starving families were moved there from Port Harrison, on the east coast of Hudson Bay. Living south of the Arctic Circle, these Inuit had never known the darkness of an arctic winter, and in order to teach them the art of survival in the far north, other experienced Inuit families were brought from Pond Inlet in northern Baffin Island to join them. Now, the settlement has grown to a community of 170 people, heavily dependent on jobs in oil and gas exploration work, and in the Polaris lead and zinc mine on Little Cornwallis Island. The community costs one million dollars a year to run, but generates no income for the federal and state governments. Four miles from the Inuit village, some 200 construction workers, engineers, scientists, meteorologists, pilots and policemen live an entirely separate life in a sprawling camp around the airport. In winter, dressed like spacemen against the cold, they struggle from centrally-heated living quarters to their place of work in the hangars, workshops, and offices. Many never bother to leave the camp for the duration of their contracts, even in summer.

The white workers have imported bulldozers and excavators, and constructed townships of identical wooden frame houses, designed by southern architects who have no conception of the requirements of arctic life. Shipped north in kit form, some houses have been built with doors which open outwards, a major problem for the occupants when snow-drifts form outside. Powdered snow blowing through the cracks freezes, warps the doors, and opens the apertures. Large windows on every side cause problems in summer, when the glare and excessive heat of the sun, low in the sky, have to be curtained off.

In winter, with triple or quadruple glazing, the heat loss is still so great that heating costs rise drastically. The designers of these houses forgot that the warmer the temperature inside, the greater the degree of moisture in the air, that when the temperature outside is −40°C., internal condensation on cold windows and walls will freeze. They also forgot that moisture will penetrate the smallest hole in the insulation panels, made perhaps by a picture hook on the wall, and that ice will form between the outer and inner walls.

For the Inuit, whose traditional housing was designed to conserve heat, the frame houses from the south were wholly unsuitable, and an economic burden. Additional fuel for heating was as necessary as gasoline for their snowmobiles, guns and bullets for hunting, white man's food as a supplement to their diet, and off-the-peg clothing to replace the skins which Inuit women could no longer chew, because a diet high in sugar content had destroyed their teeth. Although they had lived in a geographical area rich in animal oils, providing all their needs, the Inuit were suddenly struggling with a market economy which would bring about their downfall. With jobs available only to a chosen few, the rest had no alternative but to rely on rent grants, social security and other benefits for their keep, increasing the cost to the federal and provincial governments to an almost unacceptable level.

The average Inuit home is characterised by its rickety furniture, a faded religious picture on the wall, a chamber pot under the iron-frame bed and a chunk of raw seal meat on top of the television set. In contrast, the nurses, teachers, government employees and other whites live generally in suburban luxury. In the unheated entrances to their homes, where heavy clothing and footwear are left so that snow and dirt is not trodden into the fitted carpets inside the house, stands a deep freeze packed with a year's supply of meat, frozen vegetables, tv-dinners, pastries and icecream. Indoors, comfortable sofas and armchairs surround the colour television and video recorder. Pot plants thrive in the hot and humid atmosphere. Pictures and books line the walls. Direct-dial long distance telephone calls and television programmes are made available by the Telesat 'Anik D' satellite 22,000 miles above the earth.

In the kitchens of most whites, hot coffee is available day and night, a tin of Carnation cream beside it. Refrigerators are laden with beer, six-packs of Coke and jugs of fruit-flavoured drinks mixed from powder concentrates. In the larder, there is every imaginable foodstuff from Cornflakes and chilli con carne to baked beans and apple pie. Fresh vegetables, tomatoes, lettuce, and fruit are available three times a week from 'The Bay', and many householders order a year's supply of groceries by telephone from Edmonton or Yellowknife, happy to pay the additional cost of air freight, which pushes prices up three or four times higher than those in the south. These homes could be anywhere in North America: only the carvings of seals, walrus and drum dancers on the mantlepiece and bookshelves serve as a reminder of the conditions outside.

During World War Two, the North American way of life spread to Greenland, where American bases were established as a defence against the Germans. The arrival of American troops ended 250 years of isolation, during which the poverty-stricken Inuit had become totally dependent on the Danish missionaries and traders. The Greenlanders were intrigued by the American lifestyle and readily absorbed it. Suddenly the drab and meagre supplies in the stores of the Royal Greenland Trading monopoly were replaced by an infinite variety and abundance of consumer goods, eagerly snapped up by the Inuit with Danish welfare payments.

After the war, Danish authorities, worried by the financial burden the colony was imposing on them, were anxious to modernise the country, an almost impossible task because of the topography and the climate. The majority of the population lived in isolated settlements hundreds of miles apart, ice-bound for most of the year. Apart from the odd ship in summer, there were few communications. There are still no roads between the towns and settlements, and the population of many communities would fit easily into a London double-decker bus.

The Inuit lived in picturesque but poorly insulated wooden huts perched on the coastal rocks. Water was obtained by melting snow or chunks of ice. Cracks in the roof and walls were sealed with mud or chewing gum. Inside, the hot, humid atmosphere nurtured tuberculosis, which at that time claimed 180 lives a year.

The Danes decided that if the health of the nation was to improve, and Greenland was to become an economically viable country, the population must be centralised. The hunters were moved from scattered settlements into four towns of between 3,000 and 4,000 people situated on the southwest coast, where the sea is normally navigable all year. In a massive development programme, the Danes built schools, hospitals, housing estates, airfields and harbours, and established fish factories so that the populace could capitalise on the rich cod fishing in Davis Strait. The Inuit were never consulted nor were their cultural needs considered. The Danes, well-meaning but arrogant, believed that the country's welfare was best left in their hands.

In a frenzy of building, the Danes erected massive blocks of apartments 500 ft long, six storeys high, 120 apartments to each block. They differed from each other only in their numbering and lettering. There was no room for sentimentality. To function properly, the township had to be compact, so the apartments were built high and close together, not least because the foundations had to be blasted from mountain bedrock. Today, one-third of Greenland's population lives in such apartments. From a cultural standpoint, they were a disaster. Unwittingly, the Danes had created in the capital, Godthab, which the Inuit call Nuuk, a densely populated, concrete slum, more like a prison camp than the focal point of a modern town.

Bewildered hunters and their families, who owned little more than their hunting equipment, a few cooking pots and skins, and had been used to a life outdoors, suddenly found themselves in apartments with parquet flooring, flowered wallpaper, Scandinavian furniture, chiming clocks, balconies, and baths which some believed had been provided so that they could flense their seals indoors. The Inuit hung their kayaks and dried fish from the balconies, and in the anonymity of the complex, felt isolated and unwanted. Longing for the open sledge tracks and the clear views to the skerries and mountains, they were confused by the crowds and the new streets, and by the signs pointing to schools, nurseries, public works, warehouses and the fish-processing plant. It was almost inevitable that such a rapid change in lifestyle should lead to psychological problems, broken families and despair, followed by alcoholism and crime.

Alcoholism has replaced tuberculosis as the national disease. More alcohol is consumed per capita in Greenland than anywhere else in the world: 28 million cans of beer every year, shared among an adult population of 25,000 people. The Inuit are allowed to buy alcohol from the state liquor stores only at certain hours of the day. Wisely, perhaps, it is not sold on Fridays, when people are paid, or Saturdays, although some unscrupulous taxi drivers will always provide a bottle at double the price. Hotels, which hold dinner dances most evenings of the week, allow the public into the dining area after nine p.m., but the Inuit must place orders for alcohol before eleven p.m. During the last fifteen minutes, waiters are overwhelmed with orders, and it is not uncommon to see thirty bottles of beer brought to a table for two people. As the dancing ends at midnight, the rate of consumption, and inebriation, is rapid. In Nuuk, which is littered with discarded beer containers, 100,000 bottles of Danish beer are drunk every week, an average of twenty for each person above the age of fourteen, or forty per cent more than the Danes, who themselves drink more than most other countries in the west.

The damage caused by alcohol to Inuit society is frightening. Heavy drinking in communities where hunting knives and rifles are common has led to a spate of violence unparalleled in the west. One in three Inuit in Greenland dies violently. One in three deaths, mainly drownings, are alcohol-related accidents. Every twentieth person takes his own life, at an average age of 23 years, the highest suicide rate in the world and surely the most poignant of all examples of Inuit frustration and hopelessness. In Alaska, about forty per cent of violent deaths are now caused by drink. In one year, every single death in Barrow was related to excessive drinking.

In the Canadian Arctic, most communities allow beer, wines and spirits to be purchased only by mail order. Special permits must be obtained from Yellowknife, the capital of the Northwest Territories and the seat of its government. Yet the sale of alcohol remains an important source of government income. Despite the restrictions, each individual above the age of fifteen years in the Northwest Territories drinks an average of 28 pints of pure alcohol a year, half as much again as in the rest of the country. Alcohol-induced homicide, suicide, violence and accidents have been the principal cause of death among the native peoples of the Canadian Arctic for nearly two decades. Today, Inuit and Indians aged between 15 and 24 years are killing themselves at six times the national average, and in many communities, there have been suicide epidemics.

The authorities in each country have conducted intensive anti-drinking campaigns, often aimed at the Inuit sense of pride. Their success, however, has been limited, and there is now the added problem of drugs among the young. Addiction is becoming widespread in southern Greenland, and police there record about 150 violations of the Narcotics Act each year, a remarkably high figure in view of the sparse population. Greenland also consumes more penicillin than any other country in the world, but this has not protected its population from an epidemic of venereal disease. The incidence of gonorrhoea and syphilis is nearly five times that of influenza, and three-and-a-half times that of tonsillitis. Every third adult is afflicted, one of the highest incidences on earth.

The transition to modern living initially brought a radical improvement in health standards. Thirty years ago, three in every four Inuk babies died, and the life expectancy for those who survived was only 25 years, compared with 75 years in Denmark, Canada and the United States. Since then, the infant death rate has been brought down to one-sixth of the level twenty years ago, while the post-natal mortality rate has dropped to one-eighth. Black lung disease, caused by smoky oil lamps, has been eradicated. So has tuberculosis, once so widespread in arctic Canada that deaths from the disease exceeded the birth rate. Despite these advances, cardio-vascular disease, lung cancer, and other illnesses previously unknown in the Arctic are spreading rapidly. In communities where water is in short supply, hepatitis is rife. Most Inuit prefer to drink Coke and soda pop because of the risk of contaminated water. A 600 per cent increase in sugar consumption during the past twenty years had led to severe dental problems.

The traditional Inuit diet of fish and wild meat was rich in protein, but low in sugar and fat. The 500-year-old remains of an Inuit woman discovered in 1978 in a grave at Qilakitsoq, near Uumaannaq in Greenland, were found to have a near perfect set of teeth. The corpse, one of several found in a partially exposed cave, had effectively been freeze-dried, and was remarkably well-preserved. Although the woman's teeth were worn down from chewing skins, she had lost only one incisor in her lifetime, had no cavities, and there was no evidence of gum disease. During the past thirty years, the Inuit have been introduced to potato crisps, gum, chocolate, white bread, hamburgers, hot dogs, and French fries swamped in ketchup and sweet mustard.

This junk diet, high in sugar, fat and starch, has caused widespread problems for dentists, who must frequently treat children aged six years for abscesses and rotten teeth. Many have lost *all* their teeth by the time they reach their teens. Their inability to chew properly has led to chronic gastric problems. Although the introduction of fruit and vegetables has been beneficial, providing a source of vitamins in addition to *mattak*, the *qallunaat's* diet is directly responsible for a high incidence of obesity, acne, diabetes, high blood pressure, heart disease, gallstones and poor eyesight. Ophthalmia, inflamation of the eye, conjunctivitis and myopia are common. Nearly a quarter of the children in the Arctic now wear glasses, while thirty per cent suffer from ear infections.

Government and local authorities are taking steps to improve health standards in the north, but their efforts are directed only at physical illness. No attempt has been made to correct the psychological damage which stemmed from white policies, creating an abyss between the two populations. In Alaska and Canada, few whites actually *live* in the Arctic. Oil men, construction workers and technicians fly north for shifts of less than a month. Scientists, teachers and nurses sign short-term contracts, and begin counting the days to their return south almost as soon as they have arrived. Every job in the Arctic is highly paid, and most whites go there for the money, but their lifestyle creates envy, and any commitment to the Inuit usually ends with their contracts.

In Greenland, Inuit frustration is exacerbated by resident Danes, nearly one-fifth of the population, who have formed a privileged class from whose dominance the native Inuit cannot escape. Every waking moment of their lives, the Greenlanders are reminded of Danish superiority. For years, all the planning for their country was carried out by Danes in Denmark. Business is totally controlled by immigrant Danes.

None of the shops is owned by an Inuk in Nuuk. Everything that money can buy, from food to furniture, is imported from, or through, Denmark. The Danes hold not only all the best jobs, but also the best menial jobs. In the hotels, the chambermaids are Danish girls. Office windows are cleaned by Danish window cleaners. Outside, an Inuk, standing in a ditch at the side of the road, picks up the litter. Houses are designed and built by Danes, and the bulldozers on construction sites are driven by blonde, not dark-haired drivers. The Inuit are employed as labourers, dockers, miners and fish gutters.

Excusing their policy by pointing to the unreliability of Inuit workers, employers say job absenteeism is endemic. 'On a sunny day, the Inuit don't bother to turn up. They go fishing or hunting, instead. You can't run a business like that,' they complain, forgetting that the Inuit have been accustomed for thousands of years to seize every opportunity to hunt for food. The majority of Greenlanders are content with a rifle, ammunition, coffee, cigarettes and food for their families. In the per-petual daylight of the arctic summer, they eat when they are hungry, and sleep when they are tired. They could no more adapt to a nine-to-five routine than the Danes can adjust to staying up all night, every night, in the summer.

The unwillingness of the Danes to understand Inuit thinking has helped to push the unemployment rate up to twenty per cent. Soon, every third person of working age will be jobless because of the high birth rate during the 1950s and 1960s. Among the Canadian Inuit, unemployment is already at that level. In order to pay the rent and fuel, the electricity and the maintenance of their imported housing, they need to earn at least $25,000 a year. This is quite unrealistic, and many cannot pay. Powerless to rectify this, the government reduces their social welfare payments by a few token dollars, and reluctantly shoulders the financial burden.

In Greenland, the government must find 1,500 new jobs for those leaving school each year, at present an impossible task. The situation is so desperate that when shrimp stocks are depleted in winter, the manage-ment of the shrimp factory turn off the automatic peelers, slowing production almost to a standstill in order to create work. Notwithstanding these efforts, the workforce has to be halved each winter, and those who have been laid off must seek social assistance.

With little hope for the future, Inuit youngsters brought up on a diet of comics, cheap literature and second-rate television, are reduced to smoking cigarettes and drinking endless cans of beer outside the local supermarket, where they chat about the latest western or pornographic video movie. Nuuk has the highest per capita ownership of video recorders in the world. Video films like *Breakdance Explosion* quickly caught the imagination of young Inuit. Groups of teenagers danced in the streets to the deafening beat of American rock music.

When approaching winter forced the break-dancing craze indoors, more than a thousand fans packed the town's gymnasium for a marathon championship competition lasting six hours. The Prime Minister, Jonathan Motzfeldt, was asked to award the first prize, a large portable tape-recorder with multiple speakers, which teenagers balance on their shoulders and play at peak volume, inches from their ears. Members of the winning group admitted that until break-dancing became popular, they had spent most of their time getting drunk, and fighting in the streets. Now, they say, they resolve their disputes by holding break-dancing competitions, the modern substitute for the drum dance of the past.

Until the Greenlanders won Home Rule in 1979, they were mere spectators of the developments in their country. This is gradually changing, but Inuit leaders are aware that language and education are the key to a future under their own control. Language remains a serious problem. From his first day at school, an Inuk child is taught Danish, in Danish, by Danish teachers who cannot speak Inuktitut. Yet, if the child is to escape his subordinate relationship to the Danes, a higher education is vital. This is available only in Copenhagen, 2,500 miles away. Yet, on arrival, the cultural shock experienced by the Inuit is often so great that it leads immediately to alcoholism and drug abuse.

Approximately half of them become disillusioned, or find the academic work too difficult, and drop out. Inuit students in Copenhagen invariably have a bad reputation, although only an estimated ten per cent of them relapse into anti-social behaviour. Accustomed to staying up all night in the summer, these drop-outs are unaware of the need to be quiet in the small hours. They invite friends to their rooms and drink beer throughout the night, behaviour which, although infuriating, is very often due to ignorance of Danish customs. Many Danes, tired of subsidising students who they feel are abusing their generosity, become antagonistic.

Although the number of Inuit graduating from Danish universities is small, education is finally proving to be worthwhile. Greenland now has its first doctors, nurses, teachers and lawyers, the country's future leaders. In Nuuk, special technical colleges have been established, where Inuit students with a natural aptitude for mechanical and technical subjects can study engineering, metalwork and shipbuilding. Inuit leaders hope that one day the country will be self-sufficient, and finally shake off the Danish yoke. For their part, the Danes would not be sorry to reduce the continuing financial penalty paid for their former colonialism. With Greenland able to produce only ten per cent of its needs, the cost of supporting its economy is a massive 1,500 million kroner, £110 million ($165 million) annually, or £2,150 ($3,225) for each man, woman and child in the country.

Clearly, Greenland cannot return to the traditional hunting culture. Nor is there much point in trying to reduce the pace of modernisation because this would merely lengthen the period of transition into a new era, without making it less painful. The dilemma for Greenland's leaders is how to achieve the Danes' high standard of living, while avoiding financial dependence upon them. The solution may lie in the great mineral wealth beneath the icecap. Cryolite, coal, lead and zinc have all been mined successfully in the past.

The Black Angel Mine, blasted out of a sheer cliff half-a-mile above the Marmorilik Fjord in northwest Greenland, produces 140,000 tons of zinc, and 40,000 tons of lead concentrate, each year. In financial terms, this is equivalent to half Greenland's national income from the private sector. Although the present mine is expected to be exhausted in a few years, the Danish management hopes to open new seams before present stocks run out. If it is unable to do so, the mine will close and the company will be run down, to the inevitable detriment of Greenland's economy.

Nevertheless, leading politicians are pinning their hopes for the future on the exploitation of minerals. North of Nuuk, geologists have detected two billion tons of iron ore. On the east coast, they have discovered 120 million tons of molybdenum, which is used for tempering steel. In the south, there are nearly 50,000 tons of uranium, one of the richest deposits in the world. Inaccessibility, the adverse climate and transport costs may prevent extraction of some of these minerals. The Greenlanders are adamant that in order to protect the environment they will not allow the uranium to be mined. For the same reason, they have banned oil exploration on the continental shelf in Davis Strait, and have been reluctant to grant oil exploration rights in Jamesonland on the east coast, where seal hunting provides the only income for local Inuit. The government's unwillingness to allow the oil industry, with all its disruptive effects on the environment, to become established on their shores was tempered by its fervent, almost desperate, need to cast off the shackles of financial dependence. Finally, it capitulated, allowing exploration to proceed for twelve years, provided it was restricted to the land.

The Greenlanders' hopes of economic independence were fuelled by reports that the geological formation of the earth's strata beneath Jamesonland is comparable to that in Prudhoe Bay in Alaska, and the Ekofisk field in the North Sea. If oil is discovered, the question is whether its extraction would be profitable. Normally, oil transportation costs about five dollars a ton, even from the more isolated oilfields, but with east Greenland hemmed in by polar ice for most of the year, these costs could rise to as much as $40 a ton. If oil prices are depressed, the companies may decide that production costs are too high. If drilling goes ahead, the government will be required to pay the first $500 million profits to the Danes.

For the time being, the Greenlanders must rely heavily on their main industry, cod fishing. The employment of 2,500 Inuit fishermen and another 10,000 dependent on fish for their livelihoods is considered to be the only hope for sustained economic growth. During the late 1970s, the government embarked on a massive investment programme to boost the inshore fishing fleet with ocean-going stern trawlers. At precisely the same time, the catch declined, probably because of a slight fall in the temperature of the water.

Some scientists believe this may signal the beginning of a new, miniature glaciation period, which could last until the year 2050. By extracting a core of ice two miles long from the inner ice cap, they analysed the snow which has fallen on Greenland during the past 100,000 years. Compressed by the weight of each new layer, the snow formed patterns which enabled the scientists to establish the rhythms of climatic fluctuations during that period.

The deterioration in climate during the 1980s has brought enormous icebergs and field ice, which has formed a fringe along the west coast, and prevented trawlers from reaching the fishing grounds for several weeks during the summer season. It is this ice which has brought the drop in water temperature, and as the difference between life and death for cod fry is only half a degree, cod stocks have declined markedly. In 1984, the Greenlanders caught only 15,000 tons of their 50,000-ton quota.

Obliged to find other catches, the Greenlanders concentrated on the shrimp beds in Disko Bay, where the ice-strewn waters slow the rate of growth to produce what are claimed to be the finest shrimps in the world. These soon became Greenland's most valuable catch, providing an income of £21 million compared with £12 million for cod. Yet it seemed the Greenlanders were fated. Within a few years, the shrimp catches had also declined, probably from over-fishing. Apart from some sheep farming in the far south, the only other source of revenue was from seal products.

Greenland is one of the few remaining countries in the world with a significant proportion of its population dependent on aboriginal hunting, approximately 2,500 hunters who live entirely off seals, and another 7,500 people who are indirectly dependent on them for their livelihoods. Where modernisation has been much slower, about sixty of ninety remaining settlements in the north and east of the country would not exist but for their presence.

Here, seal meat continues to be the staple diet, and the hunters kill to eat. They hunt ringed seals, of which there are millions in Greenlandic waters. Keenly aware of the need to maintain stocks, they take no more than they need, and sell only the pelts for which there is no other use. What they do not eat themselves, they give to their dogs. The leftovers are ground down, and used as fish bait. The skins are still used to make whips, harnesses and traces for the sledge teams. Only then, do the Inuit hunters consider selling the remaining skins, their only hope of earning enough money to buy fuel, ammunition, coffee and cigarettes. Between them, they kill approximately 90,000 seals annually, or an average of 36 each, hardly excessive when one considers that a hunter needs at least fifty seals a year to feed himself, his wife, two children and twelve dogs, and that the indigenous seal population numbers several million.

In less than a decade, the activities of animal welfare groups, led by Greenpeace and the World Wildlife Fund, have ruined the livelihoods of 10,000 Greenlanders. Determined to halt the slaughter of hooded and harp seal pups, which were being clubbed to death by white hunters in Newfoundland, these organizations launched a simplistic but highly successful campaign aimed at public emotions. Publicity referred, for example, not to seal pups, but to 'baby' seals. Photographs showed them in their white coats, with large brown eyes gazing at the reader, beneath the caption 'Save the Seals'.

No effort was made to explain that the Greenlanders do not need to kill hooded, or harp seals, owing to the abundance of ringed seals. Cynically, many hunters believe Greenpeace and the World Wildlife Fund specifically published the most appealing pictures in order to attract voluntary contributions to their funds. One hunter, Ole Heinrich, observed: 'The campaign was good publicity for them. Every time they put a picture of a seal pup in the newspaper, it made money. In the advertisements, you always saw pups with beautiful eyes. It could not have happened with a crocodile.' If the animal welfare organisations were aware of the devastating effect such a campaign would have on the Inuit hunters, as surely they must have been, they deliberately chose to ignore it. If they were not, their actions were thoughtless and inconsiderate.

Greenpeace and their allies eventually forced a Common Market ban on imports of seal-pup products. The international market collapsed immediately. The average salary of the Greenland hunter dropped by two-thirds, from 15,000 to 5,000 Danish Kroner, or from £1,080 ($1,620) to £360 ($540) a year, and sixty per cent of that was a government subsidy. The seal hunter in Greenland, once a proud and respected member of the community, now earns one-quarter the wage of a street cleaner, and one-sixth that of a Danish labourer.

In Canada, where less than ten per cent of the seals taken by Canadian Inuit are harp seals, the sale of skins plunged from $586,000 to $76,000, and in one town, to $1,000 from $54,000 a year earlier. Although these figures may at first seem excessive for hunters who claim to be subsistence hunters, it should be remembered that the skins sold are those that can be used for no other purpose, and would otherwise be thrown away, and that in most cases they represent the only form of cash income available apart from social welfare cheques. Translated into individual terms, the fall in price represents a drop in individual income from approximately $23 to $3 per person per year. In an appeal to the United Nations, an organisation representing 150,000 hunters in the Arctic, Indigenous Survival International (ISI), described them as 'the most socio-economically depressed population in the world'. The group accused the 'fanatics' of Greenpeace of forcing the Inuit hunters off the land into menial jobs and social welfare, and blamed them for a deterioration in family and community life, as well as a significant increase in suicides.

Greenpeace charged the Greenlanders with commercial exploitation. In an interview with Independent Television News, Mark Glover, at the organisation's London headquarters, explained: 'We are not opposed to true aboriginal sealing if all the products are used by the people in their native villages, but the situation in Greenland is that the seal hunters carry out what is probably the largest seal hunt in the world. Tens and tens of thousands of seal skins are entering the market, through Europe, in the commercial sector ... You know, it is really nothing to do with us. When people start playing that game and entering fur markets, and are playing the commercial side of it, they live or die by the market, and the market has gone down, so the prices and overall income has gone down, too ... They maintain their livelihood is an aboriginal existence, but of course it is dependent more and more on a commercial existence.'

Mr Glover's apparently callous indifference was based on ignorance, rather than personal experience of Greenland or the Arctic. From the moment Greenpeace embarked on its 'Save the Seals' campaign in 1976 until the interview in July, 1984, not a single member of the organisation had taken the trouble to visit Greenland and meet the hunters whose livelihoods they were destroying.

Fourteen months later, after considerable pressure from Greenland's Home Rule government, and some adverse publicity from television, a delegation finally agreed to visit the hunters on a fact-finding mission. At the end of it, the chief organiser of the 'Save the Seals' campaign, Alan

Pickaver, admitted on local radio and television that he would have run the campaign differently 'had we known seven years ago what we know now.' Confronted by one hunter, who told him that 'the only species threatened here is man', Mr Pickaver reluctantly agreed that in the future, an appropriate slogan might be 'BUY A SEAL SKIN. SAVE A GREENLANDER.' His admission came too late. Three weeks after the tour, the Common Market agreed to extend its import ban on seal-pup products until 1989, and the European Parliament voted for a permanent ban.

Despite the desperate efforts of Greenland's leaders to preserve the old culture, the seal hunter is a disappearing species. In Nuuk, Philip Lauritzen, a Danish spokesman for the Home Rule government, and an expert on Inuit affairs, summed the situation up in this way: 'I think we could experience a very sad thing here in twenty years,' he said, 'when European anthropologists come up here to interview hunters in apartment blocks, wanting to know why they left their settlements. Then, everyone in Europe will ask, "who could ever destroy that kind of culture?" That, sadly, is actually the situation that Greenpeace, and the World Wildlife Fund, and many others have created.'

CHAPTER 13

The Sami of Lapland

Across the Atlantic, 2,500 miles from Nuuk, the Sami of Lapland are fighting a similar battle to preserve their traditions. Theirs is a rearguard action waged against legions of bureaucrats, who appear to detest everything that cannot be categorised and pigeon-holed. Striving for standardisation, these Nordic administrators provide each new-born baby with a Personal Registration Number. It follows him to the grave and must be presented in every dealing with the authorities, with banks, post offices and state liquor stores, or in the purchase of season tickets on buses and railways. It is of little account that such a practice is alien to the semi-nomadic Sami, whose livelihood and culture centres on reindeer herding in Europe's last stretch of uninterrupted wilderness. Officialdom holds that the Sami cannot be treated differently from any other Norwegians, Swedes or Finns.

Samiland, incorrectly but better known as Lapland, stretches across the crown of Europe from the Kola Peninsula in the Soviet Union, down through the national boundaries of Finland, Sweden and northern Norway to Trondheim on the Norwegian coast. Approximately 45,000 Sami live in this huge tract of forest, tundra and mountains, the greater part of which lies north of the Arctic Circle. A 500-mile border fence with watch towers and barbed wire separates them from nearly 2,000 other Sami, who live on collective farms in the Soviet Union, where reindeer husbandry is a sizeable industry.

The herders have lived in Samiland at least since the time of Christ. They have never sold their land, nor given it away, nor lost it in battle. Yet the Nordic governments, reputed to be the guardians of the world's conscience, have steadfastly refused to recognise Sami nationality. Legislators carefully avoid any reference to the Sami *people*, preferring to label them the *Sami-speaking* population, a terminology which, though legally safer, is misleading. Census officials who based their findings on the ability of individuals to speak Sami as a first language have seriously under-estimated Sami numbers, particularly in Norway, where a tradition of contempt and prejudice has forced many Sami to pose as

Norwegians, speaking their own language only in the privacy of their homes.

The Sami have been assimilated into the dominant Nordic cultures more easily than the Inuit in Canada and Alaska, not only because the climate is less hostile but also because the Nordic capitals are three times closer to the Sami heartland than Montreal is to the Canadian Arctic, or Seattle and San Francisco are to northern Alaska. Washed by the warm waters of the Gulf Stream, Norway's coastline, free of ice all year, enabled the Lutheran pastors to travel north with relative ease. Applying tactics similar to those used in Greenland, they ordered the reindeer herders to burn their drums, and banned a popular form of singing known as *joiking*. Those who disobeyed were sometimes burned alive as a warning to others.

The Sami religion was soon suppressed. Later, land taxes were imposed. In Sweden, the government adopted a policy of containment, establishing a Lapp zone in which the Sami were allowed to follow their customary way of life, provided that they herded reindeer and did not move outside its boundaries. In Norway, an active policy of assimilation was followed. Settlement in the north was encouraged, and rapid. The Sami became a minority in their own nation, the victims of outright racism. Their children were forbidden to speak their own language at school, and the Sami identity, language and colourful national costume became badges of stupidity, best concealed if any form of advancement was to be achieved.

Eager to exploit the natural resources of the Sami nation, the settlers hewed timber from the extensive forests for the paper and pulp industry, Scandinavian furniture and Swedish matches. One of the largest iron ore deposits in the world was discovered at Kiruna, in Swedish Samiland. The Sami were employed as miners, housed in apartment blocks and given sun-ray treatment because shift systems prevented underground workers from enjoying the short summer sunlight. To move the ore, a railway was built across the tundra to Narvik, a Norwegian port on the same latitude as Alaska, but free of ice in winter.

As industry expanded, ports, towns, airports, roads and more railways were built. Rivers were dammed, and valleys flooded. Power lines criss-crossed the countryside. Highly paid jobs were created, accelerating Nordic settlement of Samiland. By 1975, the process of assimilation was so far advanced that Sami delegates, flying to Canada to take part in the first assembly of the World Council of Indigenous Peoples, were dismayed to find that serious doubt was being cast on their credentials.

Not all Sami, in the past, lived off reindeer. Some, along the Norwegian coast, relied on fishing. Others worked small farms and picked berries, but the majority were herdsmen who relied on the animals for milk, and annually killed a proportion of the herd for meat. Like the Inuit, the Sami utilised all parts of the carcass: the skins for clothes and tents, the antlers for tools. Today, only ten per cent of the Sami earn their living from reindeer, annually slaughtering one-fifth of the herd for the domestic meat industry, and supplementing their income from the sale of pelts and antlers to tourists.

Such are the economics of reindeer husbandry that in order to be wholly dependent on reindeer, a Sami family would need approximately 350 animals. Most families now own fewer than 200 animals, and rely on secondary occupations to improve their income. In Norway and Sweden, only 14 families have more than 300 animals; 25 families who listed reindeer herding as their principal occupation owned no reindeer at all.

Despite this decline, reindeer husbandry remains the keystone of Sami culture, closely linked with the Sami language. Just as Inuktitut contains many words for the different characteristics of snow and ice, Sami has a rich vocabulary to describe a reindeer, words which take into account the physical condition, age, colour and shape of an animal, and the size of its antlers. The language reflects the importance of reindeer to Sami society, and acts as a cohesive element between families living in the traditional Sami lifestyle. Similarly, reindeer herding binds the families together, isolates them from outside influences, and is fundamental to the preservation of the language. The two elements are crucial to the survival of the Sami as a separate race. Both are severely threatened.

With no official status, the Sami language is rapidly succumbing to the dominant Nordic languages, which are used in administration, offices, schools and the media. Consequently, five per cent of the reindeer-herding Sami have no knowledge of their own language. A study in Sweden shows that another twenty per cent cannot speak it, forty-five per cent cannot read it, and eighty per cent cannot write it. The figures for Sami who do *not* herd reindeer are even more alarming: twenty per cent have no knowledge of the language, forty per cent cannot speak it, sixty-five per cent cannot read it, and eighty per cent cannot write it.[28]

As the language falls into disuse, reindeer husbandry, the linchpin of Sami culture, is under pressure from every quarter. Excessive forest felling, new roads and tourism have drastically reduced the grazing and, more importantly, the calving grounds. Military authorities have requisitioned forest and tundra for training zones and artillery ranges. Engineers working on hydro-electric schemes have flooded valleys, re-routed rivers and disrupted reindeer migration routes.

Further anxiety stems from plans to extend the North Sea oil fields and lay pipelines through Samiland to take natural gas to West Germany. The

effect of these actions, instigated by businessmen clearly indifferent to
the complexities of reindeer husbandry, is devastating. Indeed, the threat
is so great that unless the encroachment into Samiland is contained very
quickly, reindeer husbandry in the wild will become extinct, probably
within the next fifteen years. If that happens, the Sami culture is doomed.

The decision-makers in the south have failed to understand the
difficulties of reindeer management, and the hazards of the annual
migratory cycle of reindeer. To be economically viable, a herd must
consist of approximately 350 animals, and to keep track of them, the Sami
now use snowmobiles and two-way radios. As in Canada and Alaska, the
snowmobiles are a mixed blessing. Costing more than one quarter of the
value of a reindeer, they can seldom be driven for more than two winters,
after which they are traded in for approximately six per cent of a
reindeer's value. During the time a machine is in his possession, a
herdsman probably uses 350 gallons of fuel a season, wears out four belts
and has to pay for numerous spare parts. In one community, maintenance
and fuel for snowmobiles was estimated at ninety per cent of the total
income from reindeer husbandry.

The high cost of maintaining snowmobiles has forced some of the
Sami to take second jobs in order to keep their machines, and has led to
an increase in the slaughter of animals, particularly of calves. The effect
of this has been to saturate the meat market, force prices down and
reduce profit margins. Other difficulties arise from sudden, heavy
rainfalls followed by a sharp drop in temperature which freezes the snow,
and prevents the animals reaching their winter fodder. There have been
lean winters during which the Sami have lost half their stock, and
emergency food for the remainder has been so expensive that, by
summer, the animals have eaten their entire commercial value.

Reindeer husbandry is a hard way to earn a living. The Sami are not
instinctively nomadic. Indeed, those who live by farming and fishing are
sedentary. Reindeer herders travel along specific routes to the summer
and winter pastures, whenever possible using the same camps as for the
previous year. They follow the migratory cycle of their animals, a pattern
which takes them on long journeys to the mountains in conditions which
are often appalling, and always fraught with problems. In winter, the
reindeer roam free through the partially-forested tundra, where they dig
through snow four feet deep in order to reach the moss and lichen which
is their staple winter diet.

The snow protects the fodder from their hooves. If they lingered in
the forests after the spring melt, they would crush the lichen, which dries
out in summer and can take fifty years to flower, and destroy their principal source of winter food for the following year. By April or May, the

animals become restive and begin their instinctive migration to the calving grounds near the rivers, lakes and marshes. Here, the snow melts more quickly, revealing the first green plants of the year. Rich in proteins, these young shoots are essential for the cows, which, under-nourished after the long winter, have only a few weeks in which to gain weight and produce milk for their offspring. If they stay too long, the calves drown in rivers swollen by melting snow.

As if to spur the animals on, the mosquitoes hatch. By late May or early June, when the birch trees burst into leaf, the reindeer huddle together in an effort to escape the swarms. It is now that the Sami separate them into herds, brand the fawns and drive the animals as far as 150 miles to their summer pastures in the mountains, and along the northern coast of Norway, where the wind offers the animals some respite. Here they remain until the autumn, when they are rounded up again, and approximately one-fifth of the herd is selected for slaughter. In September and October when the rut occurs, the reindeer are driven back to their winter grazing, and allowed to disperse as the first snow falls.

The highly strung reindeer are liable to stampede at the sound of people, dogs and gunfire, vehicles and machinery. When the ground is free from snow, the herds can move faster than the herdsmen, who must be able to predict the movements of their animals, and find them in darkness, fog or blizzards. Animals mingling with other herds travelling along parallel routes in the same direction can delay the migration, with dire results for calving and rutting. If the autumn round-up is impeded, or the peace vital for a successful rut is disturbed, late pregnancies can lead to miscarriages, delays to the spring migration and the death of calves.

Reindeer are so sensitive that they will shy away from areas where they have been frightened, avoiding them for ten years, and forcing the herders to find new migratory routes. This can be a difficult if not impossible task when outside interests are continually encroaching on grazing lands. Forest felling can be particularly disruptive. The demand for timber is unceasing. Huge tracts of forest are razed to the ground, destroying the moss and lichen. In north and eastern Finland, cleared forestland stretches as far as the eye can see, a barren landscape studded with dried tree stumps.

Where replanting is carried out, the ground is first ploughed deeply, and trenched by heavy machinery. The forest floor becomes impassable, a tangle of roots and undergrowth. The growth of lichen is halted and the reindeer are frightened away, perhaps for ever. The destruction of winter grazing increases the pressure on other forestland, creating shortages of winter fodder, which may lead to the death of reindeer from starvation in the late winter and early spring. Nor is this a short-term problem. A ploughed area may be useless for decades. Whereas pine trees in the south require between sixty and seventy years to mature, the same process north of the Arctic Circle can take between 150 and 250 years. Yet, during a depression in the paper and pulp industry, Swedish businessmen deliberately increased the rate of forest clearance in order to prevent redundancies. At the same time, they postponed replanting because demand was temporarily low, a policy of incredible short-sightedness. The effect of such decisions is inevitable. Each year, the total forest area in Samiland diminishes.

More forests have been obliterated by hydro-electric schemes, especially in Norway where fast flowing rivers provide more power than in any other country. The rivers of Samiland have been dammed and regulated by more than a hundred projects, but the electricity generated is transmitted south for industrial consumption, and is of little benefit to local people, who usually continue to light their homes with oil lamps.

Further major projects are planned in all three Nordic countries. In Norwegian Samiland, the threat posed by one scheme is so great that the calving grounds, migration routes and rutting areas of 40,000 animals will be severely disrupted. Secondary chaotic effects, such as the intermingling of herds and increased pressure on other grazing lands, cannot be quantified. The scheme, known as the Alta-Kautokeino project, could jeopardise the whole future of reindeer pastoralism in the heart of Samiland, with dire effects for the Sami language and culture.

The Alta River passes through the village of Kautokeino, the unofficial capital of Samiland, in which Sami is the mother tongue of more than eighty per cent of the 2,000 villagers. Downstream, the river runs through Masi village, one of the most important centres for reindeer husbandry in the region, and one of the last in the world where Sami is spoken by the entire population. In 1970, Norway's State Water and Energy Development Authority (NVE) announced plans to dam the river and to create several reservoirs. The intention was to submerge a 25-mile stretch of river valley, including the village of Masi.

Although protests by local people, who had not been consulted, eventually forced a substantial reduction in the scheme, the plans to regulate the water course placed the livelihoods of about thirty Masi households in jeopardy, and threatened the loss of spring pasture. The acreage involved was relatively small, but the grazing land was vital because there were no other suitable calving grounds in the vicinity. Further difficulties arose from the topography of the region. With summer and winter grazing areas at opposite ends of the migration route, herds of between a few hundred and several thousand reindeer, totalling nearly 40,000 animals, had to travel through a gap far too narrow to allow them all through at the same time. To avoid congestion, the Sami stagger the movement of the herds.

This operation is especially complex after the autumn round-up. The Sami release the herds from their pens one by one, but by mid-September, with the rut approaching, it is difficult to restrain the animals. To do so indefinitely would merely cause them to stampede through the barriers, fan out and mingle with other herds in the bottleneck. The Sami prevent this by driving some of the herds into special waiting zones, until there is room enough to move them through the gap. The zones are crucial because they allow the animals to graze without fear of disturbance for several weeks prior to, and during, the rut, essential if late pregnancies and their effects are to be avoided. Yet it was precisely in these waiting areas that the NVE planners sited the Alta-Kautokeino dam and 22 miles of access roadway.

Such disruption creates insuperable problems for the herdsmen. Reindeer alarmed by noise and traffic lose valuable browsing time and expend large amounts of energy on flight, giving rise to a protein deficiency which must be replaced quickly if the cows and their offspring are to be strong enough for the spring migration. If the source of their fear remains, they are likely to desert the area and head for the hills where it is colder, and the pasture less nourishing. Malnutrition and miscarriages follow, and calves freeze to death within hours of birth. The frightened animals will not return until long after the workmen and their machines have disappeared. It was twelve years before the Sami could persuade a herd to cross the approach road to one newly constructed dam, and use prime calving grounds on the far side.

Opening approach roads to the public after completion of a hydroelectric project usually brings an influx of weekend skiers, hunters, fishermen and tundra tourists whose arrival is frequently followed by an increase in the illegal slaughter of reindeer, and the theft of their carcasses. The Alto-Kautokeino scheme posed a further threat to Sami culture. Plans to billet approximately 200 construction workers in the Masi district were likely to lead, as with similar projects elsewhere, to sexual liaisons between the two groups, illicit deals in alcohol and reindeer meat, and rapid assimilation into the dominant culture.

Previous experience indicated that some herdsmen might be given temporary jobs on the project, but that instead of using their earnings to buy reindeer, they would develop new habits and needs, and fritter the money away. When the dam was completed, the Samis would be out of work and, disillusioned and discontented, be obliged to live on social welfare.

With enforced retirement a certainty for most of the reindeer herders in the Alta River region, the Sami began to organise themselves into protest groups. Their demonstrations led to a marked reduction in the size of the scheme and the threat of flooding Masi village was removed. Nevertheless, the NVE still intended to blast tunnels through the mountainside, and build a 350-ft high dam of reinforced concrete, a power station and an approach road. But the Norwegian parliament declared Masi an area of national heritage, in consequence of which, the NVE commissioned an investigation into the harm which could result from the project, and what should be the compensation for those affected. For the NVE itself to do this was as cynical as a tobacco company setting up a study into the effects of cigarettes on health, and then determining the amount of compensation payable to the victims of cigarette-induced cancer.

The terms of reference required the investigating team to consider only the direct damages likely to result from the Alta-Kautokeino scheme. Its brief was to map and register migration routes and pasture-land, and assess the compensation for their loss. No directive was given, and no attempt was made, to find out why the area was of such importance, or to instruct parliament about the wider implications of the project for reindeer management. It has been compared with removing a stave from a wine barrel, and assessing the damage as a percentage of lost wood. Furthermore, the commission based its report on the original, more ambitious Alta-Kautokeino project. When the smaller plan was adopted, the authorities falsely assumed that the damage to reindeer pastoralism would be reduced proportionately, and thus be negligible.

The commission did note that the loss of valuable calving grounds would be 'very serious', and reported that every additional loss of pasture was likely to have catastrophic consequences, even when a loss was only for a limited period. The Norwegian parliament chose to ignore this, in a debate which minimized the problem: 'So far as reindeer pastoralism is concerned,' observed one speaker, 'the only loss would be the flooding of some pastures. Their value approximates to food for 21 reindeer for 115 days.' The compensation was calculated accordingly.

Incensed, the Sami organised a protest camp near Alta, attracting several thousand Sami, farmers and environmentalists from all over Scandinavia and Europe. Linking themselves together with chains, they halted all work on the approach road for nearly four months. In the meantime, another group of Sami travelled to Oslo, set up camp outside the parliament building, and began a hunger strike. Politically embarrassed, the Prime Minister announced that the whole project would be re-examined, but the government's attitude became apparent shortly afterwards, when an ill-informed deputy minister, quoting incorrect statistics, declared:

> There is no connection between Sami interests and the Alta-Kautokeino hydro project ... The whole project affects, as far as I can remember, no more than the equivalent of the pasture as needed by eight or ten animals over one year, and that is not much in view of the 140,000 reindeer in Finnmark [Norwegian Samiland].

The hearing by the Norwegian Court of Appraisal was most noteworthy for the discrepancies between the evidence it accepted, and the conclusions drawn from it. The court agreed that the spring pastures could not be replaced, that the calving grounds and waiting zones would be lost, and that this amounted to a serious incursion into the pattern of reindeer management in the area. With that firmly established, the court concluded:

> It seems doubltful that the incursions we have mentioned are of such proportion and of such significance as to be of any important consequence to Sami culture ... The investigation that has been undertaken is satisfactory in respect of those damages that have been considered.

As if to add insult to injury, the Court added that Masi was not an area of national heritage after all, and that the proposal to make it one had been made on the floor of parliament, not in parliamentary committee, and was therefore not legally binding.

At a subsequent hearing, the Supreme Court upheld the state on all essential points. It rejected arguments that the evidence placed before lower courts was inadequate and misleading, and ruled that the potential effect of the Alta-Kautokeino project on reindeer management was not sufficiently serious to bring parliament's decision into conflict with international common law. Compensation, it decided, should be paid only on the basis of lost acreage. The Sami affected by the project could not be considered an indigenous people because the river was being regulated in a region that came under Norwegian jurisdiction.

This was all the government needed. With the support of parliament, approval was given to commence work on the project, which had been halted for more than a year. Bitterly disappointed, about 1,000 Sami and their sympathisers returned to the protest camp. As they chained themselves to boulders strewn along the access road, the temperature dropped to −35°C. The Sami, wearing their traditional pompom hats and colourful costumes, threatened to freeze themselves to death. The government response was to embark on the biggest, and most expensive peacetime police action ever. At a cost of £100,000 a day, 600 policemen were flown to the site with their dogs in a fleet of chartered aircraft. A large passenger ferry anchored off the Norwegian coast, 25 miles away, to house them. In shifts of 200 men, the police worked day and night, cutting chains and transporting the demonstrators through the snow to the court at Alta, where they were fined about £300 each. Most of the Sami refused to pay, and returned to the camp as quickly as possible, but soon the last protestors were removed.

Later, fourteen Sami women were granted permission to discuss the issue with the Prime Minister, but dissatisfied with the government's argument that more electric power was needed to create new industry, and that the Sami would have to pay the price, they refused to leave and police were called in to remove them. At the same time, five Sami herdsmen embarked on a hunger strike which lasted 31 days. Another Sami, who had become an activist, attempted to sabotage the hydro-electric project by blowing up a bridge, but the charges detonated prematurely and he lost an eye and a hand. It was the last protest. A month before the injured Sami was due for trial, he fled to Canada. The Alta-Kautokeino dam had become a symbol of Sami defeat.

In Swedish Samiland, the Samis suffered another setback, when the Supreme Court refused to recognise the right of eleven Sami villages to ownership of approximately 4,000 square miles close to the Norwegian border. The decision concluded a court case that had lasted nineteen years, the longest in Swedish legal history. Claiming that roads, railways and increased tourism were threatening their lifestyle and culture, the Sami were seeking greater control over development of the region. Among the documentation considered by the court was a royal decree from the seventeenth century. This not only gave the Sami title to the territory, but also promised them the right to control it for all eternity. Despite this, the court held that as a semi-nomadic people they could not acquire the right of ownership over a territory which, throughout history, they had formally failed to claim.

Official thinking on Samiland was placed into perspective when the Governor of Finnmark (Norwegian Samiland) commented: 'In this day and age, the tundra areas of our province are, *first and foremost*, important as recreational areas ... particularly for the week-end tourist.' His comment underlined the rule which has enabled the industrial mono-culture to steamroll its way over lesser cultures in every part of the world – that when the advantages to the larger, urban population are greater than the disadvantages to smaller, rural groups, all schemes are socially defensible, irrespective of the damage to the individual or the countryside.

When construction on the Alta-Kautokeino dam commenced, the Sami attempted to drive their reindeer along a more northerly route to the summer pastures. As expected, the herds intermingled. During a subsequent election campaign, the Norwegian Minister for the Environment expressed the personal view that, had the effects of the dam on reindeer management and the Sami culture been fully appreciated, permission to build the dam would have been withheld.

PART THREE

Expanding Horizons

CHAPTER 14

The Road to Nunavut

From the earliest voyages of discovery and plunder, the *qallunaat* from the south seized ownership of the arctic lands, ignoring the rights of the indigenous populations. When American whalers informed the Inuit in 1867 that the United States government had purchased Alaska from the Russians for $7.2 million, the hunters could not believe that the land in which their forefathers had lived for 4,000, or perhaps 10,000 years, would belong to anyone but themselves. They had not been consulted, either by the Americans or by the Russians, nor were they offered compensation from the sale. Such indifference towards the Inuit became accepted government practice, and they suffered in much the same way as the Aborigines, Maoris, Amerindians, Cossacks and other tribes around the world. Throughout the north, land that had been neither surrendered in war nor revoked in peace was purloined by various southern governments. The Russians, Americans, Canadians, British and Scandinavians each exploited the local resources, rehoused the inhabitants and imposed upon them their own customs and beliefs.

For years, the disgruntled Inuit and Sami stood by helplessly. There seemed to be no one capable or powerful enough to overcome the despair which shadowed the entire arctic region. Yet, such a man did exist. His name was Etok, better known as Charles Edwardsen, Jr. When the U.S. fleet arrived off the Alaskan coast in 1944 to establish a naval base near Barrow, effectively bringing Alaskan isolation to an end, Etok had barely celebrated his first birthday. The son of a whaler, his earliest memories were of the differences between the conditions of the hunters, who lived in poverty with no water supply, sewage system or clinic, and those of the sailors and government officials who enjoyed the benefits of electricity, radio, television, telephones and health care.

The contrast must have seemed greater still when he was sent 1,000 miles from his home to attend a government school in the south, where he studied in centrally-heated classrooms electrically lit. Here, he luxuriated in hot baths and learned how to use a porcelain lavatory, visited the cinema and listened to the radio. As his awareness sharpened, he began to understand the plight of the Inuit people, and learned to think like a *qallunaat*. In his early twenties, Etok decided to fight back.

Realising that the Inuit had never formally surrendered the Alaskan North Slope, which lay between the mountains of the Brooks Range and the arctic coast, Etok was convinced that the solution to the frustration and anger of his people was to win back the territory that had been taken from them. If the *qallunaat* wanted to use the land, he declared, let them pay for it.

Ironically, the U.S. Atomic Energy Commission provided the catalyst Etok needed to accomplish his aim. A plan to detonate an atomic bomb and to blast a deep-water port from the bedrock at Cape Thompson, near the Inuit village of Point Hope on the Alaskan coast, was causing serious concern and bitterness amongst the Inuit. Their counsel had not been sought. Yet, contamination was expected to affect an area of nearly 50,000 square miles, with possibly devastating effects on the caribou, fish, sea mammals and birdlife upon which the Inuit were dependent for their livelihood. Local meetings were called, and Etok seized the opportunity to influence grassroots opinion on the wider issues. When details of the nuclear plan became widely known, public anger was so great that the Commission was forced to abandon the project.

A few months later, an Inuk named Johnnie Nusunginya was arrested for shooting a duck.

Although he only wanted food for his family, the Inuk hunter had knowingly contravened an international treaty controlling the hunting of migratory birds. In specifying the hunting season, the legislators had concentrated on controlling the activities of sportsmen in the south and had ignored the Inuit in the north for whom ducks and geese were an essential supplement to their diet. When the season opened legally in the autumn, most birds had flown south from the Arctic and would not return until spring, after the season had closed. If Johnnie Nusunginya and his fellow hunters wished to eat, they had no option but to disregard the law. As word spread of his arrest, 138 other Inuit took their guns, each bagged a duck, and presented themselves to the game warden for arrest. Eventually, all the charges were dropped.

Capitalising on these successes, Etok created the Arctic Slope Native Association (ASNA). He was aware that without a strong power base from which to fight a land claim, historical right counted for nothing. He therefore journeyed round Alaska to persuade other communities to form similar organisations. Stories of gas in the thin layer of earth above the permafrost spurred him on with an added sense of urgency. Despite many setbacks, he eventually welded Indian and Inuit local native associations into one body, the Alaska Federation of Natives (AFN).

Under this common umbrella, each member association formulated land claims based on past hunting traditions, and presented them to the authorities in Alaska and Washington. ASNA demanded virtually all of the North Slope, an area totalling nearly sixty million acres. As events were to prove, this was not as pointless as many people at first believed. On July 18th, 1968, at Prudhoe Bay on the north coast of Alaska, the 51st and last exploration hole that British Petroleum and its partner, Atlantic Richfield, planned to drill into the North Slope, struck oil. Suddenly, Inuit land was worth money.

Within weeks, the boom was in full swing. Oil men, adventurers and speculators descended on the area. The State of Alaska auctioned drilling concessions covering 450,000 acres in Prudhoe Bay. The winning bid for one of the new oil leases was $272 million. In a single morning, the State of Alaska sold drilling rights for $900,220,590.21. Realising the potential for gaining public support throughout the United States, Etok and a few friends patrolled outside the salesroom, carrying placards which highlighted the poverty of the Inuit, and their helplessness in trying to tackle governments and multi-national oil companies. It was a story no journalist could ignore.

With the Inuit land-claims pending, the oil men were anxious to verify the legality of their leases before building a pipeline to carry the oil from Prudhoe Bay to Fairbanks. The Secretary for the Interior at the time, Steward Udall, believed that until the issue of land ownership had been settled by Congress, the transfer of federal land, and oil and gas leases should be frozen. In Washington, the administration was eager to reach a financial settlement under which native rights would be forsworn for all eternity, but Etok and his close associates were not interested in money. They wanted land, and control over its development. It was as if the Inuit negotiators were directing their infinite patience and hunting instincts towards a new quarry, the *qallunaat.*

After much wrangling, bitter in-fighting within the AFN, and some pressure from oil companies, Congress passed the Alaskan Native Claims Settlement Act of 1971. It allowed the natives to own outright 44 million acres, or approximately ten per cent, of the land in Alaska. In return for giving up the remainder, they received a cash payment of nearly a billion dollars.

In a referendum two years later, the Inuit elected to establish the North Slope as a borough, and imposed taxes of nearly seven million dollars on the oil companies and their property. At first, the oil men refused to accept the legality of the borough and contested the levy in the courts, but were overruled by the Alaskan Supreme Court.

By the time he had celebrated his thirtieth birthday, Etok finally achieved his aim and forced the *qallunaat* to pay for the use of Inuit land. He had seen a remarkable transformation in his homeland. In the North Slope villages, where during his childhood there had been a lack of sanitation and other amenities, there were now supplies of electricity and water, as well as sewage systems, schools, clinics, modern stores and satellite telephones. The price of victory, however, was high.

The ultimate intention of the Settlement Act had always been to absorb the Inuit into the mainstream culture, and in this it was spectacularly successful. Most of the billion-dollar compensation was used to underwrite more than 200 profit-making corporations, owned and administered by a new breed of Inuit executives and shareholders. Shouldering the mantle of capitalism, the guardians of these huge investments grew to be dependent not on the land, but on its continued exploitation, and as a result were thrown into conflict with the Inuit who wished to remain hunters.

Poorly advised by white consultants and cheated by sharp businessmen, the new tycoons made many mistakes. Improvement schemes were neglected and the towns for which there had been so much hope declined into ramshackle slums. In the end, Etok's idealism appeared to have produced little more than greed and corruption, discontent and discord, followed by boredom, endless hours of television, alcoholism, violence and crime.

In 1991, the Alaskan Inuit will be free to sell their land and compensation shares. Bids could be as high as a million dollars for each individual. Such wealth has left the Alaskan Inuit torn between two lifestyles, one desperately hoping to preserve the old hunting traditions, the other anxious to retain the modern advantages brought by the land claims and the oil. Whether the future encompasses the best of both worlds, or the worst, will depend mainly on whether there is a resurgence of native pride. That, in turn, may be decided by events in Canada, Greenland and Samiland.

In Canada, the discovery of oil at Prudhoe Bay had raised hopes that huge oil and gas reserves might exist in Canadian waters, especially in the Mackenzie Delta region of the Beaufort Sea. One obstacle to exploration, however, was the Arctic Island Preserve, an area of nearly 450,000 square miles of arctic territory reserved for Inuit use by a government order of 1926.

The order represented an early attempt by the Canadians to establish sovereignty over the Northwest Passage and the arctic islands further north, but it proved particularly useful four years later when the Norwegian government supported an application to extract minerals from the islands discovered by the Norwegian explorer, Otto Sverdrup.

The Canadians replied that they were unable to help because the area had been set aside for the exclusive use of the Inuit. Forty years on, and confident that oil would be found, the federal government in Ottawa quickly thrust aside such sentiments, repealed the order and began to issue exploration concessions.

With the prospect of an oil bonanza dawning in the north, a regional government was established at Yellowknife, the capital of the Northwest Territories. It came under the authority of the Department of Indian Affairs and Northern Development (DIAND), whose dual, and conflicting, role was to assist industrial development, and at the same time safeguard the social well-being of the native people. The administrators of DIAND left no doubt as to their interpretation of the latter responsibility; the sooner the Indians and Inuit were assimilated into the Canadian culture the better, a view shared wholeheartedly by the Prime Minister, Pierre Trudeau.

The Mackenzie Delta Inuit, still recovering from the devastating effects of their encounters with American whalers at the turn of the century, realised that decisions vital to their future were being made without their knowledge. Fearful that their aboriginal rights would be swept away in a tidal wave of development, a blind Inuk called Sam Raddi hastily formed the Committee for Original Peoples' Entitlement (COPE), the first political organisation of its kind in Canada. Raddi, inspired by the successes of the Alaskan Inuit, wasted no time raising the question of land ownership.

With equal speed, Ottawa rejected the whole concept of aboriginal rights. The federal government declared that the land claims were so vague as to be questionable in law. In British Columbia, Pierre Trudeau asserted that everybody in Canada, no matter what their origins, should be equal. A single social group, he said, could not make a separate deal with the rest of society. If the Indians and Inuit were saying that they wanted to re-negotiate previous 'beads for land' agreements because they considered that they had been cheated, then so far as he was concerned, they were wasting their time. The past could not be redeemed. Instead of seeking aboriginal rights, the Prime Minister declared, they should accept that their first duty was to become Canadian, and be treated like everyone else.

Thrusting Inuit fears aside and without consulting the public, the government pushed ahead with its plans to develop the north. Lucrative tax incentives were offered to drilling companies prepared to risk exploration in the Beaufort Sea. The government insisted that these did not necessarily give them the right to extract and transport oil, but companies spending tens of millions of dollars on exploratory drilling had a powerful argument on their side. In the meantime, they could write off as much as 200 per cent of their costs. Within two years of the Prudhoe Bay discovery, the government had issued nearly 10,000 exploration permits and 450 oil leases covering 450 million acres of Inuit land.

Throngs of drilling teams descended on the Mackenzie Delta. They punched more than a hundred holes into the subsoil,, and soon found an abundance of natural gas, and later, oil. The Minister for Energy declared that there were gas reserves for 330 years, and supplies of oil for more than 920 years, enough for themselves, and plenty more for export to the United States. Alarmed by the rapid turn of events, the Indians and Inuit realised that their only hope was to negotiate from a stronger, national political base. With this in mind, they formed the Inuit Tapirisat of Canada (ITC), or the Inuit Brotherhood. In the course of time, the Inuit organisation was to become a major political force, run on government grants of a million dollars a year, and an equal amount in interest-free loans against future land claim settlements.

Although partially funded by the government, the ITC did not become subservient to the administration. One of the first lessons the Inuit leaders and their advisers learned was the importance of public relations. Lambasting the government at each hint of unfair treatment, they gained nationwide publicity. Soon, a group of independent and distinguished engineers, lawyers, scientists and businessmen, concerned about the threat to the arctic environment and Inuit culture, founded a watchdog organisation, the Canadian Arctic Resources Committee. Its purpose was to promote a balanced and responsible approach to development, to protect the north and to respect the rights of the Inuit to take part in decision making. From now on, the government had to tread more carefully.

Pierre Trudeau's forceful declaration had stunned both the Indians and the Inuit. The Nishga Indians of British Columbia argued that Canada had adopted the British judicial system, and that as British law recognised native population rights, the whole question of aboriginal rights should be tested in court. They had signed no treaties with the Canadians, and in the writ served on the provincial government they demanded that recognition must be given to their original right to the land in Nass River Valley, where their people had lived for centuries.

The case proved historic. Although the Indians lost, and the Court of Appeal upheld the ruling, six judges of the Supreme Court were evenly divided. The seventh dismissed the case on a technicality, but agreed that the Indians did have aboriginal rights, and that they had never lost them by legal means. Pierre Trudeau was quick to appreciate the significance of the ruling, which was effectively a victory by a vote of four to three for the Indians. Two weeks later, the government changed course.

Reluctantly accepting that compensation should be paid where traditional interests were adversely affected, the government let it be known that it was ready to negotiate, and vested large amounts of money in native organisations to help them fight their cause. Three months after the Nishga ruling, talks began with representatives of 7,500 Cree Indians and 4,500 Inuit living in northern Quebec to settle what was known as the James Bay dispute.

The James Bay hydro-electric project was an ambitious three-phase plan to regulate seven major rivers flowing into the east side of James Bay, some of them the largest in North America. Costing nearly $6 billion for the first phase alone, this was the largest civil engineering project in Canadian history. It was intended to probe 500 miles into the heartland of northern Quebec in a series of ten artificial lakes and more than 200 dams, with power stations, access roads and airports. The scheme would satisfy the growing demand for electricity in eastern American cities for the foreseeable future. It would generate thirty per cent of the power produced in Canada, and more than one-tenth of North America's total electricity consumption.

Although hordes of southern workers were to be assigned to the area and vast tracts of land would be flooded, the Indians and Inuit were ignored, and learned of the project only by hearsay. There had been no serious attempt to study the damage such a massive scheme might cause to the environment. Bewildered, the Cree and the Inuit, like the Nishga Indians, also turned to the courts for help. Seeking the aid of sympathetic lawyers, they applied for an injunction to halt work on the project. They argued that the scheme was in violation of their native rights and would disrupt the ecological balance of the region irrevocably. After a year of testimony and deliberation, the court ruled that changing the flow of the rivers, eroding their beds and banks, and flooding adjacent areas on such a vast scale meant that the native people would no longer be able to hunt, trap or fish in the affected areas, and granted an injunction until the issue of native rights had been settled.

The victory was short-lived. Eight days later, an Appeals Court overturned the decision. Nevertheless, the provincial government was worried that work on the project might be stopped by further appeals, and no doubt mindful of the Nishga Indian ruling three months earlier, agreed to talk. A year of hard bargaining followed, and eventually the two sides reached an agreement in principle. The Indians and Inuit were not at all happy with the proposed deal, which had been hammered out with maximum haste and under considerable pressure from the developers.

Like the Alaska Native Claims Act, it amounted to little more than an exchange of ancestral land and hunting rights for cash, with a package of social programmes thrown in for good measure.

Adopting a tough stance, the provincial government negotiators intimated that the native groups could take the offer or leave it. They warned that work on the project would continue irrespective of whether they signed the agreement or not, and added that an appeal to the Supreme Court would be prohibitively expensive and could take up to ten years to settle. By that time, the project would have been completed, and the native groups would have gained nothing.

With their backs to the wall, the Cree and the Inuit accepted $225 million compensation, the right of ownership to 1.3 per cent of their territory, and exclusive hunting, fishing and whaling rights to 14 per cent of the land. Viewed from the opposite standpoint, the James Bay Agreement had deprived them of 98.7 per cent of their native land, and 86 per cent of their hunting and fishing rights in return for approximately $18,750 for each individual. This amount was payable over several years, and depreciated rapidly owing to subsequent inflation. Nevertheless, the agreement was better than nothing, and an important lesson for Inuit elsewhere.

As the details of the James Bay agreement were being thrashed out, another development project was announced which threatened to have an even greater impact on Indian and Inuit affairs. This was a plan to build a $10 billion pipeline to transport gas from Prudhoe Bay along the north coast of Alaska and Yukon to the Mackenzie Delta. Here, it would link up with Canadian gas fields before snaking south through the Mackenzie Valley to join an American pipeline system in Alberta, a total distance of 2,625 miles.

Conservationists were particularly concerned about the inadequacies of a new government review process, which required the effects on the environment to be gauged before construction started. Although the government had laid down set guidelines, responsibility for the inquiry, and the method of assessment, was left to the firms involved. Company experts were frequently more highly qualified than the government employees who scrutinised the final reports and made the recommendations upon which a final decision would be based. It was also in the interests of developers to isolate the various aspects of a project when weighing its possibly damaging effects. A firm appraising the potential harm to the ecology from a pipeline might consider it in their own interests to conduct a separate assessment on the pumping stations. Similarly, a multinational company could concentrate on the detrimental features of a single drilling rig, fully aware that if oil was discovered the impact from a multitude of wells, pumping stations, pipelines, roads and increased ground and air traffic would be infinitely greater.

Feeling threatened by the Mackenzie Valley pipeline, the Indian and Inuit Brotherhoods lobbied urgently for a public inquiry. At the same time, the Canadian Arctic Resources Committee detailed the likely hazards of the scheme. Sympathy groups protested and the southern press rounded on the government, which had been extraordinarily secretive about its development policies for the north, particularly with regard to the granting of exploration permits and oil leases, and the publication of research work. With the growing dissent posing a potential security risk to the expensive and vulnerable pipeline, the government capitulated, and appointed a widely respected Supreme Court judge from British Columbia, Thomas Berger, to head the inquiry.

Judge Berger approached his task earnestly, and with refreshing probity. He listened to everyone who had anything to say. He travelled thousands of miles to visit witnesses who were unable to attend the main hearings in Yellowknife. In all, he heard testimony from 3,000 experts and 1,000 local inhabitants in nearly fifty towns, villages and settlements, and collected 33,353 pages of evidence. Never before had such attention been paid to the native viewpoint, nor had it been so widely publicised.

As Judge Berger journeyed across the country, he realised that the land which the government and the developers regarded only as a frontier to be conquered was a home for those who lived there. The local people were not interested in cash compensation. They wanted to keep their land and determine their own futures, and they begged for time to consider how they might protect their cultures while trying to adjust to the inexorable advance of development.

Greatly moved by the overwhelming opposition to the project, Judge Berger stressed in his findings the importance of protecting animal and birdlife, particularly the huge caribou herds and the snow geese. He suggested that instead of building a pipeline which would dissect the migratory routes of the caribou in north Yukon, the government should create a national park, in which the native population should be granted sovereign hunting rights. Finally, he recommended that the pipeline through the Mackenzie Valley should be postponed for ten years to enable native land claims to be settled before construction work began. On publication of the report, the Indians and Inuit were jubilant. In Ottawa, the government was appalled.

During the early days of the inquiry, the Indians had refused to negotiate with the federal Land Claims Office on the grounds that their land, the whole of the Northwest Territories south of the tree line from the Mackenzie River to Hudson Bay, was not for sale. Refuting the government view that the James Bay Agreement was a precedent for the settlement of all other land claims, they emphasised that their people had lived in *Denendeh*, meaning 'The Land of the People', for 30,000 years. They had no intention of relinquishing it now for what they considered to be yet another trinkets-and-blankets-for-land agreement.

Consequently, at a meeting of the Indian Brotherhood at Fort Simpson in July 1975, 300 delegates voted unanimously to adopt an historic document called 'The Dene Declaration'. For the government, which had seen its relations with six million French-speaking Canadians in Quebec deteriorate almost to the point of secession, the opening sentence verged on treason. It stated:

> We the Dene of the Northwest Territories insist on the right to be regarded by ourselves and the world as a nation.

The document continued, with touching simplicity:

> Our struggle is for the recognition of the Dene Nation by the government and people of Canada and the peoples and governments of the world.
>
> As once Europe was the exclusive homeland of the European peoples, Africa the exclusive homeland of the African peoples, the New World, North and South America, was the exclusive homeland of Aboriginal peoples of the New World, the Amerindian and the Inuit.
>
> The New World like other parts of the world has suffered the experience of colonialism and imperialism. Other peoples have occupied the land – often with force – and foreign governments have imposed themselves on our people. Ancient civilizations and ways of life have been destroyed.
>
> Colonialism and imperialism is now dead or dying. Recent years have witnessed the birth of new nations or rebirth of old nations out of the ashes of colonialism.
>
> As Europe is the place where you will find European countries with European governments for European peoples, now also you will find in Africa and Asia the existence of African and Asian countries with African and Asian governments for the African and Asian people.
>
> The African and Asian peoples – the peoples of the Third World – have fought for and won the right to self-determination, the right to recognition as distinct peoples and the recognition of themselves as nations.

But in the New World the Native peoples have not fared so well. Even in countries in South America where the native peoples are the vast majority of the population there is not one country which has Amerindian government for the Amerindian peoples.

Nowhere in the New World have the Native peoples won the right to self-determination and the right to recognition by the world as a distinct people and as nations.

While the Native people of Canada are a minority in their homeland, the Native people of the N.W.T., the Dene and the Inuit, are a majority of the population of the N.W.T.

The Dene find themselves as part of a country. That country is Canada. But the Government of Canada is not the government of the Dene. The Government of the N.W.T. is not the government of the Dene. These governments were not the choice of the Dene, they were imposed upon the Dene.

What we the Dene are struggling for is the recognition of the Dene Nation by the governments and peoples of the world.

And while there are realities we are forced to submit to, such as the existence of a country called Canada, we insist on the right to self-determination as a distinct people and the recognition of the Dene Nation.

We the Dene are part of the Fourth World. And as the peoples and nations of the world have come to recognize the existence and rights of those peoples who make up the Third World the day must come and will come when the nations of the Fourth World will come to be recognized and respected. The challenge to the Dene and the world is to find the way for the recognition of the Dene Nation.

Our plea to the world is to help us in our struggle to find a place in the world community where we can exercise our right to self-determination as a distinct people and a nation.

What we seek then is independence and self-determination within the country of Canada. This is what we mean when we call for a just settlement for the Dene Nation.

The Dene Declaration was a milestone. It created new hope for the Dene, and inspired the Inuit. Shortly afterwards, the Dene placed their relationship with the government on an entirely new footing by formally submitting a proposal for local government which would control land resources and nature conservation. Although it was repeatedly emphasised that self-determination would be within the framework of the Confederation, many Canadians viewed the proposal as a threat of secession. Pierre Trudeau refused to accept what he called an autonomous native local government based on race. The proposal is still being negotiated.

The Inuit, who had been discussing their own claims along the lines of the Alaska Native Claims Settlement Act and the James Bay Agreement, decided to withdraw from the negotiations, and begin again. Starting from the premise that their right to self-determination had never been surrendered, they pressed for political power as well as compensation for past wrongs.

Although there were no academics in their ranks, the accurate documentation of their culture was vital if critics were to be convinced that their way of life was, and always had been, inextricably bound up with vast areas of the arctic environment. With the help of the anthropologist Milton Freeman, virtually every adult hunter in the Canadian Arctic was questioned about his hunting journeys, equipment and methods. Wildlife patterns were charted and hunting grounds mapped with infinite detail. It was the most complete description of Inuit life ever undertaken.

Freeman's three-volume report proved not only that during their lifetime, many Inuit hunters travelled between 10,000 and 20,000 miles on hunting trips, but that they had occupied every part of the Arctic for at least 4,000 years, and were therefore justified in claiming ownership of approximately 770,000 square miles of land and 865,000 square miles of sea as their home. Heartened by the Alaskan settlement and the progress made on their home front, the Mackenzie Delta Inuit, known as the *Inuvialuit*, negotiated a special agreement with the government. Under it, they were guaranteed 35,000 square miles of land in perpetuity, with mineral rights to 18 per cent of it, and nearly $120 million (£60 million) compensation. Both land and cash were placed in trust so that there could be no question of selling out, as in Alaska.

Clearly influenced by the Dene Declaration, other Inuit stressed in a similar document that as they had never had a constitutional relationship with the Canadian government, they wished to form a new territory within the Canadian Confederation, to be governed by themselves under the supervision of Ottawa. It must contain all the land and sea north of the Canadian tree line, an area the size of India. They called it *Nunavut*, the Inuktitut word for 'Our Land'.

The concept of a Dene Nation and Nunavut made sense. The new territories would separate the histories, cultures and climates of the two peoples along a natural border, with the Dene occupying the forests to the south of the tree line, and the Inuit the tundra and arctic wastelands further north. It was not a question of creating separate ethnic states, but the fervent desire of the Dene and the Inuit to govern themselves, rather than be ruled by southern administrators who did not fully understand their problems, and whose seat of government at Yellowknife was hundreds of miles from many of the isolated areas whose future they were trying to decide.

Ottawa's reaction to the Nunavut proposal was predictable. Insisting that autonomous native governments based on race could not be discussed in the same context as land claims, the federal government reiterated that the James Bay Agreement was a precedent from which it would not depart. With negotiations deadlocked and the Northwest Territories in political turmoil, Pierre Trudeau attempted to cool the situation by appointing a former cabinet minister, Charles Drury, to investigate the possibility of constitutional reform in the north. Drury, however, was boycotted by native groups and the inquiry was an embarrassing political failure.

Nobody seemed to notice that the Drury report included a recommendation that the Northwest Territories should ultimately be divided into two parts, a suggestion which was subsequently endorsed in a referendum, and tentatively approved by the federal government in Ottawa. Nunavut was about to become a reality.

CHAPTER 15

Fighting Back

The Nunavut proposal sparked a renewed sense of pride among the Canadian Inuit. During a visit to North America in September, 1984, Pope John Paul II gave them what they needed more than anything else – initial recognition of the justice of their battle for self-determination. Apologising for the heavy-handed evangelising of previous Catholic missionaries, he unequivocally expressed solidarity with Canada's native people, and told thousands of Indians and Inuit at St Anne de Beaupré in Quebec: 'You must be the architects of your own future, freely and responsibly.' Pope John Paul added that further progress was needed, and said this should be negotiated 'in the increased recognition of your own decision-making power'. Afterwards, Stephen Kakfwi, the President of the Dene Nation, described the visit as the beginning of a new era.

In fact, the new era had already begun when large numbers of Inuit children were sent during the post-war period to be educated in the south. Like Etok, many of them subsequently returned home to fight the cause of their people, quickly gaining experience from government negotiations, legal actions and contacts with sympathetic liberal groups. The emerging leaders also maintained informal contacts with the Alaskan Inuit, and had been inspired by the events in Greenland where the Inuit had made even greater progress. Here, like a phoenix rising from the ashes of despair, the Inuit leadership had managed to shrug off its disillusionment, and wrested from the Danes the most comprehensive form of self-determination anywhere in the Arctic. This change in their fortunes stemmed from a decision to amend the Danish constitution in 1953. Until then, Greenland had been a Danish crown colony, governed centrally from Copenhagen. Now, it was to become an equal and integral part of the Danish Kingdom, with the Inuit representatives occupying two of the 179 seats in the Danish *Folketing*, or parliament.

Denmark's vision for the future of Greenland was a simple one. In a country where there was no agriculture or forestland, and minerals were difficult to extract, economic viability hinged on the enormous stocks of cod and shrimp off the west coast. The fishing industry would have to be modernised, fish factories built, and the hunting communities moved into the towns. Housing would be needed to accommodate the influx of people, schools would have to be provided to educate them, and hospitals to treat their illnesses. The Danes paid for all of it. They decided that if the young Inuit were to become wage-earners in the modern industrialised society, it was essential that they be taught the Danish language, but until they achieved fluency, Greenland would have to import Danish labour.

One difficulty was the necessity to offer high salaries to Danish workers to induce them to work in the Arctic. If Inuit labourers were paid equally well, the high cost could negate the whole purpose of the experiment, which was to nurse the country to economic health. The *Folketing* solved this dilemma by enacting a law which permitted Danes to be paid higher salaries than the Inuit for exactly the same jobs. Appreciating the need for progress, many Inuit politicians supported the Danish approach and reluctantly accepted the discriminatory pay law as a necessary evil, but the majority of the population voiced their intense displeasure. In their view, the Danish dream was a recipe for disaster, and their complaints did not go unheard.

In the municipal councils, a new breed of politician was emerging. These were the Inuit leaders who dissociated themselves from policies which forced hunters to abandon their hunting traditions, and humiliated their people with inferior wages. They were angered that Danish was the principal teaching medium in the schools and outraged that students should be obliged to travel to Denmark for further education. Seeing no gain in centralising the population, they rebelled against the control wielded by the Danes over every aspect of their lives.

The new political generation pictured the Danish dream as a nightmare in which the Greenlandic language, community spirit and Inuit culture were slowly being extinguished. Soon, these angry young Inuit would become the elected representatives to the Provincial Council, the national advisory body to the Danish *Folketing*. Eventually, their voices would be heard in the *Folketing* itself, and in time, they would achieve what no Inuk had dared to believe possible.

As Etok negotiated the final draft of the Alaska Native Claims Act, and the Cree and Canadian Inuit sought to stop the James Bay project, three Greenlanders, a poet, a teacher and a clergyman, joined together and became a formidable political force. The poet, Moses Olsen, agitated for the opportunity to let Greenlanders solve their own problems. The teacher, Lars Emil Johansen, warned of cultural genocide at the hands of the Danes, and Jonathan Motzfeldt, the clergyman, demanded the abolition of the discriminatory pay policy. The three men sat on Greenland's Provincial Council, and two of them, Olsen and Johansen, were elected to the Danish *Folketing*. In 1973, Jonathan Motzfeldt formally demanded that the Greenlanders be granted Home Rule.

The Danes were stunned. The Copenhagen government could not conceive that the vast amounts of money spent on helping Greenland into the modern world was in anything but the best interests of the Inuit. Many Danes publicly denounced them for being ungrateful. Deeply wounded and genuinely concerned that its good intentions might have been misguided, the government eventually set up a commission to discuss the issue. The numbers were evenly divided between Danes and Greenlanders, the first time the Inuit had been accepted on an equal basis.

As the commission settled down to its task, Moses Olsen made one more demand. With the discoveries of Alaskan and Canadian oil assuming new importance following the quadrupling of world oil prices in 1973, he insisted that Home Rule should also incorporate recognition of the Inuit's original right to own Greenland's subsoil, and any mineral wealth it might contain. The Danes, like the Canadians, refused outright. If that was the Inuit's wish, the Danish Prime Minister warned, the Greenlanders would have to abandon their ties with Denmark. Knowing this to be economically impossible, the Inuit compromised, accepting *fundamental* rights to mineral and oil resources, rather than the right of ownership. The Danes neglected to define the term, but the Inuit were reasonably happy, having won the right to veto any decision to extract resources.

After five years of discussion, the Greenlanders voted by 70 per cent to 26 per cent to adopt Home Rule. This was ratified soon afterwards by the *Folketing*. The 51,000 Greenlanders, of whom more than 9,000 are of Danish extraction, are now responsible for every aspect of home affairs, including education, employment, trade and industry, fishing, hunting, and country planning, as well as taxation, broadcasting, hospitals and the Church. The Danes, however, retain control of the foreign and defence policies, the police and the courts.

One of the first areas the Inuit tackled was education. Inuktitut immediately became the principal language in the schools, with Danish taught as a second language. Soon, approximately 12,000 children, more than a quarter of the Greenland-born population, were attending 100 schools, an average of 120 pupils to each school compared with 850 in Copenhagen. Traditional hunting and fishing methods were taught to ensure that the skills would not be lost, but these lessons were combined with classes on modern ecological and environmental theory so that natural resources would be farmed carefully. Many courses for further education were moved from Copenhagen to Greenland towns; training colleges for nursing, teaching, building, fisheries and sheep farming were established. (A tiny but important industry, with approximately 23,000 ewes in southern Greenland, sheep farming supports 500 people, including a hundred independent farmers; some 20,000 lambs are slaughtered annually.)

With international contacts between the Arctic nations increasing, the Greenlanders' progress was followed particularly closely in Canada and Samiland, where education, language and communications were vitally important in the battle to restore native pride. In Canada, the government had convinced most Inuit parents that unless their children were given an English-language education, they would be hard pressed to secure a decent future for them in the modern world. The awakening of Inuit political consciousness in the 1970s proved that this was far from true.

Demands for more lessons in Inuktitut and government support for Inuit teacher-training programmes quickly gained ground. The number of native students who continued their education after secondary school leapt from 16 to 154 in five years, and is still increasing. A one million dollar Indigenous Language Development Fund was established to help teachers design language courses and modernise Inuktitut. New words were invented to describe technological advances. The word for 'satellite', for example, became *qangattaqtitausimajug*, meaning 'it has been made to fly'.

When domestic communications satellites linked the Arctic to Canadian radio and television networks, the Inuit soon demanded their own programmes. Today, nearly half the output at the Canadian Broadcasting Corporation stations at Frobisher Bay and Rankin Inlet are in Inuktitut. Having learned the techniques of television, the Inuit formed their own broadcasting corporation, and were soon generating five hours of current affairs, cultural and sports programmes each week. Their ultimate ambition is to establish a circumpolar radio and television station which would beam programmes to Alaska and Greenland.

A constant theme in the Inuit programmes is the urgent need to protect the environment. This issue is so pervasive in the north that the Home Rule government in Greenland cited it as the principal reason for refusing to allow any form of offshore oil exploration in Greenlandic waters, although it agreed to drilling on land in eastern Greenland subject to stringent conditions. Reiterating that Greenlanders alone should own the country's natural resources, the new government signalled to the Danes that it would eventually wish to re-negotiate the terms of their agreement on mineral and oil resources.

The Greenlanders' immediate priority, however, was to extricate themselves from the European Economic Community (EEC). When Denmark joined the market in 1973, the colony automatically became a member as well. To the Greenlanders, who hunted seals from kayaks and lived in a country which was ninety per cent ice, the rules and regulations of the bureaucrats in Brussels seemed irrelevant and absurd. What was the purpose of common transport charges, they argued, when there were no roads, buses or trains, and the population of 50,000 was scattered in towns and settlements hundreds of miles apart? With almost no farming of their own, it would have been cheaper to buy agricultural products on the world market than be bound by the Community's Common Agricultural Policy. Similarly, the European Coal and Steel Union merely raised the prices for imported EEC steel to exorbitant levels.

In virtually every aspect, the wishes of the Inuit were at variance with EEC rules. The Community advocated free movement of labour between member countries. The Inuit were anxious to restrict the influx of foreign labour, especially from Denmark. The Common Market encouraged centralisation, the Greenlanders were eager to de-centralise. The European Atomic Energy Community, Euratom, stipulated that where extractable uranium existed, it should be mined to the advantage of its members. The Inuit, who were sitting on one of the largest uranium reserves in the world, refused because of the potential hazard to the environment.

The Inuits' greatest concern was the protection of the sea. Its teeming waters were their lifeblood, their only major resource. Yet the rules laid down by the policy-makers in Brussels were a strait-jacket. As long as the Greenlanders remained members of the Community, they could never be granted exclusive fishing rights in their own waters. To their annoyance, the catches of EEC fishermen were worth five times as much as the subsidies they received from Community. 'It is intolerable', Moses Olsen told a conference in Denmark, 'to have to ask permission in Brussels to catch our own fish, especially as over and over again, we experience Community fishermen taking advantages in our waters beyond the granted quotas.'

Community fishermen persistently caught more fish than they were allowed. As experience in the Arctic had shown so many times before, stocks inevitably declined. The depletion was so severe that reported catches dropped from 32,000 tons in 1971 to 6,000 tons four years later, but these figures were frequently manipulated. The International Council for the Exploration of the Sea reported that EEC fishermen sometimes took up to eight times the reported catch. Between 1977 and

1982, catches from east Greenland waters were logged at 50,000 tons, although 133,000 tons of fish were actually taken.

Marine biologists warned that the level of spawning stock was so low that the cod would stop reproducing off East Greenland unless catches were urgently reduced, but fishing continued unabated. The Greenlanders pointed to the West Germans as the only EEC nation with a deep-sea fleet large enough for exploitation on such a scale. They were equally angry at the EEC administrators, who in 1982 ignored a recommended maximum allowable catch of 62,000 tons in Greenlandic waters, and set the limit at 75,000 tons. When the scientists urged a reduction to 56,000 tons the following year, the EEC maintained the quota at the same level, but by now, the Greenlanders had had enough. In a special referendum, the Inuit voted by 52 per cent to 46 per cent to leave the Community, with spoiled or blank votes accounting for the other two per cent. The turn-out was 75 per cent of the 32,385 people entitled to vote.

Negotiations for withdrawal were long and difficult. West Germany warned that it would exact a high price for the Greenlanders' departure. Not to be trifled with, the Inuit drove their own hard bargain. In return for allowing Community fishermen to take 68,000 tons of fish a year from their waters, they demanded an annual payment of £16 million, and won the status of an overseas associated country, which meant that they could sell their own fish on the European market without being tied by EEC red tape.

Until the last moment, like children squabbling over a box of chocolates, the ten member nations quarrelled about the terms of the withdrawal, and how the proportions of cod quotas should be shared. The date set for Greenland's departure was January 1st, 1985. In a last-minute protest, the French petulantly exercised their veto, claiming that a special arrangement for Greenland could create difficulties in the Pacific, where the inhabitants of New Caledonia were rebelling against French colonial rule. This extraordinary decision was followed by another bizarre incident when, despite repeated reminders, the Irish parliament 'forgot' to give formal approval to the agreement before the Christmas holidays. As a result, Greenland's withdrawal was delayed by one month.

Exasperation turned to anger. Jonathan Motzfeldt, the genial Lutheran clergyman who had become Greenland's Prime Minister, issued a stern warning. If by the end of the month the Community did not formally approve the terms agreed and pay the first cash payment, due on New Year's Day, he would call on the Danish navy to repel EEC fishermen from Greenlandic waters. Failing that, he added ominously, he would make alternative arrangements with the Soviet Union.

Within 24 hours, the difficulties had been smoothed away, and on February 1st, 1985, Greenland became the first nation to leave the European Economic Community.

Although eager to maintain contact with Europe, the Greenlanders had always considered themselves an arctic, rather than a European, people. Their history, culture and temperament bound them to Alaska and Canada with whom they shared a common environment and similar aims. Not surprisingly, as the Inuit in the three countries engaged in their separate struggles, the bonds between them strengthened.

In July, 1977, hunters and community leaders from every part of Greenland converged on Sondre Stromfjord, an American air base on the west coast, where a chartered French-Canadian Boeing 737 was waiting to fly them across Davis Strait. After a brief flight to Frobisher Bay on Baffin Island, they were joined by a group of Canadian Inuit, each of whom had travelled separately from Labrador, Quebec, Baffin Island and Keewatin on the northwestern edge of Hudson Bay.

Taking off again, the Boeing, its bright blue fuselage gleaming in the summer sunlight, headed across Hudson Bay and over the Dene Nation. Somewhere ahead, a chartered Twin Otter packed with Inuit from villages and settlements in the western Arctic was flying along the same route, northwest along the Mackenzie River and across north Yukon towards Alaska. Their destination was Barrow, the northernmost tip of the North American continent. Here, for the first time in their history, one of the oldest races in the world met together as one people.

On arrival, the Greenlanders were elated to discover that although 3,000 miles separated them from the Alaskans, with whom they had virtually lost contact for 4,000 years, they had no difficulty talking to the Inuit of Barrow. Elsewhere, the centuries had left their mark, and the various groups were able to communicate with each other only when they spoke very slowly. Nevertheless, their common tongue was Inuktitut, and this was the official language at the meeting.

The Inuit resolved to call the assembly the Inuit Circumpolar Conference (ICC). They proposed a charter which would preserve their language and culture, improve transportation and communications, and safeguard Inuit resources. It would include scientific game management and the improvement of living conditions in the north. Formally constituting the ICC, the charter was adopted unanimously. The delegates shook hands, hugged each other and then burst into song. After centuries of isolation, the Inuit had become a united political force.

They lost no time in settling down to work. Every aspect of arctic life was discussed: language, education and health care, land ownership, conservation and the encroachment of southern development. One of the most significant resolutions was that of an arctic peace zone, in which nuclear weapons, weapons testing, military bases and manoeuvres would be prohibited, together with the disposal of chemical, biological and nuclear waste. After vigorous debate, this proposal was adopted by an overwhelming majority.

Throughout the conference, the first concern of the delegates was to preserve the equilibrium of the arctic environment. In 1980, when they met again at Nuuk, the Inuit were horrified to learn of a Canadian plan to ship huge quantities of highly explosive liquefied natural gas in two super tankers from the High Arctic to southeastern Canada. Each ship would be more than a quarter of a mile long, with a beam the width of an ice-hockey rink. Fitted with 150,000 hp engines, they would smash through ice seven feet thick. No mention was made of the pressure ridges, which could be as much as 60 feet thick.

The plan, called the Arctic Pilot Project (APP), anticipated that on every voyage each vessel would carry approximately 140,000 cubic metres of liquefied natural gas, more than Greenland used in a year. The shuttle service involved sixteen round trips a year through the icefields of the Northwest Passage, Baffin Bay and Davis Strait, a total of 64 voyages within 100 miles of the west Greenland coast. Financing the project were four major companies, including Canada's state-owned national oil and gas company, Petro Canada, and Dome Petroleum. With huge financial investments at stake, a titanic struggle looked inevitable.

The Inuits' main objection to the project was the danger to marine life. Experts called to public hearings before the National Energy Board in Ottawa testified that the noise from the powerful engines of the gas carriers, the largest ships in the world, would disrupt the sonar communication system of whales, and endanger their survival. There would be equally damning evidence from Greenlandic hunters. Attempts by APP executives to prevent them giving evidence were blocked by the Board, which ruled that their testimony was relevant and could be heard before the Canadian lawyer in the magistrates' court at Nuuk.

The first witness was Uusaqqaq Qujaakitsoq, a seal hunter and deputy mayor of Qaanaaq, the home of the Polar Inuit, who live further north than any other population on earth. He explained that when a police vessel sailed into Inglefield Bay during the beluga hunting season in 1979, the whales disappeared for the rest of the season. Similarly, when Inuit at Siorapaluk obtained snowmobiles, there was a marked decline in the number of seals in the district. The local council was so concerned, he added, that it had been forced to ban the use of snowmobiles for all but the summer months, when the seals retreat to the open water.

Pavia Nielsen, a hunter and fisherman from Uummannaq, described the difficulties encountered by hunters attempting to catch sea mammals. 'In my own experience of hunting in kayaks, I know that the only reason I can get near the animals is because the kayak is silent,' he began. 'As soon as I make any noise, the animals disappear. I recall hunters who were approaching a narwhal, and knocked the side of their kayak with their paddle. As soon as that happened, the narwhal became alarmed by the noise and swam away.' The problem, Nielsen explained, was that when one seal, narwhal or whale was alarmed, it communicated with the others, and within a few minutes the fjord would be empty. The animals, he continued, were also sensitive to noise from ships.

> In 1975, when the Greenex company [a Danish subsidiary 100% owned by Vestgron Mines Ltd, which is in turn 62.5% owned by the Canadian Corporation, Cominco Ltd.] began to mine zinc near Uummannaq, it sailed icebreakers through one of our good hunting areas.
>
> As a result, the animals went away from that area and the hunters had to hunt elsewhere. The whole fjord was affected for several months, until the community protested and put a stop to these icebreaking ships. There are now no icebreakers there, and so the animals have returned and we can hunt.
>
> If the APP goes ahead, we are afraid our entire way of life as hunters and fishermen will be completely destroyed. Furthermore, the APP is very dangerous because as a pilot project it will inevitably lead to other projects, and increased shipping in the area. This is what frightens us most.

With three-quarters of the Greenland population dependent on hunting and fishing for their subsistence, the Home Rule government was unanimous in its condemnation of the project. Greenland's representative in the European Parliament, Finn Lynge, wondered whether the Canadians realised the extent of the threat, and if they did, whether they cared. Fearful that the pilot project would lead to several supertankers a day breaking up the ice on a year round basis, his message to the Canadians was clear:

> You simply cannot gamble in this way with the major livelihood of the majority of our population. Unless it is proven beyond a doubt that there is no danger at all, then the APP is unacceptable.
>
> We are extremely concerned that the APP will break up the ice of the Lancaster Sound, which is the biological basis of life in Baffin Bay and Davis Strait, and disrupt the ecological food chains there.

We have some of the world's finest shrimp banks in Davis Strait. If there was a major supertanker accident, it would destroy these shrimp beds, and the entire industry.

Even if all the game does not go away, there is a grave danger that the stocks will be diminished to such a degree that we may have to depopulate vast areas of our country.

Clearly, the Canadians had given no thought to such dangers. Six months after the hearings began, the Arctic Pilot Project was shelved indefinitely. The decision was hailed as victory for circumpolar co-operation. In ten years, the Inuit had fought back from a position of isolation, helplessness and despair, and won back their pride. More importantly, they had gained the increasing respect of the *qallunaat* in the south as tough negotiators genuinely intent on preserving their way of life. In the years to come, they would need all the influence and stamina they could muster to combat the new, and infinitely greater dangers looming on the arctic horizon.

CHAPTER 16

The Wilderness Polluted

When hurricane force winds swept across the Kola Peninsula in the Soviet Union in 1983, the clear blue skies of the glorious arctic summer darkened without warning into a polar nightmare. For two days, clouds of stinging black dust blotted out the sun. In the city of Apatity on the shores of Lake Imandra, approximately eighty miles from the Finnish border, pedestrians were forced to protect their faces with handkerchiefs, hats, scarves and newspapers – anything they could find to avoid choking. Windows in every building remained firmly shut. Engineers switched off the ventilation plants in apartment blocks. Not until the gales had died down and the tiny particles of industrial waste had settled, did the people venture outdoors again.

The phenomenon was not unexpected. For years, officials had been discussing what to do with the industrial waste on the outskirts of the city. Over the years, the dumps had grown to 300 million tons, covering 1,375 acres. Each year, ten per cent of the waste from the ore-processing plant nearby was pumped into Lake Imandra. Another ten per cent was carried by the winds into the atmosphere. Samples of soil analysed by Soviet scientists showed that the thin layer of earth above the permafrost in this part of the Kola Peninsula was not only contaminated, but becoming saturated with chemicals.

In the industrial heartland of the Soviet north, massive quantities of sulphur dioxide, carbon monoxide, nitric oxides and other harmful substances are expelled from thousands of factory chimneys into the atmosphere. Pollutants from non-ferrous metal industries, which treat only one third of their harmful emissions, have been found in soil fifty miles away. Soviet executives in the metallurgy and mineral fertiliser industries of Murmansk province have been publicly castigated for showing too little concern for the environment. Some factory managements have been fined millions of roubles. So grave is the level of pollution that in one seven-year period, 30,000 acres of forest were laid waste, much of it part of a nature conservancy area in Soviet Samiland. Another 180,000 acres were poisoned to such a degree that they may never be saved.

With its economy based primarily on steel production and the use of coal, the Soviet Union is generally regarded as the principal source of pollution in the Arctic, closely followed by West Germany and the United Kingdom. Although the air in the polar regions is commonly believed to be the cleanest in the world, recent studies show that it contains as many impurities as in some suburban areas in the south. For years, the Inuit have been puzzled by the gradual whitening of traditionally deep blue skies. Now, scientists have identified the phenomenon as 'Arctic haze'. Hanging listlessly over millions of square miles of the Arctic, in layers as high as 25,000 feet, it is laden with sulphates and hydrocarbons from coal, oil and petroleum products, and a chemical, perchloreothylene, often used in dry-cleaning solutions.

The amount of chemicals in the polar air can be gauged by comparing hair samples taken from modern Greenlanders with those from the bodies of a group of Inuit found remarkably well preserved in a grave at Qilakitsoq, in northwest Greenland. Carbon dating established that the Inuit had lived more than 500 years ago, long before industrial pollution. Analysis showed that the present-day Inuit were carrying significant quantities of cadmium, a metal unknown when the Inuit family was alive in 1450. The level of mercury, which has always been prevalent in the Arctic, is 300 per cent greater in today's Inuit, the copper content is 350 per cent higher, and lead shows an increase of 700 per cent. The researchers warned that a continued increase of poisonous metals in the atmosphere, combined with the lack of important nutrients in some western food, would eventually result in the diminished health of Greenland's population.

First noticed by pilots in the 1950s, Arctic haze extends from Norway to the North Slope of Alaska. Scientists flying into it found that it was reddish-brown, and much heavier and denser than at first believed. The pollutants are extremely acidic, and most noticeable during winter, when there is little rain or snow to wash them from the air. As a result, they remain airborne for longer and travel further. Now, the atmosphere is contaminated all the way to the North Pole.

The soot particles absorb the sun's radiation, give off heat and raise the temperature of the lower atmosphere. Many scientists believe that the haze traps this excess warmth, creating a greenhouse effect. Computer predictions indicate that if the pollution continues unchecked, weather patterns across the northern hemisphere could be distorted. Natural vegetation and crop patterns would change. The icecap would begin to melt, raising the level of the oceans. Ultimately, many ports and low-lying coastal areas could be flooded. If this scenario seems far-fetched, it should be remembered that carbon dioxide levels in the atmosphere are increasing at the rate of one per cent a year, and that industry in the Soviet bloc, western Europe and North America discharges approximately 100 million *tons* of sulphur dioxide every year.

The enormity of this is difficult to grasp. By comparison, emissions of sulphur dioxide from Mount St Helens in 1980 and 1981 totalled only 300,000 tons. Expressed even more starkly, 100 million tons is equivalent to every single man, woman and child in the Soviet Union, East and West Europe, Scandinavia, Canada and the United States throwing a two-pound (one-kilogram) bag of sulphur dioxide into the air every day of their lives.

In addition to sulphur dioxide emissions, tens of millions of tons of nitric oxides and trace gases, many used in refrigeration and aerosol propellants, are discharged into the atmosphere. Recent studies show that if the emissions continue at their present level, the temperature of the atmosphere will rise as much as five degrees C. by the year 2050.

As the winds carrying these pollutants do not recognise boundaries, friction is created between nations. The Scandinavians are incensed because poisonous waste from Britain is affecting their forests and lakes, but Britain refuses to join formal international efforts to reduce the emissions. Canada and the United States are similarly at loggerheads.

When, in Helsinki in July 1985, ministers from nineteen countries signed a protocol to reduce sulphur dioxide emission by thirty per cent by 1993, Britain – which releases 3.5 million tons a year – refused to sign the document on the grounds that the percentage was arbitrary, and that in the 1980s it had cut emissions by 24 per cent. This compares with 37 per cent for France, 19 per cent for Italy and six per cent for West Germany. The average reduction for EEC countries is only seven per cent.

American researchers calculate that seventy per cent of airborne pollution in the Arctic emanates from Europe and the Soviet Union. This cannot be confirmed because Moscow has refused to cooperate with the study. Although some Soviet scientists have expressed concern that higher carbon dioxide levels may be melting the permafrost in Siberia, others apparently do not subscribe to the greenhouse theory, but suggest that the Arctic is becoming cooler rather than warmer.

Pointing to a marked increase of approximately 250,000 square miles in the amount of sea ice between Greenland and eastern Siberia, they say the mean temperature in some areas of the Soviet Arctic has fallen by 3°C. To some extent, this is borne out by the unusually severe ice conditions which have prevented Greenland's trawlermen reaching their fishing grounds. It is also supported by scientific projections of a new mini-glaciation period, based on the ice cores extracted from the Greenland icecap, and a thirty-day reduction in the time during which shipping can penetrate Soviet arctic sea routes.

A cause of equal concern in the West is a £10 billion Soviet plan to reverse the northerly flow of the Irtysh and Ob Rivers, which feed the Arctic Ocean with fresh water, diverting them so that they run southwards through a 1,500-mile canal to irrigate dry but densely populated desert zones. Advocates of the scheme dismiss arguments that the climate in the northern hemisphere could be adversely affected, although the effects cannot be established with certainty until after the event. The Soviet leader, Mikhail Gorbachev, has since indicated that he considers the scheme too grandiose, and may not permit it to go ahead. Rivers have already been polluted by industry throughout the Soviet Arctic, Samiland, and the North American sub-arctic regions. The water in Norway's River Tana is unfit to drink. Elsewhere, millions of salmon and trout have been killed.

In Quebec, excess water at a hydro-electric plant spilled into a swollen river, drowning thousands of migrating caribou. The animals, a prime source of meat for the Inuit, belonged to the 300,000-strong George River herd. Ranging across Quebec, the caribou migrate from the barren lands of Labrador, across the George and Caniapiscau Rivers, to the forests on the banks of Hudson Bay, a route they have taken for centuries. Fording the rivers is risky. Each year fast currents claim the lives of between 200 and 300 animals.

In September, 1984, torrential rains transformed the Caniapiscau River into a foaming torrent. Although the water level was twice as high as usual, the caribou plunged into the surging rapids as they had always done, driven by the need to reach their winter feeding grounds. So great was the force and weight of the current, that the hapless animals were swept downstream in a churning mass of bodies to Limestone Falls. There were few survivors. The carcasses were strewn along a thirty-mile stretch of river, heaped six deep along the bends, creating a major pollution threat to aquatic life, fish and game.

Altogether, 9,600 animals died. The Department of the Environment called in a fleet of helicopters to remove the rotting corpses. Fearful that another heard of 3,000 caribou heading in the same direction would meet the same fate, the Quebec Transport Department attempted to divert them by ordering aircraft to bomb the animals with water. As the extent of the calamity become known, the Inuit accused Quebec's power authority, Hydro-Quebec, and the James Bay Energy Corporation of causing the disaster. The Inuit alleged that the power authorities had allowed massive amounts of surplus water to flow into the river from the floodgates of a dam which was part of the James Bay hydro-electric project. The charge was denied vigorously. Hydro-Quebec officials answered that there had been twice as much rain as normally recorded for September, and declared the drowning to be an Act of God.

Subsequent investigation, however, disclosed that after the heavy rain, nearly 2,000 cubic yards of surplus water a second were released from the reservoir directly into the Caniapiscau River, more than doubling the flow. This appeared to be preferable to generating excess electricity that could not be sold, or to bypassing the turbines along a spillway into James Bay. The decision was taken despite specific assurances, given when the Cree and Inuit signed the James Bay Agreement, that excess water would be released into the river only in an emergency, an assurance which, since completion of the reservoir in 1981, has been breached on many occasions.

Reports that the floodgates were first opened on September 4th made a nonsense of Hydro-Quebec's claim that the high level of water was due to heavy rain, which fell later in the month. Twenty-one days later, on the 25th, the Inuit appealed to the power board to reduce the spillage. As they did so, the caribou plunged into the water. The volume of water gushing down Limestone Falls that day was nearly 3,700 cubic yards a second, more than half of it from the reservoir upstream. Four days later, or two days after the full extent of the calamity was realised, the flow rate was cut back to 1,300 cubic yards. A Canadian government report five months after the tragedy stated that human error was not to blame, and a provincial official claimed that caribou were frequently attracted to waterfalls because they sounded like a herd on the run.

Hundreds more caribou, the victims of traffic and hunters, were killed the previous winter after migrating too close to a temporary ice road, which had been built to service an isolated Canadian mine. Indeed, the construction of roads presents a serious threat to the people and wildlife of the tundras and barren lands. In Scandinavia, Samiland is marketed by government tourist agencies as 'The Last Great Wilderness of Europe', but tourists must have roads to reach the wilderness. Their arrival inevitably brings noise and disruption, and soon the wilderness is no more. In Canada, roads built to supply pumping stations along the oil and gas pipelines to the north carry a steady stream of haulage trucks, security patrols and personnel. When the roads are opened to the public, there is an immediate demand for refuelling stations, fast food restaurants, hotels and lodges. For all of them, the greatest problem is getting rid of rubbish and sewage.

Before the *qallunaat* conquered the Arctic, waste was unknown. The few remnants of an animal's carcass left by Inuit hunters were eaten by other predators. Remaining food scraps were taken by arctic foxes, human excrement by the sledge dogs. Nothing was discarded. By contrast, in every village and settlement north of the tree line, the imported lifestyle from the south has left a trail of tin cans, abandoned vehicles, fuel drums, plastics, packaging and polythene bags. Attempts are made to burn the rubbish, but this is not possible with glass, metals and some of the plastics.

In the north, a little pollution goes a long way. Bin liners snatched by high winds from arctic rubbish dumps can be found hundreds of miles from the nearest settlement. The dry atmosphere preserves everything. On countless beaches, tin cans and old barrels from the stores of whaling ships wrecked in the 1840s can still be found. A chocolate bar paper wrapper, which could be expected to disintegrate within a year in a southerly climate, might still be blowing about the Arctic twenty years later. A plastic toy carelessly lost could provide a source of amusement to an Inuit child in 500 years time.

Attempts to bury waste are usually frustrated by the lack of soil. In the far north, Nature takes 2,000 years to break down the sedimentary rock and create one foot of earth. In Greenland, Inuit in some of the coastal towns must bury their dead in graves hewn from solid granite. In areas where the permafrost is covered with only a thin layer of fragmented rock, the spring thaw forces the coffins back to the surface, so that the dead must be frequently re-buried or covered with a slab of concrete.

Evidence of pollution can be found in every village. Pepsi, Coke and beer cans litter the streets. Mounting piles of junk blight the exterior of virtually every home in the Arctic. Soggy packaging and insulation materials lie like mounds of rotting whale blubber a few feet from the front steps. In Grise Fiord, on Ellesmere Island, the discarded head of a musk ox, perched on an old box, looks down on a scene familiar throughout the Arctic, a tangle of old metal – the rusting frames of beach buggies, snowmobiles, washing machines, refrigerators, freezers – the latter being visible evidence that the ice-cream salesmen from the south really *have* conquered the Arctic. Descending to the road, frozen rivers of dish water make walking almost impossible. Sometimes, though less frequently now, black polythene bags tied carefully by the necks are stacked against the wooden houses, and await collection by council workmen. Known as 'honey bags', they line the pails gracing the corner of most bathrooms, and are filled with frozen household sewage.

Eventually, 'honey bags' are taken to a dump on the outskirts of the village. Here, they may be torn open by an arctic fox, polar bear or sledge dog on the loose. In low temperatures, the brittle polythene splits easily. When the temperature rises above freezing in early summer, the contents of winter ooze slowly into the sea. Similarly, the melting snow reveals the accumulated dog droppings deposited during eight months of polar darkness. In the meantime, the lethal rinks of frozen dish and bath water melt to form stagnant pools covered with the scum of detergents.

In Greenland, sewage disposal is more efficient, although the cost of installation and maintenance is frequently higher than the price of the house itself. The waste is carried along a network of pipes housed in insulated wooden tunnels which, raised above ground level, zigzag through the town to the local treatment plant. The sewage is prevented from freezing by a second pipe, carrying hot water for central heating. In smaller towns it is dumped directly into the sea.

The sea is also the recipient of effluent from the Black Angel lead and zinc mine run by the Danish company, Greenex A/S, at Marmorilik, in northwest Greenland. Concentrations of dissolved metals in Marmorilik fjord rose to such worrying levels that the Danish government ordered the company to examine alternative methods for the disposal of its tailings. The Greenland Fisheries Research Department found a marked increase in the lead and cadmium content in shrimps, seaweed, some whole fish and fish livers. The company made serious efforts to cleanse the effluent, with measurable success, but the amount of lead in mussels was later found to be unacceptable, and a ban was imposed on mussel harvesting within twenty miles of the mine.

The threat posed to the Arctic by pollution, trade, shipping and industry is incalculable. The region is protected by fewer international conservation agreements than Antarctica, which, although similarly threatened, has no indigenous population. The Arctic Ocean, the fourth largest ocean in the world, acts as a thermostat controlling the temperature of the atmosphere. Reflecting seventy per cent of the sun's rays back into space, the icepack ensures that the waters of the ocean do not become too warm in summer, and prevents the sea warming the atmosphere in winter.

Apart from a few restricted openings, such as the Bering Strait, this huge landlocked sea, like the Mediterranean, has only one entrance deep enough to permit a sufficient circulation of water. The passage lies between Svalbard and Greenland, and allows the warm waters of the Atlantic to flow northwards into the Arctic Ocean, while drifting ice and cold water are expelled back into the Atlantic. The dual flow system keeps the water of the Arctic and Atlantic Oceans at a steady temperature, and is therefore of paramount importance for the weather system, dictating not only the climate in the United States, Canada, Greenland, Iceland, and Europe, but also the ecological chain in which polar cod is the key link. If anything happened to the cod, which are very sensitive to temperature changes, there would be an immediate effect on the birds, seals, walrus, polar bears, foxes and every other species, including man. Yet, through this vital passage, the powerful flow of warm water carries with it not only oil spillage but millions of tons of chemical and industrial waste from western Europe and the eastern seaboard of north America. Once deposited in the ocean, the pollutants accumulate, trapped by the narrow exit.

Although strict international regulations have curtailed the deliberate pollution of the oceans, mariners secretly continue to flush out the tanks of their ships and dump oily bilge water at sea, rather than waste time and money in port. Tanker accidents are another major source of oil contamination. When the *Torrey Canyon* broke up off Britain in March, 1967, the oil spill affected 100 miles of British coastline, killed approximately 25,000 sea birds and severely disrupted the marine ecology for a decade. In February, 1970, nine million litres of bunker oil from the tanker *Arrow* covered nearly 200 miles of Nova Scotia coastline. The supertanker, *Amoco Cadiz*, which broke up off the Brittany coast in the spring of 1978, spewed 200 million litres of crude and bunker oil into the sea over more than two weeks. Like blackened chewing gum, the oil clung to 180 miles of coastline, and devastated the salt marshes which are essential to migrating birds. Some of the oil eventually drifted northwards with the currents into the Arctic Ocean.

Anxious to ship oil from Prudhoe Bay and the Beaufort Sea through the Northwest Passage, the U.S. government in co-operation with the oil companies undertook an experimental voyage to test the feasibility of oil shipments in the rigorous conditions of massed icefloes. In 1969, the captain of the largest commercial ship flying the American flag, the 150,000-ton *S.S. Manhattan*, pointed its armoured prow north through Davis Strait and Baffin Bay, and headed for Lancaster Sound. As events turned out, it was fortunate that the supertanker, propelled by 43,000-hp turbines, was accompanied by icebreakers.

In the course of bearing down on one floe approximately a mile wide and nearly sixty feet thick, chunks of ice the size of railway carriages split off, screeched along the underside of the ship, and smashed into the propellers. The noise was so terrifying that the engine-room crew were said to have felt like deserting their posts. Trapped by pack ice on several occasions, the *Manhattan* reversed and rammed the ice for up to twelve hours without making progress. Had the ship been carrying oil, there would have been considerable cause for alarm. Nevertheless, with the help of the icebreakers and helicopters, the supertanker did become the first commercial vessel to force a route through the Northwest Passage.

The Canadians had not been consulted about the voyage, and viewed it as a threat to the sovereignty they had unilaterally assumed over the

Northwest Passage, waters which the Americans regarded as international. Shortly after the voyage, the Canadian parliament passed the Arctic Waters Pollution Prevention Act. Imposing strict security measures on ships sailing through the passage, it rendered their owners liable for compensation in the event of an accident. The Act also declared 'Canada's responsibility for the welfare of the Eskimo and the preservation of the very special ecological balance which exists today'.

A year later, in a speech in Toronto, Pierre Trudeau warned that the oil industry posed an incalculable threat to the Arctic. An accident would cause untold damage, he said, because oil spillage would not decompose in the cold climate, and for thousands of square miles would harm food sources for the Inuit and for wildlife. Trudeau's concern, however, did not prevent his government from issuing exploration permits, nor restrain it from allowing Dome Petroleum to drill for four years before assessing the potential hazards to the environment. This was hardly surprising. As the largest shareholder in Panarctic Oil Ltd, a consortium of 37 companies, the government had a vested interest in the oil industry, and has repeatedly been accused of suppressing reports detailing the high risks of drilling in the Beaufort Sea.

While complaining bitterly about industrial pollution emanating from the United States, the Canadian government stubbornly refuses to act on environmental issues in the Arctic. Despite the urgent need for huge areas to be set aside to protect wildlife from pollution, Judge Thomas Berger's recommendation for a national wilderness park in north Yukon has still not been formally accepted. Similarly, the Canadian government has ignored proposals for the International Biological Programme, which identified more than 151 specific areas in the Canadian Arctic as being crucial to wildlife and in need of preservation. In the entire Canadian Arctic, only one national wildlife area, Polar Bear Pass on Bathurst Island, has been established. After interminable investigation and discussion, the authorities are still debating whether to designate a second national wildlife park near Lake Hazen, on northern Ellesmere Island.

Similarly, when the Beaufort Environmental Assessment Review Panel, after three years of research and public meetings, recommended small-scale and phased development of arctic oil, the federal government chose to ignore the report. A member of a parliamentary standing committee on Indian Affairs and Northern Development, Keith Penner, admitted: 'If there is a big [oil] find, it will be hard to avoid megaprojects.'

The Canadian government's hunger for the profits from arctic oil apparently outweighs any desire to prevent an environmental disaster. The reason is clear: exploited fully, the vast reserves of oil and natural gas in the Beaufort Sea, estimated at four billion barrels and 300 trillion cubic feet, could revitalise the Canadian economy.

The dependence of the western world during the 1970s on potentially unstable Arab nations for its oil imports is another explanation for Canada's dismal environmental record. With price control and production rates dictated at the whim of Middle Eastern oil sheiks, the Americans and Canadians resolved to take steps to become more self-reliant. Together, they got through nearly seven billion barrels of oil a year, half of which was imported. Proven reserves in Prudhoe Bay amounted to nearly ten billion barrels of oil and 25 trillion cubic feet of natural gas, making it the sixth largest oil field in the world. Panarctic, funded by the Canadian government, had drilled 173 wells at a cost of $750 million. It now expected to extract 2.5 billion barrels of oil in the coming decade. Suddenly, the ability to ship oil from the Arctic assumed new importance.

On February 6th, 1985, sixteen years after the pioneering voyage of *S.S. Manhattan*, Canada's Northern Affairs Minister, David Crombie, announced that the first crude oil would be shipped out of the High Arctic in September, 1985, when the winter ice was thickening. With the express permission of the Canadian cabinet, 100,000 barrels would be moved from Panartic Oil's Bent Horn field on Cameron Island, close to the Magnetic North Pole.

The ice-breaking bulk carrier assigned to the task was the *M.V. Arctic*, the heaviest vessel of its class in Canada. Improvements to the ship had cost the owners three million dollars, but at the time of the announcement it still failed to meet government standards for arctic shipping. Further modifications were undertaken to replace the bow and strengthen the hull. As work began, the federal government commissioned a $1.2 million study of High Arctic ice conditions, the first step in mapping a safe shipping lane for ships carrying oil through the harshest environment in the world.

CHAPTER 17

Black Ice

Notorious fluctuations in weather patterns and the unpredictability of the ice present huge, perhaps unacceptable risks to shipowners contemplating regular oil shipments through the Arctic. Ice is a formidable enemy. A floe can be five miles across with a keel as deep as a ten-storey office block. Floating on currents, travelling between one and fifteen miles a day, depending on the time of year, drifting pack ice can crush the armoured hull of a ship as relentlessly as a steamroller squashes a beer can. The danger is greatest during blizzards and fog. If a ship the size of *S.S. Manhattan*, twice the size of the *Queen Elizabeth II*, can run into difficulties, it is easy to imagine the hazards for smaller vessels. A margin of safety is achieved only with the assistance of the most powerful icebreakers, but the six ships of Canada's ice-breaking fleet are of insufficient tonnage to cope with more than the three-month summer shipping season.

The older the ice, the harder its consistency. Polar pack ice several years old, crashing irresistibly into immovable shorefast ice, creates what is known as the shear zone. Creaking and grinding under the tremendous pressure, chunks of cobalt-blue ice like boiled mints finally crack and break off, refreezing in a chaotic jumble of pressure ridges. The resulting formation of channels of open water, *polynyas*, attract colonies of seals and thousands of birds. Exposed to the colder air temperature, the surface water vaporises, reducing visibility, and grounds ice-patrol aircraft. It is in precisely such a hostile region that some of the oil men have elected to drill.

Drilling is usually conducted from ships or artificial islands. These, instantly recognisable by their drilling towers and bright red hulls, are usually protected by supply tugs which, with reinforced bows, push threatening icefloes out of the way, not always a simple manoeuvre. A floe six feet deep, a quarter of a mile in diameter and weighing more than two million tons takes some stopping, even when moving at one mile an hour. A momentum of five, or ten miles an hour, would pose a serious problem for the captain of a drillship. The process of abandoning a rig, and making sure that the well is safe, can take between eight and twelve hours. Yet, the decision to cut loose from the anchors holding his ship above the drillhole would have to be made quickly, and could cost his company more than a million pounds. So great are the dangers that the drilling season is restricted to three months a year. Ships are required to leave their drilling sites by early October. Then, the ice re-freezes so quickly that some captains, leaving their departure to the last minute, are lucky to make port without icebreaker assistance.

Artificial islands are safer, but not without problems. The earliest was created by cutting out of the ice a hole the size of two ice-hockey rinks. This was filled with sand and gravel, brought in by endless convoys of trucks along ice roads from the mainland. When the surrounding ice melted in the spring, the island remained. Known as sacrificial beach islands, they were built in less than 65 feet of water, and were protected from summer storms by sandbags. Their long, shelving beaches dissipate the energy of the waves. In winter, the ice broke up on the beaches, forming a barrier of protective rubble.

When the oilmen needed to move into deeper waters, engineers designed a sturdier platform. Dredging an underwater hill from the sea bed, they filled with sand and gravel four concrete barges, or *caissons*, each weighing 5,300 tons, and sank them onto the summit of the hill. Locked together to form a square, the *caissons* acted as a perimeter reinforcement for the creation of the island, which was completed by pouring more sand and gravel into the hollow square. Later designs included artificial drilling islands linked by sub-sea pipelines to production atolls. These were large enough to accommodate four drilling rigs, oil storage facilities and a harbour from which ice-breaking tankers could ship the oil south.

Drilling is always risky. More than anywhere else, in the Arctic oilmen fear a blowout. This occurs when the subterranean pressure is so great that the mud in the drillpipe cannot contain the oil, gas or water being forced to the surface. When their instruments indicate a serious rise in pressure, engineers can seal the drillpipe with a preventer, but if friction from drilling melts the permafrost, the seal between the drillpipe and the frozen ground may be loosened, and leaks make the preventer useless.

An oil blowout in the arctic environment would be a catastrophe. Impossible to deal with in late August or September when the ice is forming, it would have to wait until the following May. During these nine months, a moderate blowout would spill approximately 500,000 barrels of oil into the sea. A severe blowout could release more than eight *million* barrels, contaminating the ice for hundreds of square miles, making oily pressure ridges in the shear zones. Chemical dispersal of that oil would not be practicable. The gushing well would blacken the underside of the continually moving ice, and oil spreading outwards from the well-head would broaden into a huge stain. Moving at three miles an hour, the discoloured ice would travel 840 miles in nine months.

In such a case the havoc to wildlife would be incalculable. The bird population in August is densest at the beginning of the drilling season. Approximately 100 species congregate in the deltas and open leads in readiness for their migration south. The Mackenzie Delta is particularly vulnerable. Oil drifting onto the mudflats and beaches would irreparably damage the feeding grounds for tens of millions of birds.

Great numbers of guillemots and auks would drown. These birds must leave the Arctic earlier than the other seabirds as their new feathers are insufficiently grown after the summer moult to enable them to fly by the time the ice re-forms. They swim instead, all the way from Lancaster Sound across Baffin Bay south to Greenland. Should they be caught in an oil slick, their oiled feathers would deprive them of insulation, and death would result from the cold or from drowning. A bird reaching land, in its attempts to preen the oil from its feathers, would probably die from asphyxiation or poisoning.

Equally appalling would be the effect on the marine food chain. During the first two weeks of summer, when the sun first appears above the horizon, the light seeping through the ice encourages the growth of plankton and krill, enough to feed every fish, bird and sea mammal throughout the season. An oil slick would annihilate this essential food source and lamentably affect the bowhead whales, beluga whales, narwhals, walrus, tens of thousands of seals, and millions of fish and crustaceans. Oil-covered seal would be inedible, and toxic to polar bears and arctic fox. The environment could take fifty years to recover.

Recognising that a large oil spill over thousands of square miles would destroy the primary source of food for both the Inuit and the carnivores, in 1970 Pierre Trudeau said that 'the continued existence [of the Arctic] in unspoiled form is vital to all mankind.' Four years later, the Canadian government approved offshore drilling in the Beaufort Sea, fully aware that the oil companies did not have the capability for cleaning up a major oil spill. Evidently concerned about the risks, the government set up an organisation called the Arctic Marine Oil Spill Programme to investigate the problem. It concluded that the oil could be burned.

The inadequacy of such a plan became evident in 1979 when an offshore well poured 220,000 gallons of oil a day into the Gulf of Mexico. Every conceivable type of control, from booms to detergents, was tried with little success. Some of the oil was burned, but after five months the sea had been polluted with 82 million gallons of oil, the largest oil spill in history. The disaster highlighted the Canadian government's dilemma. If the oil companies could not contain the oil from a blowout in one of the world's most temperate climates, how could they hope to do so in the Arctic, during the months when the weather was at its most unpredictable?

Without answers, the Canadians pushed ahead with their master plan for dealing with an arctic spill. Hordes of bureaucrats would be galvanised into action, despatching teams of workers north to drill through the ice, and to ignite the oil bubbling to the surface. The heat would create basins into which more oil could ooze and be burned off, forming even larger basins. Squadrons of helicopters would drop firebombs onto the oil in a scenario that would do justice to a Hollywood farce. No thought was given to the environmental consequences, although the nightmare effects of such a proposal are not difficult to imagine. For miles without number across the Arctic, thick columns of black smoke would rise into the atmosphere, eventually dumping the hydro-carbons onto the ice, into the sea or onto the tundra, polluting the plant life which plays as important a role on land as the plankton and krill in the sea. The process would be repeated in the spring, when the single-year ice began to melt. Black oil attracting the heat of the sun would accelerate the melting process and lessen the time available for burning the oil before the ice became too thin to walk on.

The chances of complete success during such a cleaning operation are slender. The most optimistic assessment indicates that about 85 per cent of the oil could be burned off. The residue, like the ice trapped in multi-year ice, would have to be ignored. As it is thicker, this ice melts on the surface and freezes undernearth. Oil trapped by the new layer of ice might not be released to the surface for a decade.

Officially, oil companies describe the chances of a blowout in the Arctic as minimal. Some tout odds of a million to one. Others, more realistically, put the chances at about one in 500. With arctic drilling carried out in areas of exceptionally high subterranean pressure, experts admit privately that if exploration and production continue unimpeded, an oil blowout is a statistical certainty.

The prognosis is based on the numerous gas and water blowouts that have already occured in the Arctic. Dome Petroleum, drilling in the Beaufort Sea, has experienced water blowouts at three wells. In 1969, Panarctic was forced to remove a rig when hot water gushed out of the drillpipe to form a tower of ice hundreds of feet high. Shortly afterwards, another Panarctic project, at Drake Point on Melville Island, blew out of control after boring into a high-pressure gas deposit. Drilling engineers fought for two weeks to cap the well, which blew again a month later.

Despite heroic efforts, experts were unable to stem this second jet for a year, and nearly thirty million cubic metres of gas were lost. Within twelve months, a third Panarctic well, on King Christian Island near the Magnetic North Pole, caught fire. The 350-ft-high flame, the base of which was 100 feet above the gound, indicated the force of the jet. For three months, the fire burned nearly three million cubic metres of gas a day, and served as a beacon for pilots flying 100 miles away in the winter darkness.

Accidents are not as uncommon as one might imagine. Although offshore oil rigs are expected to withstand the 'hundred year storm', a severe arctic gale in September, 1985, forced Esso Resources (Canada) Limited to evacuate 87 men from Minuk I–53, an artificial island in the Beaufort Sea. They were just in time. Seven hours later, the rig, described by the company as one of its most modern, toppled over. Within a month, on the other side of the Atlantic, another eighty men had to be evacuated after a gas blowout ignited and killed a man on a Norwegian rig. Following a similar blowout less than a month later, tugs towed a second Norwegian rig away from a well operated by the same company, the government-owned Statoil.

Still haunted by the *Alexander Kjelland* disaster in March, 1980, when 123 men died in the North Sea after a leg snapped off and capsized the rig, Statoil immediately reviewed safety equipment and emergency procedures. The Norwegian Ministry of Justice appointed a special commission to report on the accidents. Trades Union leaders suggested that the Norwegian offshore oil industry was sacrificing safety for growth, a criticism which Statoil dismissed as nonsense, although it admitted that there could be no absolute guarantees against accidents in the oil industry.

Sounding remarkably like the Quebec-Hydro official who declared the deaths of nearly 10,000 caribou an Act of God, the company's spokesman claimed that the blowouts represented statistical averages, and suggested that 'it just happened to be our turn'. This nonchalant attitude was not reflected by the Norwegian Oil Directorate, which immediately reversed a previous decision to allow the first exploratory drilling in arctic waters during winter.

Oil companies have no specific code to follow in the event of a blowout. Each makes its own rules. These may be submitted to a government for approval, but governments seldom have personnel with sufficient technical knowledge to deal with highly complex problems, there are too few experts available to check too many procedures. As a result, safety precautions are sometimes waived, the rules bent to suit the circumstances. Although oil companies may establish strict rules, operators at the scene frequently ignore them. Spillage of more than five gallons, for example, should be reported to the authorities, but when approximately 1,500 gallons of P50 diesel oil overflowed from an experimental rig in the Beaufort Sea, no report was made.

Hundreds of similar incidents, including fires, go unreported. When one million gallons of diesel oil were accidentally spilled at Little Cornwallis Island, the Departments of the Environment, Northern Affairs, Fisheries and Oceans all failed to press charges. Despite warnings from federal officers, no action was taken. One oilman said: 'It was a perfect example of the government turning its back on environmental damage in the north. The oil industry is very skilful at playing off one department against another. The polluters are hardly ever punished. Only one or two cases a year are taken to court, although prosecution would have been warranted in a hundred cases.'

Despite the risks, the oil industry is set to transform the Arctic into a source of wealth greater than that in the Middle East. Expansion is planned on every front. Both Norway and the Soviet Union, the world's largest oil producer, are pushing the hunt for oil and natural gas north to Spitsbergen in the hostile waters of the Barents Sea, one of the stormiest seas in the world.

Here, the oil men have to contend with more than ice and storms. Frozen fog, sleet and rain cling to the exposed derricks. Radar masts, helicopter decks and the superstructure of oil rigs are equally vulnerable. Sea spray coats the bracings, moorings and chains of semi-submersible rigs. Intense cold reduces the efficiency of workers and freezes ballast water, fuels, firefighting equipment and sewage systems. The effect of extremely low temperatures on drilling equipment is still not fully understood. Yet, with North Sea production expected to decline sharply early in the twenty-first century, the Norwegian government is committed to find new oil and gas wells to maintain output. Suddenly, Svalbard, the collective name for the islands around Spitsbergen, has sprung to prominence. Under the 1920 Treaty of Paris, 41 signatory nations have equal maritime, industrial, mining and commercial rights on the islands, subject to Norwegian law.

The Soviet state oil company, Trust Arktigkugol, has already begun exploratory drilling at Vassdalen, on the north side of Van Mijen Fjord in the Svalbard Islands, and a joint Norwegian-Swedish search for high-quality gas is being intensified along the western edge of the islands. The chances of success are high. Soviet oilmen have discovered at least twenty new deposits of oil and gas in the Barents Sea, and are now operating their first semi-submersible rig off Kolgiyev Island. Although ships towing the rig to its position were delayed for several months by pack ice, the head of the arctic drilling operation, Ostap Sheremeta, was quoted as saying that he placed 'great stock in the reliability of the equipment and the eighty crew'.

The Norwegians are also operating a semi-submersible oil rig equipped with sophisticated data processing, said to be the first in the world which can operate round the year in the harsh arctic conditions. The Japanese manufacturer, Hitachi Shipbuilding, is renting the rig to Norsk Hydro, a government-financed concern which will now be able to drill to nearly 20,000 feet close to the North Pole.

If the oil companies strike lucky in Svalbard, which is 800 miles north of the Arctic Circle, they will be faced with the same nagging, and costly, problem as the Canadians: how best to transport the oil to refineries in the south. Norsk Hydro is planning to build a huge offshore factory in the Arctic Sea. Natural gas from production wells nearby would be converted to liquefied gas at a $5 billion terminal constructed on a concrete pillar attached to the sea bed. Shaped like a mushroom, the processing plant would be equipped with a sheltered harbour at its base, enabling liquefied natural gas (LNG) carriers to load the gas for export to Europe and the United States.

In Canada, serious consideration was given to a $6.1 billion pipeline, three and a half feet in diameter, from the High Arctic islands a few hundred miles from the North Pole to Ontario, a distance of 2,338 miles. The pipeline would be buried in the permafrost, carry enough gas in a day to satisfy the whole of Canada and cross several sections of sea, one of them deep enough to cover a 68-storey skyscraper. Although market conditions later forced a reduction in the scale of the project, which is due to be completed in 1991, the original concept remains unchanged. Should such a pipeline rupture, engineers would be faced with enormous problems. If it was carrying oil, the damage would be inestimable.

Designers wrestling with the knotty problem of transporting oil and gas through the Arctic have produced a range of futuristic solutions. One proposal, from Boeing, called for a fleet of gigantic aircraft to load 1,000 tons of oil in special pods slung under the wings, each pod to be the size of a Boeing 747 jumbo jet. Flying twenty hours a day, these monsters of the sky would be powered by no fewer than twelve jet engines. In Japan, engineers are working on the prototype of a supership driven by electro-magnets. With no propellers, shafts or rudder, it would be capable of 100 knots on or underneath the sea, and result in a fifty per cent saving on fuel costs.

General Dynamics, the American company which builds Trident submarines and conventional gas tankers, put ten years' research into the development of a fleet of sixteen nuclear-powered cargo submarines. Each one would be capable of carrying more than a million barrels of oil from Prudhoe Bay, beneath the icefields of the Northwest Passage, to the eastern ports of America. The oil companies, apparently wary of the horrendous potential for disaster, preferred to build the trans-Alaska pipeline.

After the first Arab oil embargo, the idea of nuclear cargo submarines was reviewed. New designs provided for the construction of submarine tankers the length of ten football fields, with a storage capacity of up to a million *tons* of oil. A study commissioned by the U.S. Department of Commerce concluded that such ships, costing $725 million each, were technically feasible and viable economically.

German designers preferred conventional submarines with strengthened hulls, towing a chain of clamp-on underwater barges. These, they claimed, would be particularly useful in *polynyas* and in the shallow waters of the Mackenzie Delta. Yet, apart from the effects on wildlife in the area, the underwater craft would be difficult to navigate in Davis Strait and other waters, in which icebergs as tall as electric power pylons have keels so deep that they frequently nudge the sea bed.

Oilmen tend to favour schemes above the surface. Dome Petroleum asked the world's foremost icebreaker experts from Finland to design a vessel that could operate in virtually any ice conditions. Having spent so much money on exploration in the Beaufort Sea that its $6 billion overdraft nearly wrecked the Canadian banking system, the company was anxious to solve the problem of transportation before the 1990s, when it hopes to start large-scale production. The Finns produced plans for a 150,000 horsepower tanker called an Arctic Marine Locomotive, which would be twice as powerful as the biggest icebreaker currently in service.

Despite these rapid developments, not even a nuclear icebreaker was able to help one of the ninety Soviet ships caught in sixty-foot-thick multi-year ice off the northeastern coast of Siberia in 1983. Among the trapped ships were smaller icebreakers which had been unable to force a channel for the other stranded vessels. Altogether, 26 ships found themselves in serious difficulty. Several were badly holed and in danger of sinking. When the ice cracked the hull and flooded the hold of the cargo ship *Nina Sagaidak*, the crew had to be rescued by the helicopter and flown to Vladivostock. The ship sank shortly afterwards.

Apart from the Finns, who have built sixty per cent of the world's icebreakers and operate its most advanced arctic research laboratory, the Soviets probably have a greater knowledge of arctic conditions than any other industrial nation. Their Finnish-built nuclear icebreakers are the most powerful on earth. The icebreakers of the future may keep arctic shipping lanes open, but accidents can, and do, happen. The danger is that as the icebreaking capacity increases, the temptation to extend the drilling season in the arctic oil fields will become irresistible.

CHAPTER 18

Untapped Treasure

Icebreakers are the key to the exploitation of arctic riches. New discoveries of oil and gas off Svalbard, or in the Bering Sea, will increase the need for a regular icebreaking escort service for tankers and re-supply ships sailing between deep-water rigs, artificial islands and offshore factories. The huge mineral deposits in the North can be properly exploited only when icebreakers are able to keep regular shipping lanes open all the year. Without icebreakers, Canada's efforts to establish sovereignty over the arctic islands are little more than empty posturing.

The Canadian government, embarrassed by its inability to patrol for nine months of the year the icebound waters to which it lays claim, has ordered the construction of one of the most powerful icebreakers on earth. Due for completion in the 1990s, the $500 million 102,000 horsepower *Polar Eight* will operate in the Northwest Passage round the year, ploughing through eight feet of first-year ice at a steady three knots. With two-inch steel plates in the bow, it will be capable of ramming through sixty-foot thick ridges. In the words of one Cabinet document: 'The commitment of funds, construction and deployment of the *Polar Eight* will be a dramatic signal to Canadians and to the rest of the world that the government is serious about Canadian sovereignty in arctic waters.'

At the Arctic Research Centre in Helsinki, Finnish designers have proved that it is theoretically possible for ships of the future to smash through ice ridges measuring ninety feet from tip to keel, the equivalent of five London double-decker buses stacked one on top of the other. Arctic experts at Finland's Wartsila Shipyard anticipate the building of 210,000 horsepower icebreakers equipped with three rudders and three propellers, each thirty feet high with 70,000 shaft horsepower. The crucial difficulty is the $450 million price tag. Nevertheless, Wartsila engineers say there is now virtually no problem in the Arctic with which they cannot cope. Canada's *Polar Eight*, and a series of shallow-draught nuclear icebreakers being built by Finland for the Soviet Union, are a strong indication of future developments.

Icebreakers have transformed Finland's own trading patterns. Until the 1970s, winter ice in the Gulf of Bothnia and the Baltic Sea closed the northern ports of Kemi, Oulu, Raahe and Vasa, denying Finnish industry access to the world's oceans. The only link across the Gulf was a temporary ice road from Vasa to Umea in Sweden. A decade of heavy investment not only gave the country an unrivalled lead in icebreaker technology, but enabled it to develop the paper, pulp, chemical and steel industries at its northern ports, which are now open every month of the year.

In the next decade, arctic shipping will flourish. The forward propellers on icebreakers will be replaced by air bubbling systems which reduce friction between the hull and the ice. Satellites in polar orbit will enable icebreaker captains to plot within a few feet the channels of least resistance. Air cushion vehicles, or hovercraft, with specially designed skirts for use in abrasive ice and low temperatures, will transport cargo and relief workers to offshore oil rigs, or skim over the permafrost and river estuaries of Siberia.

Soviet designers have produced plans for an underwater icebreaker which might have been conceived by Jules Verne. With the body of the ship immediately beneath the surface, steel teeth along the top of the hull could cut through the ice as a diamond cuts glass. At the stern, the control tower and a helipad are perched on top of a sixty-foot wedge-shaped pylon, which would slice through the broken ice like a snowplough cutting through a snowdrift. The ship would submerge repeatedly if the ice was too thick and surface like a whale at play, smashing the underside of the ice with the upper, armoured part of its hull.

Each winter, Soviet convoys in the Arctic Ocean push further east towards the Chukchi Peninsula, where the multi-year polar icepack extends almost to the shoreline. Despite the constant hazards, but aware for thirty years of the enormous potential of the Arctic, the Soviets invested in their first atomic icebreaker, *Lenin*, which has since escorted ships for more than a million miles. Later additions to the nuclear fleet opened up year-round shipping lanes from Murmansk to the Yenisei River, along which hundreds of vessels annually move approximately five million tons of cargo.

Soon, a new generation of ships will be in service, shallow-draught icebreakers designed for use in river estuaries, a fleet of icebreaking cargo ships and huge nuclear tugs capable of towing more than seventy barges with a load of 1,300 containers. During the 1990s, the ancient dream of opening trade routes through the Northwest and Northeast Passages to China, Japan and Asia is almost certain to be fulfilled.

The untapped treasure of the North extends right across the Arctic.

There are massive deposits of lead and zinc, copper, nickel, iron, manganese and uranium, and waiting to be mined a treasure store of platinum, gold, silver and diamonds. The North Slope of Alaska has reserves of 150 billion tons of coal, with eager buyers in Taiwan and Japan, which are approximately the same distance from Barrow as San Francisco. Until recently, these riches were inaccessible. Now, there is the manpower, the money and the means to extract and transport them to the South.

Siberia, 4,000 miles wide, stretching east from the Urals to the Pacific, is twice the area of the United States and contains half the earth's hydro-carbon reserves. There is enough coal to supply the world for 600 years. The region provides 65 per cent of the Soviet Union's oil, 82 per cent of its natural gas, 30 per cent of its timber, paper and cardboard, 20 per cent of its electricity, and 73 per cent of its mineral resources. By comparison, mineral production from Canada's Northwest Territories is approximately eight per cent of the Canadian total. The Soviet Union will soon be the world's largest exporter of natural gas. More than 20,000 million cubic metres are transported annually along the world's longest trans-continental gas pipeline from Urengoi, in the far north, to western Europe, a distance of 2,700 miles.

Huge supplies of natural gas in eastern Siberia and Yakutia, a province of the size of Portugal wedged between Siberia and the Soviet Far East, are thought to exceed all those known in the Middle East. Eventually, Yakutian gas will be piped thousands of miles for export to Japan from a Pacific Ocean port still to be built. Yakutia, the coldest region in the northern hemisphere with winter temperatures dropping to $-70°C$. is so rich in mineral resources that according to local legend, when God flew over the region distributing riches over the earth, His hands froze and He dropped them all. These resources include the largest gold and platinum deposits on earth (the largest nugget found in Yakutia weighed approximately 21 lbs.), and diamond fields so large that the Soviet Union is now the second largest producer in the world after South Africa. Such wealth makes Siberia and Yakutia the mightiest industrial area of the future, with the potential to transform the Soviet Union into the world's richest country by the end of the century.

Largely ignored by the west, the taming of Siberia, Yakutia and the Soviet Far East is a story of remarkable human achievement. No longer the preserve of hunters, trappers and reindeer breeders, these icy wastelands are the key to the future economic health of the nation. To supplement the countless citizens drafted into the mines for alleged infractions of the law, hundreds of thousands of workers are being enticed into mines, hydro-electric plants and industrial complexes, attracted by earnings two-and-a-half times the Soviet average. Siberian workers receive longer holidays and every third year a free return ticket to any destination in the Soviet Union. After fifteen years' arctic service, they are entitled to a full pension five years earlier than other employees (Soviet men normally retire at sixty, women at fifty-five), an inducement which has helped to halve the number of families leaving the region, and encouraged immigrants to settle in the remotest towns. Some leading Soviet economists, however, claim that the number of workers moving north is declining, and believe that new ways must be found to motivate potential migrants.

Apart from the climate, life in the Arctic is similar to that in other parts of the Soviet Union. When the former Canadian premier, Pierre Trudeau, visited Norilsk, a modern city close to the copper, nickel and cobalt mines east of the Yenisei River, he described it as the eighth wonder of the world. Here, in temperatures well below the freezing point of mercury, the 270,000 metallurgists, miners, researchers, industrial workers and their families (who between 1974 and 1984 helped to double the city's population) enjoy all the amenities of other Soviet towns.

Norilsk has nearly 2,000 apartment blocks, many of them thirteen storeys high, served by the city's own hydro-electric plant. There are colleges, secondary schools and nursery groups, hospitals, clinics and about 1,000 doctors. Each year, 3,000 couples get married and 4,000 children are born. For recreation, there are theatres, cinemas, libraries, a concert hall and an art gallery, and restaurants, cafés and bars. The city has forty streets, twelve supermarkets, hotels, and health centres with evergreen plants, aquariums and exotic birds from South America.

Throughout the winter, the inhabitants of Norilsk compete in gymnasiums at the Arktika Palace of Sports, which boasts several swimming pools, heated to 36°C. In good weather, thousands of people take part in ski races on illuminated courses through the surrounding tundra. Similar Siberian towns have built a total of approximately 9,000 gymnasiums, 400 stadiums and more than 100 swimming pools, many of them of Olympic standard.

Apartment blocks in Siberia are built on beds of deep gravel or on piles, which allow cooling winds to blow freely underneath the buildings. As in Greenland, central-heating pipes are carried above ground in insulated ducts. Protection against storms is maximised by placing buildings close to each other in semi-circles. The areas between them have transparent roofs, beneath which there are winter gardens, children's playgrounds, fountains and tropical plants. The lower floors are reserved for public use to give the inhabitants covered access to schools, kindergartens, clinics, shops, cafés and other facilities. Town planners try to reduce the risk of frostbite out of doors by ensuring that the distance from any one apartment to a bus stop is no more than 300 yards.

Fierce winds, freezing temperatures and the permafrost have forced Soviet construction engineers to adopt new building techniques and planning concepts. In such extreme temperatures, drills snap, tools break, machinery breaks down, fuel freezes, rubber crumbles, synthetic materials split and concrete must be steam-heated before use. Permafrost creates special problems. Poorly-designed houses built directly on the frozen ground generate too much warmth, melt the sub-surface ice and eventually disappear into holes of their own making. Similarly, a subterranean hot-water pipe not only melts the permafrost, but creates streams of melting water, which cut through the ice so rapidly that in a few months a pipe one foot in diameter could gouge a trench six feet deep and ten feet wide.

So sensitive is the arctic environment that the driver of a single vehicle crossing the frozen tundra could unwittingly leave behind a trail of swampy pits and craters hundreds of miles long. Churning up the thin layer of moss and lichen, the wheels can expose the soil beneath, which, unlike the ice which reflects the sun's rays back into the atmosphere, will attract its heat and melt the permafrost. Within weeks, the tracks will subside into wide, muddy channels, scars which could remain for decades.

This phenomenon is the principal reason for the lack of roads in the north. Foundations of rock or concrete, unavailable locally, must be five feet thick, making construction usually impracticable owing to high transportation costs. Some areas of permafrost have been damaged permanently, partly due to excessive timber felling. Soviet scientists believe another reason may be the high concentrations of carbon dioxide in the atmosphere raising the temperature of the air close to the earth's surface. This is a matter of grave concern. Should the permafrost thaw on a large scale, the scientists believe there could be widespread disruption to roads, railways, building projects, and by implication, the entire future of the Soviet economy.

Serious problems undoubtedly remain. The development of Siberia is dogged not only by the climate and terrain, but by bureaucracy and greed. The Communist party newspaper, *Pravda*, recently criticised factory managers in the central and southern regions for despatching shoddy and unrequested goods to Siberia and the Soviet Far East, fully aware that it would not be possible to return them once the supply routes were closed. Some factories were allegedly despatching thousands of unordered women's coats and hats to the north. 'Generally speaking, these goods are old models and of poor quality,' *Pravda* noted. 'The managers do it to fulfil their production plans.' When local people attempted to return stock the following spring, the newspaper reported that officials in Moscow refused to supply them with containers, with the result that in some remote settlements the shops, filled with unsolicited and unsold goods, looked more like warehouses.

A survey by a leading sociologist at the Novosibirsk Economic Institute, home to some of the Soviet Union's most radical official theorists, indicates that ninety per cent of the managers and eighty-four per cent of the workers believe changes in the centralised economy would increase local responsibilities and boost efficiency. Theorists suggest that the present system, which is dominated by ministries in Moscow, encourages laziness and indifference, the production of defective goods and the concealment of losses in production. Anxious to rejuvenate the economy, some Soviet economists are now calling for younger, more dynamic management and business schools run on lines similar to those in the west.

Feeding Siberia's multiplying population is another nagging difficulty. Most of the land in the north is poorly drained. Soils are acidic and deficient in soluble plant foods. Crops can grow only in protected soil. Consequently, most of the 150 million acres of cultivated land are in southern Siberia where the average annual rainfall is low, and crops must rely on irrigation. With food-producing areas representing less than three per cent of Siberia's total acreage, approximately ninety-five per cent of its food must be obtained from other regions.

Reindeer herds are a useful supply of meat, although the lack of a comprehensive road network makes transportation slow and costly. There are some sheep and goats, but pigs, poultry and dairy animals are rare, and great distances prevent the regular distribution of milk, eggs and vegetables from the south. Yet, if the riches of Siberia and the Soviet Far East are to be fully exploited and the region successfully populated, the provision of a reliable food source is of paramount importance. For this reason, the role of the agronomist has become crucial to Siberia's future.

At the Agricultural Research Centre near Novosibirsk, Siberia's largest city, researchers at ten institutes and eleven experimental farms are grappling with every aspect of arctic plant breeding, fertilisation, fodder and livestock farming. Their latest findings indicate that more than 330 million acres of new land can eventually be cultivated. Experimental fields in western Siberia are said to have produced high yields of cabbages, carrots and radishes. Agronomists have developed a new type of tomato, nicknamed 'Speedy' because of its rapid growth rate in northern latitudes. Land improvement is expected to provide extensive new acreage for potato and green vegetable crops.

In Yakutia, other seedlings raised under glass are reported to have produced yields per acre of up to sixteen tons for cucumbers, twenty tons for tomatoes and twenty-four tons for cabbages. During the brief summer, cabbages exposed to continual sunlight grew larger leaves than the same varieties in the south, a remarkable achievement in a country in which the winter temperature is so extreme that exhaled breath freezes instantly into a fog of minute, needle-sharp ice particles.

At Tomsk, in northwestern Siberia, a ninety-acre state farm feeds 500,000 people. Imported poultry and pigs provide a hundred million eggs and hundreds of tons of meat a year. This, however, is an exception. Although each town grows its own tomatoes, cucumbers, radishes, potatoes, cauliflowers, carrots and other root crops in extensive hotbeds and hothouses, farming in Siberia provides little more than five per cent of the region's food, and many more farms like the one in Tomsk are needed urgently.

Adapting hardy crops to the extreme climate is not the Soviet authorities' only concern. Eventually, they hope to be able to control the weather, prevent the formation of ice and tap vast sources of energy from volcanic heat zones deep beneath the permafrost. Tens of thousands of experts at fifty research and design institutes are conducting an impressive array of scientific studies. These include research on mineral, forest and water resources, on health, and ecology and the effects of industrial complexes on permafrost. Under the auspices of the prestigious Academy of Sciences, the findings are pooled into the 'Siberia Programme', the nation's top-priority research project. Essential to the country's future economic health, its purpose is to transform the icy wastelands of Siberia into the key fuel and energy base for the whole of the Soviet Union.

Such importance is attached to Siberia that in recent years Soviet authorities have channelled more than 10,000 students through the Arctic College in Leningrad into scientific research communities at Novosibirsk, Irkutsk, Yakutsk, Krasnoyarsk and Tomsk. The largest of these science cities is Akademgorodok, fifteen miles south of Novosibirsk, a city of more than a million people. Here, some of the best minds in the country, supported by 15,000 researchers, technicians and staff, are tackling the present and future problems of Siberia. Their efforts have already produced new welding techniques and fine-grained metals with a high degree of plasticity and greater resistance to extreme cold.

Soviet scientists predict that in the future, plastics will play an increasingly important role in the Arctic, especially in housing. Pre-moulded walls, window and door frames will replace bricks and concrete, and improve insulation. Lightweight plastics will be easier and cheaper to transport, and mass production will reduce labour costs. In the opening decades of the twenty-first century, a major feature of the North will be the self-sufficient plastic towns covered by translucent domes, with a micro-climate supplied by natural gas. In other developments, new railways are being built and engineers are studying the feasibility of building roads supported by hopper-carrying girders. The piles would be used for supporting power lines, telephone cables, and possibly oil and gas pipelines.

By reversing the flow of Siberian rivers, and by regulating and diverting them, another great source of power will be available. Dozens of hydro-electric plants are planned or under construction, each one the nucleus for a constellation of towns, mines and power-intensive industries. The mighty River Yenisei, nearly 2,000 miles long, is able to support power stations with an aggregate capacity of 70 million kilowatts. The twelve generators of the Krasnoyarsk station, until recently the largest in the world, produce six million kw, more than two and a half times the output of the Grand Coulee Dam, the largest plant in the United States. A second colossus on the Yenisei is producing 6.4 million kw. Similar projects are in progress on other rivers, notably the 1,200-mile Kolyma River in the extreme north east of the country.

Water polluted by industry is a central anxiety. Icebound for as much as eight months a year, northern rivers receive too little sunlight, are low in oxygen content and easy to pollute. It is ten times more difficult to clean an arctic river, which must flow 1,250 miles to purify itself, than a temperate-zone river, which will cleanse itself in 125 miles. Soviet authorities appear to be increasingly aware of the dangers. Although local managements are frequently insensitive to the environment, conservationists are gradually winning the battle to educate them, proving that a sound ecological approach can be beneficial.

The city of Norilsk, pride of the Soviet Arctic, is a typical example. For years, the metal industry had contaminated the city air with sulphur dioxide, until researchers discovered that the gas could be trapped by an efficient filtering system, and converted into sulphuric acid which was in short supply. Gradually, a heightened awareness of the environmental effects of industrial projects is permeating the bureaucracy. Permission to build hydro-electric plants is no longer automatic. A proposal for a massive power complex on the River Ob was recently defeated after scientists pointed out that the reservoir would attract heat from the sun, thaw out vast plains in the north and destroy the regional climate. The government accepted this view, and cancelled the project.

With such an enormous demand for power, the advent of nuclear energy in the Arctic was inevitable. An atomic plant at Bilibino, hundreds of miles north of the Arctic Circle in the hostile region near the East Siberian Sea, is the most northerly in the world. Nuclear power is being exported from a network of atomic plants on the Kola Peninsula. More atomic power stations are intended for northern Siberia. Determined to meet growing energy demands, Soviet authorities are now planning the country's first tidal power plant, which will harness the waves along the coast of the Kola Peninsula. Three similar plants, with a total capacity of more than 100 million kilowatts, will be built on the shores of the Okhotsk Sea, in the Soviet Far East.

The scale of development in Siberia during the past 35 years can be gauged by the growth of Bratsk, which in 1951 was a typical village of 4,000 people living in huts, tents and wooden cottages. Today, it is a bleak metropolis of approximately 300,000 people sprawled round a hydro-electric plant, which supplies timber processing factories, industrial complexes and an aluminium works, the annual output of which surpasses production for the whole of western Europe.

Moving goods and people across the vast distances of the Soviet Arctic is a daunting task. Roads are almost non-existent. Siberia's only main highway, running between its largest cities, Yakutsk and Norilsk, is a nightmare. In summer, drivers motoring through dense clouds of mosquitoes are obliged to stop every few miles to clean windscreens blackened by tiny corpses. Autumn and winter blizzards bring convoys to a halt. Frost breaks up the surface. Other routes are not roads at all, but unmarked, seasonal tracks across frozen swamps or on river ice. Driving calls for expert map-reading, navigation and eyesight. In spring, patches of thin ice are a hazard, sometimes costing a driver his life, and at others forcing him to abandon his load until it can be retrieved by helicopters or by another truck.

Siberian rivers offer a more convenient method of transport. Each year, ships ferry hundreds of thousands of passengers and more than 100 million tons of freight along approximately 42,000 miles of navigable waterways. Unfortunately for Soviet planners, most of these critical arteries, like the roads, are open only for a few months a year, and whereas the movement of passengers and freight tends to be in an east-west direction, the majority of rivers flow from south to north.

For many northern towns, the one lifeline is air travel. More than a third of all mail and cargo carried annually in the Soviet Union is destined for Siberia and the Far East. At many smaller towns, pilots land on dirt runways or the ice. Unpredictable weather makes schedules uncertain. As in the west, the expression 'Hurry up and wait' applies. Frustrating though this may be, without regular flights passengers would need weeks to reach their destinations and business would come to a standstill.

Helicopters play an equally important role, delivering food and mail, evacuating the sick, ferrying equipment to mines and factories, and gas pipelines and rail tracks to isolated outposts.

Railways, which run south of the arctic zone, but provide essential staging posts for Siberian exports, are by far the most reliable form of transport. Until the 5,778-mile Trans-Siberian railway was built in 1897, the sledge journey between Moscow and Vladivostok took nearly a year. Today, freight trains laden with food, clothing and machinery complete the run in seven days, returning with minerals, coal and timber. For European manufacturers, shipping goods to Leningrad, across Siberia by rail, and from the Soviet Pacific coast by sea to Japan and Hong Kong can be twenty days faster and forty per cent cheaper than using traditional sea routes through the Suez and Panama canals.

Keenly aware of this, Soviet authorities sanctioned a second major rail link to the Pacific, the Baikal-Amur Mainline railway, affectionately known as BAM. The 2,000 miles of double track, of enormous economic importance, runs 200 miles north of the old, over-burdened Trans-Siberian line, which was deemed to be too close to the Chinese border for the peace of mind of the defence strategists. Opening up 600,000 square miles of virgin territory, BAM gives access to a treasure trove larger than the combined land mass of Britain, France and Italy. Rich in asbestos, salt, copper, gold and other precious metals, it contains 45 billion tons of coal, 21 billion tons of iron ore and more than half the Soviet Union's timber and fresh water resources.

Hailed as the construction project of the century, BAM and its builders provided the national press with an abundance of statistics and innumerable stories of heroic Soviet workers struggling against impossible odds to the greater glory of Socialism. Conditions for the 132,000-strong workforce were indeed appalling. Lured to Siberia by pay packets as much as four times the national average and the promise of rising to the top of long waiting lists to buy a car, many workers and their families were forced to live in cramped, poorly-insulated railway carriages in temperatures below −50°C. Army engineers equipped with dynamite and flame throwers were repeatedly called in to force a route through deep snow and ice, blocks of which were sometimes 1,000 feet thick.

Working in atrocious weather, engineers laid two-thirds of the track on permafrost and forged a route through one of the world's worst earthquake zones, in which as many as 2,500 tremors are recorded each year. With some tremors registering between seven and eight on the Richter scale (the March 1960 earthquake at Agadir which killed twelve thousand measured 6.6) the ultimate frustration must have been having to tunnel eighteen miles through solid rock. One tunnel was nine miles long. In another, the rock fractured twenty times in a 300-yard section, with some fissures thirty feet wide. Despite the difficulties, engineers pushed BAM across seven mountain ranges and built more than 2,000 bridges, of which 142 crossed fast-flowing rivers hundreds of yards across, an average of one bridge or tunnel for every mile of track.

After ten years' labour, the £5 billion railway was completed. Within months, construction began on a new line linking BAM to Yakutsk, 500 miles further north. The spur, due to be finished in 1995, will require 700 bridges. Seventy million cubic metres of earth must be transported to the track-laying site to make the foundations in the permafrost. Eventually, more than one million people are expected to settle in new towns along the railways, and a new industrial belt will be born.

Having invested £140 billion in Siberia since World War Two, Soviet authorities during the next decade intend to build more than 350 new towns, most of them with resident populations of up to 200,000 people. Siberia's current population of approximately 27 million is expected to swell to 100 million by the end of the century. By comparison, Canada's Northwest Territories, which are three times smaller, have a population of 50,000. There is little doubt that this imported population will learn to survive the Siberian climate.

The effect on the native peoples of Siberia is a different matter. Concern for the ethnic minorities in the Soviet Union has always been minimal. Long before the 1917 Revolution, corrupt Tsarist officials introduced drunkenness and disease, and exploited Siberian natives by forcing them to pay a fur tribute, or tax. The Tsarists, however, made no attempt to educate them, improve their medical welfare or to interfere with the structure of the ethnic communities.

This was in contrast to the Bolsheviks, who regarded the Siberian natives as backward and in need of political enlightenment. In the course of providing this, they successfully eliminated much of their traditional way of life. In today's highly politicised one-party state, an influx of workers on the scale envisaged cannot help but have a detrimental effect on the remaining traditions of such boreal ethnic groups as the Sami, Nenets, Nganasany and Dolgans, or in Siberia and the Soviet Far East, the Yakut, Yukagirs, Eveny, Chukchi and Siberian Inuit. The real issue, however, is whether the Arctic itself can cope with such an onslaught.

CHAPTER 19

Cold War Games

Increasing populations, the resources of the north and the post-war realisation that maps drawn on Mercator's projection create a false impression, have all transformed the Arctic into an area of immense strategic importance. Suddenly, arctic wealth has become a military liability. In political terms, oil, gas, uranium and other valuable minerals, in addition to the growing number of arctic residents, must be defended. Oil installations and pipelines are tempting targets for terrorists and saboteurs. Tankers and liquefied natural gas carriers operating in northern seas are vulnerable in times of war. Communications and supply lines to isolated cities must be protected. Yet, the preparation of defences leads inevitably to the formulation of plans for attack and counter-attack, an unwritten law which has impelled defence chiefs in the United States, Canada, Scandinavia and the Soviet Union to develop the Arctic as the decisive battleground in the event of a future world war.

Viewed from the North Pole, the shortest distance between the superpowers is across the polar icecap, rather than across the Atlantic and Pacific Oceans as suggested by Mercator. Indeed, the northern coasts of Alaska and Canada are closer to the Soviet Union than they are to Washington and Ottawa. At their closest, between the Diomede Islands in Bering Strait, East and West are separated by only three miles of water. (Visitors to the Aleutian Islands, west of Alaska, are frequently reminded that the Soviet Union and China are in the west, Canada and the United States in the east!) The East-West battle lines are drawn between the Soviet Union on one shore of the Arctic Ocean, and on the other by four members of the North Atlantic Treaty Organisation, NATO, the United States, Canada, Greenland and Norway. A fifth NATO country, Iceland, guards the entrance to the ocean.

The proximity of the superpowers to each other is a headache to defence chiefs, who are aware that the polar ice offers no protection against long-range bombers and ballistic missiles. National insecurity, and the international tension deriving from it, have been heightened both by the search for oil and gas, and by the lack of defined boundaries in the

Arctic. Economic zones, territorial claims and questions of sovereignty have caused friction between neighbouring countries and among NATO allies. Britain and Iceland have engaged in naval conflict over cod fishing limits. Canada and the United States have failed to resolve the question of drilling rights in the Beaufort Sea. The sovereignty of the Northwest Passage remains at issue. Greenland is in dispute with Canada and Norway over the ownership of the High Arctic islands, and Norway is at loggerheads with the Soviet Union over fishing, oil and gas rights in the Barents Sea. No one was happy, during the 1960s, about the Soviet nuclear testing programme on Novaya Zemlya, the islands which separate the Barents Sea and Kara Sea, and were home to millions of little auks and other seabirds.

In the arctic game plan, the Barents Sea and the polar icepack are of immense tactical importance to Soviet naval planners. Three of the five ice-free coastlines from which Soviet ships can operate are easily blockaded. Warships guarding the Bosphorus or Dardanelles could prevent the Soviet Navy leaving the Black Sea. The narrow entrance to the Baltic could be closed with little difficulty. Patrols across Korea Strait and the channels between the Japanese islands would contain ships based at Vladivostok in the Sea of Japan.

A fourth naval base, on the Kamchatka Peninsula, lacks road and rail links to the rest of the Soviet Union, and can only be supplied by air and sea. The alternative is the Kola Peninsula. Here, communications with Moscow and other Soviet cities are excellent. The coastline is washed by the warm waters of the Gulf Stream, and the open waters of the North Atlantic can be reached after a short voyage through the Barents Sea.

Soviet strategists were not slow to capitalise on these advantages. Knowing that the shortest flight path to the North American targets was from the Kola Peninsula, they established in its forests and tundra one of the mightiest arrays of military power on earth, a secret world of missile pads, airports, naval shipyards, submarine pens and vast ammunition dumps. Here, sophisticated early-warning radar systems are supported by more than 100 jet interceptors. Another 300 military aircraft, including long-distance bombers and modern Backfire bombers are on standby at sixteen major airfields. A new addition to this aerial power is almost certainly the latest bomber, the swing-wing supersonic Blackjack, its estimated range of 4,400 miles sufficient to allow it without refuelling to bomb any city in the United States.

Along the Finnish and Norwegian borders north of the Arctic Circle, a brigade of naval infantry, an airborne division, and two motorized infantry divisions equipped with more than 500 modern battle tanks are poised to strike across Samiland. Within ten days of a decision to go to war, another twelve to fourteen divisions would be rushed north to reinforce them. The military arsenal on the Kola Peninsula contains enough firepower to blow up the entire world. Most of the country's 1,400 inter-continental ballistic missiles and 6,400 warheads are based here, all pointing westwards.

So horrifying is the potential destruction from such weaponry that military experts from both east and west continue to plan for a conventional war, which they believe will be won in the North Atlantic. The arctic war games pre-suppose that Soviet troops and aircrft would move out of their bases on the Kola Peninsula and sweep across Scandinavia, intent on capturing the harbours and airports of northern Norway. The Norwegians, who do not permit foreign troops to be based on their soil, would be reinforced by three divisions of NATO forces travelling by sea from the United States, Canada and Britain. On arrival, these troops would be issued with millions of dollars' worth of weapons and equipment, stored in huge underground chambers gouged from the Norwegian mountains, and if they were not too late, endeavour to contain an attack by the Soviet forces.

NATO's cause was not helped by the construction of a 110-mile, two-lane paved road between the Swedish mining town of Kiruna and the port of Narvik, in northwestern Norway. In an attempt to attract tourism and reduce unemployment in Samiland, politicians of both countries ignored the protests of the Sami, who were fearful of a tourist invasion, and military experts, who were furious that political expediency should provide the Soviet army with a convenient highway to its top priority target area. Prior to the official opening ceremony, defence staff hatched secret plans to mine the road at the first sign of an invasion.

Supporting the Soviet army and airforce in their advance across Samiland, the Soviet Navy would sail out of the Barents Sea, round the North Cape and into the Norwegian Sea in an attempt to prevent the NATO ships reaching their destination. Success in this mission would leave Norwegian troops hopelessly outnumbered, with approximately four-fifths of the NATO forces and supplies stranded at sea. In such circumstances, the Soviet divisions would have gained a forward base from which to protect their supply lines, sever Europe's lifeline to North America and achieve the domination of Europe.

The outcome of this battle for supremacy would depend largely on the effectiveness of the Soviet Navy. Such importance is attached to its role that Moscow has assigned to the northern fleet two-thirds of its latest combat ships and anti-submarine forces. Spearheaded by three nuclear-powered aircraft carriers bristling with high-performance combat aircraft and rocketry, the armada includes the 37,000-ton *Kiev*, the 28,000-ton nuclear cruiser *Kirov* and 80 other destroyers, cruisers and frigates.

Apart from denying NATO ships access to the Norwegian coast, the principal task of these ships is to protect the massive submarine forces at Severomorsk, near Murmansk, and at Severodvinsk, on the White Sea, the world's largest submarine building yard. Nearly seventy per cent of the Soviet Union's nuclear attack and ballistic missile submarines are based here, the largest concentration of such ships on earth. (The remainder operate from the base at Petropavlovsk, on the Kamchatka Peninsula in the Soviet Far East. The International Institute for Strategic Affairs in London estimates that 116 of the Soviet Union's 371 submarines are based on the Kola Peninsula. In 1986, the Soviet Union had 42 nuclear ballistic missile submarines [SSBNs] and 132 nuclear attack missile submarines [SSNs] compared with NATO's 31 SSBNs and 135 SSNs.) Carrying approximately 1,000 missiles and 2,650 warheads, this deadly armada includes submarines built specifically to launch cruise missiles. Recently equipped with advanced navigational equipment, these missiles can now be guided along a pre-determined course across the featureless polar icecap.

Initially, poor accuracy and the short range of early nuclear submarines posed a host of problems for Soviet strategists. In order to threaten U.S. targets, submariners were obliged to avoid the ears and eyes of the West, a sophisticated network of underwater microphones feeding back information to the anti-submarine warfare headquarters at Norfolk, Virginia. Inter-connected, these ultra-sensitive sonic detectors identify submarines by the individual sound of their engines and track their progress as they slip out of the Barents Sea or through the open water known as the Greenland-Iceland-UK (GIUK) Gap. (This is occasionally referred to as GIN, the Greenland-Iceland-Norway gap. Another network of hydrophones stretches from Alaska, north of the Aleutian Islands, to the Kamchatka Peninsula.) Submarines attempting to pass through Denmark Strait between East Greenland and Iceland are also threatened by captor mines. Having detected and identified the sound and vibrations of a passing enemy submarine, the mines launch torpedoes which, fitted with homing devices on their warheads, are unlikely to miss their targets.

For some time, superior western technology seriously hampered the mobility of the Soviet underwater fleet. Partially boxed into the Barents Sea, the submarines turned northwards under the polar icecap. Admiral James Watkins, the Chief of Naval Operations at the U.S. Naval Institute, declared: 'The Russians must not be allowed to build a sanctuary underneath the ice. The battle of the North Pole has started.' Imperceptibly, the Arctic Ocean had become a new theatre of nuclear conflict.

The success of the hydrophones nudged Soviet designers into producing a new submarine, with greater range and accuracy. The result was the 24,000-ton, 200-yard long *Typhoon*, the world's largest underwater craft, carrying twenty missiles, each with nine warheads. By the mid-1990s, eight of these ships will be patrolling the northern oceans, adding a further 1,440 warheads to the Soviet stockpile. The nuclear hunter-killer submarines were fitted with external tiles similar to those on the U.S. space shuttle, in order to reduce echo and the risk of detection by newer, more sensitive hydrophones. The development of fine-grain metals and advanced welding techniques, particularly with titanium, allowed Soviet submarines to operate in deeper waters. Equipped with heated fins, periscopes and communications masts, they patrol the silent depths beneath the ice, communicating with their headquarters on ultra-low radio frequencies. Beacons planted on the arctic sea bed mark the exact position from which they should fire their missiles.

The peculiar conical fairing round the squat base of the *Typhoon's* fin suggested that it had been specifically designed to smash through the polar ice cap. In March, 1984, an American Landsat weather satellite orbiting above Wrangel Island in the East Siberian Sea photographed what appeared to be a hole in the ice, ringed by the vapour trails of two circling jet aircraft. Analysts later indicated that the jets had been observing a Soviet missile-firing submarine punching a hole through the pack ice. If true, this was a significant breakthrough. Acoustic sensors were unable to decipher the chaotic echoes rebounding off the uneven keels of grinding and cracking ice floes. The apparent ability of Soviet submarines to surface through ice several feet thick was a serious threat, specifically because the 5,600-mile range of the *Typhoon* would enable it to hit a target in the American Midwest from anywhere in the Arctic Ocean.

Soon after the Landsat pictures were published, the Pentagon announced that it had begun a 'significant development effort' to match Soviet technological advances. Submarine hulls would be strengthened. Researchers would study the feasibility of laser detection systems and ground sensors which could be scattered across the ice like seeds, and locate lurking submarines. In April, 1985, the U.S. space shuttle, Spacelab-3, quietly deployed an unusually small satellite, in an experiment to test the possibility of relaying signals from the sonic 'seeds' back to the anti-submarine warfare headquarters in Virginia.

By this time, the crew of western hunter-killer submarines had begun extensive training under the ice and were stalking their Soviet counterparts in the ocean darkness. Registering the sounds of their reactors and engines, and testing the defences of Soviet naval bases, they shadowed the Soviet submarines constantly in a deadly game of hide-and-seek.

The risks hardly bear contemplation. Navy commanders have not forgotten the collision in 1969 between a Soviet submarine armed with ballistic missiles and the USS *Gato*, which was probing the under-sea defences outside Soviet bases on the White Sea. Slightly damaged, the Soviet submarine was forced to surface. The *Gato* escaped into the Atlantic. Later, it was learned that in the event of an attack during this extremely sensitive mission, the American skipper had been ordered to fire his nuclear torpedoes and sink the assailant.

Equally disturbing is the possibility of a political misunderstanding or an accident leading to the despatch of nuclear missiles across the polar icecap. Banks of manned radar stations, stretching across a 6,500-mile frontier from Alaska to Greenland and on to Iceland and Britain, continually scan the skies for just such an eventuality. Known as the Distant Early Warning (DEW) Line, the system was prompted by the Cold War during the 1950s. The 31 radar stations cost $3 billion and took eleven years to build, but gave western defence staff an hour's warning of approaching Soviet bomber aircraft, sufficient for them to scramble jet interceptors. Subsequent improvements and additions provided the Pentagon with fifteen minutes' advance warning in the event of a missile attack, long enough for American generals to retaliate with their own nuclear salvos.

The staggering array of weaponry directed at North American targets spurred the United States and Canada to announce in 1985 a $4 billion programme to modernise their northern defences. Fifteen squadrons of F–15 and F–16 fighter-interceptor jets and twelve more AWAC (Airborne Warning and Control) aircraft, with huge radar discs above the fuselage, were made available. The DEW line, outdated by advanced technology and low-flying cruise missiles, was to be replaced by a 'Northern Warning system', a new chain of 33 unmanned robot stations and 52 microwave radars. Due to be in service by 1992, this $1,200 million network will locate and track cruise missiles flying at extremely low altitudes, and is said to be so sensitive that a radar sited in Washington could pinpoint an orange thrown into the air in Florida.

Shortly after the modernisation programme was announced, USAF F–15 jets intercepted four Soviet bombers flying in pairs off Alaska. Two of the four-engined turboprop Bear-G aircraft, which are designed to carry air-to-ground missiles, were no more than forty miles from the coast. The other, more sophisticated Bear-H bombers, capable of launching long-range cruise missiles, were sighted about a hundred miles offshore. Fired from this position, the missiles would need less than fifteen minutes to reach targets in the United States. Air Force officials were subsequently quoted as saying that pilots based in Alaska are scrambled to intercept Soviet aircraft at least once a month, 'especially on Sundays and holidays', although the Soviet pilots are careful not to violate U.S. airspace, which extends three miles from the Alaskan coastline.

At the strategic bomber airbase at Zavitinsk, northwest of Khabarovsk, in Siberia, runways have been extended and new maintenance facilities and ammunition dumps built to equip and service the latest TU–26 Backfire bombers. Flying supersonically at low level, these aircraft have a range of 6,000 miles and could fire cruise missiles from holding areas over the Arctic Ocean or the Canadian archipelago.

Caught in a vicious cycle from which there seems to be no escape, military strategists from both East and West are turning to increasingly futuristic solutions in the battle for arctic supremacy. New 'over-the-horizon' radar systems are being developed. The United States government has proposed a missile defence system, popularly known as 'Star Wars', which would use lasers to detect and destroy missiles raining down across the polar wastes. This concept clearly worried Soviet leaders, who embarked on an international campaign to alienate the European populace from American thinking, portraying Star Wars as a madcap idea of a right-wing President, Ronald Reagan.

In Britain, the Prime Minister, Mrs Thatcher, gave her unreserved support to the idea, but more than 6,500 scientists in the United States signed a pledge of non-participation, declaring that they would not accept any money from the research funds for President Reagan's plan, officially known as the Strategic Defence Initiative, SDI. The scientists, who included fifteen Nobel laureates and the majority of professors in the leading university physics departments in the United States, described SDI as 'ill-conceived and dangerous'. They made no mention, however, of the 10,000 scientists and engineers in Siberia who are reported to be carrying out research into a laser defence system which would not only destroy missiles, but demolish American satellites with laser guns orbiting in space. This could be a reality by 1996.

Predictably, the eternal struggle for advantage has caused friction between the superpowers and among the western allies. The Soviet Union and the United States fight endless propaganda battles over the numbers and types of ballistic missiles held by each side. International tension has been heightened by fear and mistrust over the Northern Warning System, Star Wars and the true purpose of a highly advanced radar station near Krasnoyarsk, in Siberia. The Soviets claim this is merely a satellite-tracking station. The Americans say it is a space battle-management control centre. The British disagree.

Denouncing the U.S.-Canadian agreement to update the DEW line, the Soviet Union accused Canada of being an accomplice in the American 'Star Wars' programme. In Canada, opposition parties demanded guarantees that the new radar system would not be linked to Star Wars. The Prime Minister assured them that this was not the case, which may have surprised the U.S. Defense Secretary, Caspar Weinberger, who had previously indicated that anti-missile bases in Canada might be essential to a Star Wars programme.

Echoing the views of his premier, the Canadian Defence Minister, Erik Nielsen, observed that as Canada was paying forty per cent of the cost and would be responsible for the maintenance of the Northern Warning System, Canada would at last exercise full sovereignty over its territory and airspace. This remark was undoubtedly intended to remind the Americans of Canada's determination to achieve sovereignty over the Northwest Passage.

Relations between the two countries had been frosty since August, 1965, when the Americans caused an international incident by instructing the U.S. icebreaker *Polar Sea* to sail through the disputed waterway. Refusing on principle to seek permission to travel through waters which they consider international, the Americans insisted that they were not trying to stir up the sovereignty issue. Arguing that the ship was merely taking the direct route from Greenland to Alaska, they explained that sailing through the Panama Canal would have taken a month longer, and added $500,000 to their fuel costs.

The Canadians were outraged. In a display of patriotism, demonstrators flew hundreds of miles to drop a Canadian flag and protest leaflets onto the deck of the American ship. Another group declared the voyage 'insulting and demeaning to Canadian citizens'. Unconvinced by the American protestations, the Canadian government despatched a terse note to the State Department in Washington. Expressing deep regret that no attempt had been made to seek authorisation for the voyage, it stated:

> The government of Canada has made clear that the waters of the arctic archipelago, including the Northwest Passage, are internal waters of Canada and fall within Canadian sovereignty.

It was the first time the Canadian government had laid claim to the Northwest Passage and the islands of the High Arctic in such unequivocal terms.

Hours later, Canada announced that it would increase military surveillance flights in the High Arctic to support its position. At the same time, the government indicated that Soviet submarines had already sailed beneath the North Pole, chosen suitable sites for anti-submarine mines in the Northwest Passage and penetrated Baffin Bay and Davis Strait on their way to the North Atlantic. In these circumstances, the Canadians observed cannily, it would hardly be prudent to establish the Northwest Passage as an international waterway, to which Soviet submarines would have legitimate access.

Clearly worried by the growing threat, the Pentagon prepared contingency plans to attack Soviet nuclear missile submarines even in the event of a purely conventional war, and deploy U.S. warships armed with nuclear weapons close to the Soviet coast. Admiral Watkins suggested that such aggressive tactics could benefit the United States by adjusting the nuclear balance before either side had fired nuclear weapons. Recognising that such a policy might escalate into a full-scale nuclear war, the Admiral added that he did not believe that this was likely 'solely as a result of actions at sea'.

Dicing with such appalling possibilities caused bewilderment amongst the American public, and brought into dispute officials within the Defense Department who saw the strategy as unduly provocative. Advocates of the policy lambasted critics as defeatists. The Secretary for the Navy, John Lehman, explained that plans to build a fleet of 600 ships to engage Soviet warships in the Barents Sea, and attack Murmansk, Severomorsk and other northern Soviet ports, were essential to protect NATO's northern flank. His opponents believed that the American fleet could sustain serious losses and urged a defensive posture across the Greenland-Iceland-UK gap, but this, Admiral Watkins argued, would be tantamount to sacrificing Norway, a NATO ally, to dubious military expediency.

Friction resulting from arctic war games is equally evident in northern Europe. Naval exercises in the Norwegian Sea, and military manoeuvres on Norwegian soil, the fortification of the Kola Peninsula, and suspicions about Soviet intentions on Svalbard have all contributed to a marked deterioration in relations between Norway and the Soviet Union, its northern neighbour.

Military bases on Svalbard are forbidden under the Treaty of 1920, but a naval yard on the islands would be of undeniable value to Soviet submarines preparing to journey under the polar icecap. In 1978, without prior notice, Soviet engineers enlarged a helicopter pad at Barentsburg, on Spitsbergen, to accommodate five MI–8 helicopters. NATO analysts had for years harboured doubts about the true purpose of an unprofitable coal mine employing 2,000 people in the vicinity, and suspected this new move to be a ploy to establish a secret military foothold on the island. This soon gave rise to rumours that the Kremlin was planning to take over the islands to test NATO's military resolve and alter the strategic balance at the entrance to the Barents Sea. Norwegian protests about the helicopters were countered with objections from Moscow to the presence of Norwegian troops on the islands during celebrations to mark the sixtieth anniversary of the signing of the 1920 Treaty.

As the war of words continued, a NATO exercise called 'Anorak Express', involving more than 18,000 troops from seven western countries, prompted a spate of attacks and blunt warnings from the Soviet Union. Accusing the Norwegians of helping to create an 'arc of crisis' on the frontier between the two countries, the Soviet leadership protested that the Norwegians were allowing themselves to be drawn into unfriendly acts against the Soviet Union, without paying heed to the possible implications.

Five years later, in July 1985, the Soviet Navy itself staged the biggest naval exercise in its history, with more than 100 ships cruising into the Norwegian Sea and North Atlantic. The Norwegians were particularly disturbed to see among the convoys amphibious attack vessels, which in their view proved beyond doubt that in wartime the Soviet leadership intended to gain control of Norwegian territory. Within weeks, the display of Soviet force was matched by the most ambitious naval exercise ever organised by NATO, with 165 ships and submarines, and hundreds of aircraft, patrolling the North Atlantic.

During this period, Soviet and Norwegian negotiators laboured to reach an agreement on a boundary across the continental shelf in the Barents Sea. Norway believed that in accordance with international law the dividing line should be equidistant from the two countries. The Soviet Union insisted that it should be drawn from the land frontier to the North Pole, a ploy viewed by Norway as a flagrant attempt to secure the major share of the oil and natural gas fields. The talks were still deadlocked when a former Norwegian diplomat, Arne Treholt, was sentenced in June, 1985, to twenty years imprisonment for betraying to the Soviet Union secret plans for the defence of northern Norway.

Across the border, the late Prime Minister of neutral Sweden, Olof Palme, announced that his government had been unable to reduce defence expenditure owing to increased NATO activity in northern Norway and the continued arms build-up on the Kola Peninsula. Speaking with unprecedented severity, he declared:

> The Cold War continues. We are not militaristic, but all around us there is an entirely senseless arms race ... Our neutrality stands

firm, but we must be sufficiently self-confident to look the super-powers in the eye. We do not shrink from criticising the Soviet Union ...

Although Sweden maintains a formidable defence to protect its neutrality, the effectiveness of its forces is an unknown quantity. During the past twenty years, the Swedish government has reduced military, naval and air capacity by half. The ability of Swedish forces to mobilise quickly is doubtful. They have an unenviable record of embarrassing errors.

In one incident, enthusiastic naval gunners firing an anti-aircraft gun scored a direct hit on the bridge of their own ship. In another, a group of conscripts inadvertently sparked off a series of fires which engulfed thousands of acres of forest, causing consternation in Stockholm's northern suburbs. An ill-trained army patrol blew up a coastal artillery gun, killing one conscript and injuring eight others. Finally, a guardsman on parade outside the Royal Palace dropped his sub-machine gun, which spun round, emptied its magazine across the cobbled courtyard and shot three of his colleagues in the legs.

On hearing this list of disasters, one military attaché in Stockholm remarked that Soviet troops advancing on Norway might be wise to bypass Sweden. The joke was ambiguous. Sweden maintains a strong airforce, and in wartime would defend its northern borders with four well-equipped, highly mobile infantry brigades.

Invading Soviet forces are far more likely to pass through Finland, where commandos of the Finnish 'Jaeger' (Hunter) Brigade would engage them in a closely co-ordinated guerrilla war. A Soviet spearhead crossing the 300-yard swathe of cleared forest which marks the border with northern Finland would soon run into trouble. Tanks and heavy trucks would be halted by forests, marshlands and innumerable lakes. In winter, the progress of a mechanised army would be hampered by freezing vehicles and fuel. Darkness and cold would sap the strength of soldiers unused to such extreme conditions. Moscow is unlikely to have forgotten the Winter War of 1939, when a hopelessly outnumbered but disciplined Finnish army inflicted 700,000 casualties on the invading Soviet Army. Finnish roads, which run from south to north, provide ideal supply lines for Finnish troops, but the single dirt road traversing the country in an east-westerly direction is an easy target for the 'Jaeger' Brigade.

Mobile, lightly armed and superbly trained, the 'Jaeger' ski patrols can live off the land for extended periods at the coldest time of the year. So expert are they in the art of camouflage that, at ten yards, observers who have been primed about their probable positions are frequently unable to pinpoint them. Based at Soedankyla, ninety miles from the Soviet border, most of the commandos are selected from reindeer herders, hunters and local people accustomed to the harsh climate. In a crisis, the Finns could raise an army of 700,000 people, and requisition 250,000 reindeer for reserve food, clothing and transport. Soviet troops advancing through Finland might reach Norwegian territory, but marauding commandos would undoubtedly sever their supply lines.

Despite these preparations, and the pervasive awareness that the nuclear arsenals on the Kola Peninsula are less than 100 miles away, Finland desires peaceful relations with its eastern neighbour. In his New Year speech in 1985, the country's gentle and philosophic President, Mauno Koivisto, appealed to the superpowers to dismantle their cruise missiles in Europe and 'to stabilise the overall situation in the northern hemisphere'. Worried that NATO missiles could be fired at Soviet targets through Finnish airspace, the Finns had already served notice that they would shoot down any western missiles fired across their territory. Advanced radar systems were installed, and aerial surveillance increased. President Koivisto declared: 'We must arm ourselves so that we can stop violations of our territory and our airspace.'

Within 24 hours of Finnish television screening his speech, the Norwegian defence staff announced that its radar operators had tracked a short-range missile streaking across northern Norway. Travelling faster than the speed of sound, it had been fired from a Soviet warship in the Barents Sea and had disappeared thirty seconds later into Finnish territory, where it crashed through the ice on Lake Inari. (Whether President Koivisto was aware of the details is unknown, but it is probable. The missile was detected on December 28th, 1984, three days before the television speech.) Officials in Helsinki confirmed that a 'foreign unidentified flying object' had crossed its borders, but were careful not to describe it as a missile or implicate their Soviet neighbours. In Washington, U.S. intelligence confirmed the violation. The Ministry of Defence in London voiced its deep concern, and said it was in touch with Norway and other NATO allies. In Moscow, the Defence Ministry refused to comment. A week later the Kremlin apologised, explaining that the missile was of an older type used for target practice and that a malfunction had caused it to stray off course during a naval exercise.

Fortunately, the drone was not armed, although if it had been, this would not have been the first time that nuclear weapons had been involved in an accident in the Arctic. In May, 1984, western seismologists recorded a blast so powerful that it was at first thought to have been a nuclear explosion. Ignored in the Soviet press, it is believed to have destroyed a third of the ground-to-air and cruise missiles stockpiled for the northern fleet at the submarine base at Severomorsk.

Diplomats in Moscow subsequently heard repeated accounts of a huge, radioactive cloud drifting from the base towards the densely-populated city of Murmansk. The explosion was said to be the latest in a series of similar incidents at Soviet military installations. In Washington, U.S. Navy officials, who doubtless regarded the Soviet setbacks with an element of glee, voiced concern that if the main ammunition dump at Severomorsk had been demolished, it did not augur well for Soviet safety procedures or quality control.

Exactly two years after the Severomorsk explosion, in May, 1986, a similar blast in one of four nuclear reactors at Chernobyl, near Kiev, raised further doubts about Soviet safety standards. With southeasterly and easterly winds carrying radio-active dust thousands of miles across the Soviet Union, Europe and Scandinavia, it emerged that the Soviet nuclear authorities had not considered necessary the secondary containment of the reactor, standard procedure for similar reactors in the west.

With the risk of a nuclear accident or a war continually increasing, no fewer than seven arctic nations declared their opposition to nuclear weapons on their soil. As details of the 'Star Wars' proposal emerged, Canada's External Affairs Minister Joe Clark told parliament: 'There will be no nuclear weapons stationed on Canadian soil. That can be taken as categoric.' Greenland's parliament voted unanimously to declare the country a nuclear-free zone in both peace and war, taking the Danes, who are responsible for Greenland's foreign and defence policies, by surprise. The Greenlanders also demanded a full investigation into the activities of American bases on their territory, particularly the huge U.S. base at Thule, in northwest Greenland.

In Iceland, the Foreign Minister noted that while 85 per cent of his countrymen were in favour of NATO membership, anti-nuclear sentiment was overwhelming. Ships carrying nuclear arms, including those from NATO countries, would not be allowed into Icelandic territorial waters. 'We are not storing any nuclear weapons here. That is a definite policy,' the Foreign Minister declared. A few months later, more than a hundred legislators with other officials from Iceland, Denmark, Norway, Sweden and Finland convened in Copenhagen to re-examine a proposal to ban nuclear weapons in all the Nordic countries. The Soviet Union had first suggested such a zone in 1958, and had subsequently agitated for Europe to follow suit. Delegates to the conference noted that an ideal gesture of Soviet support would be the removal of nuclear weapons from the Kola Peninsula.

CHAPTER 20

The Arctic Challenge

In the scramble to unlock and protect the arctic treasure chest, the Inuit and the other natives of the Far North have been overwhelmed and forgotten. The attitudes of miners, oil men, politicians and military chiefs are in essence no different from those of the whalers and traders, or the explorers, missionaries and Danes. None of them intended to undermine the livelihoods of the happy and gifted peoples with whom they came into contact. The brawling whalers, accustomed to the rough and tumble of shipboard life, are unlikely to have given a second thought to the effects of their violence on a peaceful society. The missionaries, impervious to all but the spread of Christianity, simply did not understand that female infanticide, suicide and the desertion of the old and sick were, if evil, a necessary evil for the survival of the group. The Danes were thoughtless in their dealings with the Inuit, rather than malicious. Yet, like water eroding the bank of a stream, the *qallunaat* have trickled through the Arctic, and worn away a culture.

The stream became a torrent with the construction of the DEW line in the 1950s. In a few short weeks, hunters accustomed to hoarding the smallest scraps of food saw more waste than they or their ancestors had known in 4,000 years. Uninvited and without warning, ships, helicopters and pot-bellied transport planes appeared over the horizon. In Greenland, to the amazement of the 118 descendants of Robert Peary's Inuit at Thule, the convoys and aircraft dumped hordes of fresh-faced men and countless tons of cargo barely a harpoon's cast from their traditional hunting grounds and houses of turf and stone.

Intrigued, excited and bewildered, the Inuit stood by their dog teams and watched the intruders drive heavy trucks and bulldozers down the ramps. Innumerable sheets of corrugated iron were unloaded. In a single day the strangers bolted them together to create a city of tunnel-shaped huts and hangars. Soon, soldiers had flattened a 10,000-foot runway along the valley. More aircraft circled overhead, and on landing disgorged drums of fuel and crates of food, which were stockpiled in the unloading bays, a store greater than the impoverished Inuit had seen, or heard of, in a lifetime. White radar domes, like giant golfballs, took shape, followed by a radar scanner so huge that it was likened to a football pitch tipped on its side. Nearby, a communications mast only slightly shorter than the Empire State Building rose into the sky. Before the Inuit could discover what was happening, the listening post for Armageddon had been established.

In two years, 20,000 men passed through Thule, which grew into one of the biggest air bases in the world. The resident staff of 3,000 men carved tunnels in the ice, abandoned or burned trucks which failed to function in the cold and littered the landscape with discarded packets of chewing gum and Camel cigarettes. Heaps of uneaten food were left for the foxes. Whipped by the high winds, empty barrels of fuel trundled across the valley or out to sea. After a year, the Danish Minister for Greenland announced that the Inuit had voted to leave Thule for Qaanaaq, 100 miles further north. From that time on, the U.S. airbase and its environs were out of bounds.

Thirty-one years later, in 1985, the Greenland Home Rule government demanded from Washington between three and five million dollars, compensation with which to support the hunters Peary had called 'my eskimos', and replace the 27 poorly-insulated, one-room wooden shacks built for them after their expulsion from Thule. At the time of writing, the compensation had not been paid.

There can be no return to the old life. The *qallunaat*'s damage is done. The Inuit cannot divorce themselves from the modern ways of the world, or from the nuclear age. Tens of thousands of Inuit, Sami and other arctic dwellers are more secure now than they have ever been. Survival is no longer a central issue. The Inuit no longer face starvation. Materially, if not spiritually, there has been a vast improvement in their lives. Improved housing and health facilities, and lower infant mortality, have increased their numbers, but game stocks are no longer sufficient to support their hunting traditions. In truth, few indigenous northern dwellers would wish to face the rigours of the past. Softened by southern comfort and welfare, it is unlikely that the young are tough enough to live off the land and endure the hardships suffered by their ancestors. The hunting culture, and with it the old customs, will disappear.

The danger is that the peoples of the north will become human animals in a cultural zoo, mere objects of curiosity for adventurous southerners wealthy enough to enjoy the temptations of glossy travel magazines, luxury cruises through the icebergs, reindeer round-ups or photographic safaris among walrus and polar bears. For £1,000, travel agents in London sell tours of East Greenland, during which travellers are encouraged to 'experience the unique world of icebergs and glaciers, gasp at magnificent landscapes of snow-clad mountains, cross majestic frozen white lakes on skis and try the marvellous time-worn way of travel by husky dogsledge.'

Perpetuating the images of Nanook, the Midnight Sun and Europe's Last Great Wilderness, travel promoters talk excitedly about tourism in the north, which they say is at last taking off. Flying supersonically, Concorde recently transported day trippers from Britain to Christmas lunch with the 'Lapps' in Samiland. After roaring into Rovaniemi, a medium-sized Finnish university town on the Arctic Circle, passengers who had paid £965 for the privilege were driven to a forest lodge for reindeer meat and red whortleberries, champagne and snapshots of 'Lapps' in red and blue tunics and pom-pom hats.

Reindeer round-ups and safaris are a major attraction in the Nordic countries. In winter, customers encased in thermal underwear, sweaters and down-filled anoraks don fur hats with ear muffs, are tucked snugly into individual *pulkas* and drawn across the snow-clad fells of Finland to the sound of tinkling reindeer bells. In the evenings, they relax in forest hunting lodges, luxuriate communally in saunas, and eat smoked salmon or reindeer delicacies in front of log fires of birch and pine.

Samiland's growing popularity has provided an additional source of income in an area of high unemployment. The Nordic Council, hoping to create more jobs, wants to study and breed wolves and bears, lynxes and rare arctic species at a zoo exhibiting 600 animals. The guides and ticket collectors would doubtless be Sami in traditional costume.

Herdsmen in Norway and Sweden, where tourism is more highly developed, would prefer tighter controls on visitors, who tramp over the vegetation and frighten the reindeer, often when the cows are giving birth or gaining weight for winter. A common complaint is that tourists drive too quickly. Intent on reaching the North Cape to see the midnight sun, they hurriedly photograph a passing Sami or buy a pair of reindeer boots, but show little interest in Sami culture. 'When tourists come here,' the herders say, 'they look at us like animals on a reservation.'

In the Canadian Arctic, the impact of tourism is equally disturbing. The government of the Northwest Territories, which publishes a 98-page *Official Explorers' Guide* listing available package tours, proudly observes that in ten years the number of guest lodges and outfitters has doubled. Today, the government is spending nearly a million dollars a year to promote the region in the United States and Europe.

Tourists can fish and hunt at Great Bear Lake, back-pack on Baffin Island or travel for ten days with a dog team on the sea ice of Foxe Basin. Drum dancing, 'igloo' building and dog teams are available at a price – $100 an hour at Grise Fiord on Ellesmere Island. For $7,500 (U.S.), tour operators offer a week-long package which includes a snowmobile trip to Beechey Island, four days' camping on Ellesmere Island, and an insufferably boring sixteen-hour return flight for the questionable bonus of a thirty-minute stopover at the North Pole for photographs and champagne. Pilots try to land within ten miles of the Pole, but weather or ice conditions may impose restrictions. As there is nothing but ice at the Pole, the photographs could just as well be taken one mile from Resolute Bay.

Throughout the Arctic, the volume of air traffic is increasing dramatically. Airlines fly polar routes to save time and fuel. Helicopters, light aircraft and Twin Otters from forty Canadian air charter companies continually ferry personnel and supplies. Pilots swoop down on animals so that tourists can photograph them, or scientists spray them with paint. Snow geese feeding in the Mackenzie Delta before migrating south may take fright at low-flying light aircraft and leave the Arctic prematurely. Unable to build up sufficient reserves of fat, they die before reaching their destinations.

Providing they are paid the going rate, Inuit on snowmobiles will tow visitors over the ice in a *U-doo*, a sledge covered with plywood and perspex, to hunt seals. (The word was first used by Bezal Jesudason in Resolute Bay, who explained: 'It is just something "U-doo" to give the passenger more protection from windchill when the sledge is towed by Ski-doos, which are much faster than dogs.') Gone are the days when an Inuk sat for 36 hours patiently waiting for his quarry to appear at a blowhole. Now, young Inuit spy a seal basking on the ice, gun the engines of their Nordic or Yamaha snowmobiles, race at top speed towards it, and are frustrated to find that the seal has taken fright and slipped quietly into the depths. For every kill, old rifles and poor marksmanship account for a second seal which slithers wounded beneath the ice, probably to die underwater.

Without thought for the susceptibility of the game, one tourist company plans to ferry American and Japanese tourists to the icefloes off Canada's Atlantic coast. Here, they will be able to photograph the harp seal pups which, prior to animal rights campaigns, were clubbed to death for their fur by white hunters. With equal insensitivity, Canada's *Official Explorers' Guide* proclaims that 'caribou, polar bears, grizzlies, seals and whales can all be seen by lucky travellers.' Ensuring that these visitors receive value for money, Inuit snowmobiles buzz like angry wasps across the snow, round up herds of musk oxen and drive them towards the waiting bands of photographers. Knowing that polar bears can be frightened by the noise of snowmobile engines, Inuit guides illegally chase them for miles, until the exhausted bears amble placidly past the battery of tripods and long lenses.

Clearly, visitors must be primed about the possible consequences of their actions *before* they embark on journeys through the Arctic. The tide of tourism cannot be stemmed but, approached wisely, it can provide jobs and generate income without disrupting local communities or wildlife. If the sole motive for developing arctic tourism is instant profit, the result can only be an environmental disaster.

The future development of the Arctic cannot be halted. It is too late for that. Industrial man is here to stay, but the exploration and exploitation of natural resources cannot be allowed to advance unchecked. It should be subjected to stricter controls. Industry, too, needs to undergo a change of heart, and channel as much energy into the conservation of the environment, as it has, until now, into its rape.

The assessment of environmental damage from a single oil rig is meaningless when it is obvious that if oil is discovered, dozens of wells will be sunk, pipelines built, and motor and air traffic increased throughout the region. Future estimates of possible damage should be examined in the light of the harm inflicted in the past, with assessments based on completed projects, rather than on their isolated features. Every industrial scheme in the Arctic, including the extraction of oil, should be separately mapped, with yearly additions on transparent film. At a glance, the annual rate of industrial expansion could be assessed, and where necessary curtailed. It is ludicrous to fell vast areas of forest in order to provide short-term employment. Hydro-electric plants which have an adverse effect on reindeer pastoralism may provide cheap electricity for the cities of the South, but the resulting loss of livelihood among the Sami could incur, for the Nordic governments, infinitely greater expense in social welfare and job-creation schemes. The transportation of oil and natural gas through Baffin Bay, in the event of an accident, may result in astronomical costs for cleaning operations, legal battles and compensation. The benefits of the oil shipments would indeed be short-lived if Greenland's shrimp beds and cod fishing grounds were contaminated, and the population along the west coast had to be evacuated.

Profitability and political expediency can no longer be the only deciding factors. It is nonsensical to grant oil exploration permits on the basis of environmental assessments compiled by the industrial groups applying for them, in which government agencies may have a financial stake; it is also an insult to the public intelligence.

Applications for every development in the Arctic need reviewing by councils of independent experts drawn from industry, commerce, government and opposition parties, and ecological and conservation organisations. Their recommendations should be binding, subject to appeal through the courts. Changes can be achieved only through public awareness of the complex issues involved, and by intensifying pressure to such a degree on those in positions of authority that it becomes more expedient to heed the warnings, than to ignore them. Most of all, justice demands that the peoples whose homelands are affected should have a voice – and a decisive one – in such councils.

Government and industry can no longer pretend that wildlife preserves are none of their business. Protection of the arctic environment is everybody's business. The Canadian government ought to be publicly castigated for its dogged refusal to establish nature reserves. The total acreage of the 151 sites suggested as wildlife sanctuaries by the International Biological Programme is infinitesimal in comparison with the vastness of the Arctic. Yet, in contrast to the hundreds of exploration and exploitation permits issued to oil companies, the extent of the Canadian government's concern for the environment has gone no further than to establish two national parks, which will promote tourism, and to impose a temporary moratorium on drilling in the Lancaster Sound.

This sound is an essential part of the ecological food chain in Baffin Bay and Davis Strait. For countless marine and land mammals, and millions of sea birds, it is one of the most important breeding grounds and migration routes in the High Arctic. As the entrance to the Northwest Passage, it is equally significant for international shipping. Panarctic Oils, in which the Canadian government has a sizeable stake, proposes to ship crude oil through this channel, where other companies already have long-standing applications for permission to drill wildcat oil wells.

Hard decisions will have to be made to resolve the conflict of interests, and thought given to the advisability, rather than the feasibility, of oil shipments and of drilling in waters so unpredictable that there are years when the ice does not break up. Until all the available evidence is collated, past damage and future risks assessed, the Department of Indian Affairs and Northern Development (DIAND) in Canada should impose on all developments, for a minimum of twenty years, an immediate moratorium.

That is one solution. If it is accepted, there are many during this time who may feel that greater benefit would be achieved by establishing industrial and tourist parks, rather than wildlife reserves. This scheme is already in operation on a small scale in Finland. Here, national parkland is divided into three zones. Tourists are restricted to specific sightseeing areas, where amenities for barbecues and camping are provided, and trails clearly marked. In the 'wilderness' zones, strict regulations govern camping and hunting, and there are no organised hiking services. The 'natural' zone, by far the largest of the three, is sealed off and retained in its original state.

Industry and tourism in the Arctic could be contained in the same way within designated pockets of activity, beyond which only aboriginal hunting, research and emergency work would be permitted. Organisations such as Greenpeace and the World Wildlife Fund have an enormous contribution to make in achieving such a goal. The 'Save the Seals' campaign is destroying the livelihood of thousands of Inuit hunters. Less than ten per cent of the seals taken by Canadian Inuit are the harp seals pictured in the anti-sealing campaigns, which so effectively destroyed the European fur market. Hoping to counter the disastrous effects for the hunters, a new international organisation, Indigenous Survival International (ISI), has been constituted. Its purpose is to defend the traditional harvesting activities of indigenous peoples, and to develop a comprehensive arctic environmental strategy which can be used as a guideline by governments and industry. Hitherto, conservationists have balked at the intricacy of the Arctic ecology and its development. A 'Save the Arctic' campaign now would be an admirable way for the animal rights groups to redeem themselves.

The need for such a campaign is urgent. If Nunavut is soon to be a reality, and the Inuit are to have greater responsibility for the management of northern resources, they must be given the capability to conduct, and profit from, research without which no amount of campaigning will save the Arctic. Science can serve the northern populations, but greater mutual advantage will stem from their full involvement in basic research, which properly funded, should be expanded to provide improved facilities for applied research.

The Arctic is of significance to every country in the northern hemisphere, and plays an indispensable role in global climatic patterns. Yet, little is known about the exchange of energy between the sea, the ice and the atmosphere. The downward movement of cold water in the arctic oceans appears to be the only truly effective mechanism for removing carbon dioxide from the atmosphere, but unless there is a more profound understanding of such processes, it will be impossible to calculate how much atmospheric pollution the oceans can safely absorb. Nor can we discover the degree of change pollutants are likely to cause to the climate of Europe and North America, or whether the icecaps will melt. Who better to study such mysteries than the Inuit?

Investigation into the microscopic organisms which adapt so successfully to the arctic cold, the long winter darkness and the continual summer daylight may produce information which will directly benefit human health. Understanding the natural biorhythms of animals in the polar regions may assist us in judging human reactions to arctic conditions, and help to create working routines to improve productivity.

Extensive programmes need to be undertaken to find ways to minimise noise in offshore developments, and to reduce the impact of pipelines, causeways and roads.

The most pressing task for researchers is to find new ways of reducing to zero the industrial emissions of sulphur dioxide and air pollutants, to investigate the long-range transportation of soot and chemicals, and evaluate the dangers of climatic changes as a result of burning fossil fuels. Man needs to know what are the prevailing physical and chemical conditions in the North Atlantic and Arctic Oceans, into which falls the bulk of the industrial pollution of Europe and North America. The causes and potential effects of unexpectedly high levels of heavy metals in marine mammals off the coast of Greenland require urgent attention.

Industrial emissions must be reduced at a quickening pace, in view of the industrial expansion in Siberia. The British government will have to join the rest of Europe and sign the Helsinki Protocol on sulphur dioxide emissions, or take rapid action against those industries which produce the contaminants.

International cooperation is solving the problems of the Arctic, and the mutual exchange of information, will provide excellent opportunities for dispelling some of the mistrust between east and west. American and Canadian expertise in business and management techniques could be pooled with Soviet advances in metal welding, building processes, and plant and vegetable breeding. Each nation with territory north of the 66th parallel, assisted by the indigenous populations, should formulate an arctic policy in which protection of the land and its peoples is paramount.

The makers of arctic policy ought to give greater responsibility to northern peoples, who have no wish to live in the past, and no desire to be mere objects of southern curiosity. Now is the time to help to restore their confidence and pride. The Inuit and the Sami harbour no secret longings to threaten the sovereignty of the Canadian or Nordic governments. Their goal is to control the new developments, and to guarantee the future growth of their cultures. The Canadian government is to be commended for beginning the process of negotiating native claims, and for lending millions of dollars to the Inuit to fight their cause. What is required now is to nurture the Inuit's self-respect.

Inuit organisations have already shown themselves to be responsible, politically astute bodies. Decisions on resource development, tourism, housing, employment and social policies should be taken with their participation. Involvement in these issues will provide local people with the necessary training before they shoulder their full responsibilities.

The Inuit communities should be given their fair share of the royalties from oil, gas and minerals. They could be channelled into health and education, social and economic projects and small-scale industries for the arctic market. Local ventures will motivate the Inuit, and provide work in each community for those who cannot hunt. Initially, government subsidies may be required, but hand-outs tend to promote discontent and a sense of hopelessness. Far better that Inuit projects are funded with income from generous royalties and land-claim settlements, while government finance is used to support research into improving arctic productivity.

Soviet scientists have shown that the potential for agriculture and horticulture in the north is greater than is generally supposed. One day, millions of acres of arable land in the Mackenzie Valley and the Yukon will be ploughed to grow grain and root crops. In time, each community in the north will be self-sufficient in fruit and vegetables, eggs, milk and a variety of nutritious foods. Shrimp, arctic char and seafood products can be harvested and exported to the south, earning millions of dollars a year. Commercial fisheries and vegetable farms will cut the crippling costs of transportation, and help to improve diet. If tomatoes and cabbages which are resistant to the cold can be grown larger in Siberia than on the banks of the Volga, the Inuit of Grise Fiord, Resolute Bay and Pond Inlet should not have to pay for fresh supplies to be flown in from Edmonton.

The opportunities are limitless. Musk oxen can be bred and farmed for their lightweight wool, which is in great demand in the south. In Asia, where powdered elephant and rhinoceros tusks are sold as aphrodisiacs, there are ready markets for caribou and reindeer antlers, which are renewed annually. The oil industry could make a valuable contribution by providing, in part payment of royalties and development taxes, transport for raw materials, and surplus heat for technical schools and workshops – an insurance for the Inuit. They could then harness their adaptive and inventive abilities, sell their arts and crafts, manufacture clothing, footwear, furniture and pre-moulded goods, and each community would specialise in its own product or products.

The requirement for achieving these dreams is political will. Conservation of the north, and the helping hand which has to be extended to its peoples, will prove to be expensive. The Arctic is too important to be ignored. It is our heritage, and should be preserved for future generations. From now on, the Inuit and the *qallunaat* must work together, as partners.

EPILOGUE

Shortly after the nuclear accident at Chernobyl, in the Soviet Union, in May 1986, the Norwegian Health Directorate announced that the levels of radioactive caesium discovered in arctic char in northern Norway were more than ten times the permitted maximum, and warned the public not to eat freshwater fish.

As in other European countries, thousands of tons of vegetable crops were destroyed. Radioactive strontium was detected in milk. One month after the explosion, Norwegian scientists detected over a wide area of Samiland high levels of radioactive fall-out, especially in lichen, upon which the reindeer herds are dependent for food.

Closer inspection showed that reindeer meat in the central breeding grounds of Scandinavia registered between 15,000 and 40,000 becquerels a kilo of caesium 137 and caesium 134, which are among the most dangerous radioactive isotopes. These readings compared with a Norwegian safety level for contamination of 600 becquerels a kilo. The Swedish limit is 300 becquerels a kilo.

Immediately, Norwegian and Swedish authorities declared the reindeer herds unfit for slaughter, and banned lake fishing and berry-picking, the two supplementary means of subsistence available to Sami herders. Agents for the Swedish confectionery industry cancelled their orders for berries, and prohibited their sale in the region.

The Sami were told that of the animals due for slaughter in the autumn of 1986, nearly 210,000 animals in Norway, and twice as many in Sweden, would have to be put down and buried in trenches ten feet deep.

During the next five years, the entire stock of the Central Sami, nearly 200,000 reindeer, will meet the same fate.

Officials in both countries admit that they have no idea how to solve the problem, and that government compensation, however generous, will be of little value. The cultural damage is likely to be so great as to cause the disintegration of the Sami, who, ironically, have always opposed nuclear and hydro-electric power in Samiland.

* * *

As the Scandinavian authorities were beginning to realise the extent of the radiation, leading scientists in Washington expressed to a Senate committee their fears that within fifteen years man-made pollutants creating a greenhouse effect would force the temperature in the atmosphere to rise 'to a level which has not existed on earth in the past 100,000 years'.

The scientists told the committee that serious over-heating of the earth's atmosphere is now a reality, and that it may already be too late to avert major climatic changes which could result in floods, droughts and an increase in skin cancer.

Sherwood Roland, a chemist from the University of California, was quoted as saying that if the chemical destruction of the atmosphere by carbon dioxide and other man-made pollutants is allowed to continue indefinitely, the temperature will rise to such a high level that all human life on earth could be extinguished in as little as 500 years.

* * *

Shortly after these predictions, delegates to the Inuit Circumpolar Conference at Kotzebue, in Alaska, criticised the use of oil tankers in the Arctic Ocean and condemned increased military activities in the Far North. Then, for the first time, the Inuit unanimously elected a woman, Mary Simon from Kuujjuaq in northern Quebec, to lead the organisation.

* * *

ACKNOWLEDGMENTS

This book would not have been written had it not been for Vernon Mann, a reporter for Independent Television News (ITN) Ltd., in London, who, as duty Foreign Editor in May, 1983, assigned me to cover the voyage of a replica Viking ship across the North Sea. Before the passage was successfully completed, we twice lost a steering oar, and were towed a hundred miles back to shore in a Force Eight wind, in constant danger of capsizing owing to an insecure mast.

I was in expert hands, however. The skipper of *Saga Siglar*, Ragnar Thorseth, had previously crossed the North Sea in a canoe, sailed through the Northwest Passage in a cabin cruiser, and with my cameraman, Trygve Berge, in 1982 had become the first Norwegian to reach the North Pole. With Max Vinner of the Vikingeskibsmuseet in Vanloese, Denmark, who extended unlimited moral support during the voyage, they stirred a latent interest in the Vikings, and introduced me to Eiriksfjord and the Viking settlements in Greenland.

In Nuuk, I was fortunate to meet and befriend Philip Lauritzen, then the Head of Information for Greenland's Home Rule government. More than anyone, he opened up for me an arctic world, of which I knew nothing. My thanks are also due to Jan Drent and Ole Heinrich at Tusarliivik, Fleming Christenssen and his colleagues at the Ice Patrol headquarters at Narssarssuaq, and Peter Lind, for his gargantuan efforts in re-arranging my travel plans at 24 hours' notice.

Moses Olsen, Greenland's Deputy Prime Minister, and Dr Robert Petersen, the renowned eskimologist, deserve special thanks for their time and help, and for the valuable insights they gave me into the psychological and political background of the Greenlanders. The same applies to Joseph Motzfeldt, who shared with me his remaining food and offered me lodging during the process of leaving his home in Uummaannaq, prior to taking up his new position as Greenland's Minister of Education in Nuuk. I am equally grateful to the management of Greenex A/S, who helicoptered me hundreds of miles across Greenland, and welcomed me to stay at the Black Angel Mine at Marmoriliik.

The hospitality of Bezal and Terry Jesudason in Resolute Bay is well known among arctic travellers, and during the writing of this book, my thoughts have frequently returned to them. I am also grateful to Dennis Hillman of the Baffin Cooperative Society, Jamie MacKendrick, Senior Development Officer of the NWT government in Yellowknife, Rev. Jim Bell of Baffin Island, and to the staff of The Inuit Circumpolar Conference, DIAND, the Canadian Wildlife Service, the Resolute Weather Bureau and the RCMP. Although far too numerous to mention individually, hundreds of officials, oil workers and Inuit throughout the Arctic gave me their time and hospitality during nearly three years' research. Special mention must be made of Tony Manik and Larry Audlaluk at Resolute, who taught me so much, and Paul Kasudluak and Elijah Nutarra (E.9912) of Grise Fiord, whose soapstone carvings are a constant reminder of our times together on the ice.

I would like to acknowledge my debt to my good friend of more than twenty years' standing in Scandinavia, Mr Tom Soederman of the Finnish Foreign Ministry and Mr Lasse Lehtinen at the London Embassy. Another great 'Finnfriend', is Mr Matti Kohva, of Finnfacts in Helsinki, with whom I shared many happy saunas and struggled through the snows of Samiland in search of reindeer and Finnish soldiers. Mr Teuvo Tikkanen, also of Finnfacts, and Captain Tom Artela offered unlimited assistance during our sub-zero voyage on board the icebreaker, *Urho*. I am indebted to Mr Tankmar Horn, the Chairman of Wartsila Shipyard in Helsinki, Mr Harri Soininen, the manager for Wartsila Consulting Engineering and Mr Goran Wilkman, the Head of Wartsila's Arctic Research Centre. Their expertise and patience with my naive questions was invaluable. Thanks are also due to Oystein Dalland and Philip Hayes, in Norway, for their assistance on the Alta affair. Among the Sami, Aslak Magga, Maaret-Anne and Inga Magga deserve special mention.

In Britain, David Nicholas, the Editor of ITN, was generous in allowing me several weeks off work to travel to the High Arctic. I should also like to express my warmest thanks to Jim Green, Ian Lomas, Mike Chandler, John Davies, and Ian Aldridge, Bob Learmonth, Doug Fenner, John Wroe and Stuart Maskell, of ITN's News Information Library, who helped me to find elusive details on a variety of subjects. Mrs Pam Barlow at The Society for Cultural Relations with the USSR, was equally tireless in her efforts to assist. Additionally, my knowledge of birdlife improved greatly with the assistance of the ornithologist, Mr Roger Durman, who took such an interest in my project, and checked the manuscript for factual errors.

To my dear wife, my love and thanks for living with my obsession, for enduring my depressive moods when words would not come or my word processor failed, for helping to acquire books long out of print, and for understanding my need to travel in such inhospitable regions. My warmest thanks go also to her mother, Mrs Marion Higgins, who not only corrected the manuscript, but with infinite patience, kindness and wisdom taught me discipline in language, and showed me the difference between writing for television news and for a publisher. Without her invaluable help and encouragement, this first book might never have been completed.

Above all others, my thanks go to the Inuit, the Sami and the peoples of the North.

S.H.

NOTES ON PUBLISHED SOURCES

1 Finn Gad, *The History of Greenland*, Vol. II, pp. 278, 382.
2 A. H. Markham, *A Whaling Cruise to Baffin's Bay*.
3 D. Murray Smith, *Early Arctic Expeditions*.
4 D. Murray Smith, *op. cit.*
5 D. Murray Smith, *op. cit.*
6 A. H. Markham, *op. cit.*
7 A. H. Markham, *op. cit.*
8 D. Murray Smith, *op. cit.*
9 Peter Freuchen and Finn Salomonsen, *The Arctic Year*, p. 199.
10 Jean Malaurie, *The Last Kings of Thule*, p. 234.
11 Robert E. Peary, *The Discovery of the North Pole*.
12 Robert E. Peary, *op. cit.*
13 Robert E. Peary, *op. cit.*
14 Finn Gad, *op. cit.*, Vol. III, pp. 232, 418.
15 Finn Gad, *op. cit.*, Vol. II, p. 300.
16 D. Murray Smith, *Arctic Expeditions from British and Foreign Shores*, p. 29.
17 E. E. Rich, *Hudson's Bay Company, 1670–1763*, Vol. I, p. 441.
18 Hudson's Bay Record Society, *Andrew Graham's Observations on Hudson's Bay, 1767–91*, Vol. XXVII, p. 237.
19 Hudson's Bay Record Society, *Northern Quebec and Labrador Journals and Correspondence, 1819–1835*, Vol. XXIV, p. 123.
20 Jean Malaurie, *op. cit.*, pp. 200–1.
21 Fritjiof Nansen, *Eskimo Life*, p. 316.
22 Finn Gad, *op. cit.*, Vol. II, p. 86.
23 Fritjiof Nansen, *op. cit.*, p. 307.
24 Fritjiof Nansen, *op. cit.*, p. 307.
25 Poul Egede, *Relationer fra Groenland*, 1741, *Meddelser om Groenland*, Vol. 54, and *Efterretninger om Groenland*, pp. 117, 162.
26 Hans Egede, *Efterretninger om Groenland*, pp. 230–6.
27 Fritjiof Nansen, *op. cit.*, pp. 339–40.
28 Erkki Asp, *The Lapps and the Lappish Culture*, p. 17.

Permission to quote from the Hudson's Bay Record Society volumes has been received from the Keeper, Hudson's Bay Company Archives, provincial Archives of Manitoba. Permission to quote from Jean Malaurie, *The Last Kings of Thule*, has come from Messrs Jonathan Cape and E. P. Dutton (English translation © 1982 by Jonathan Cape and E. P. Dutton). Permission to quote from Robert E. Peary, *The Discovery of the North Pole*, has come from Messrs Hodder & Stoughton. To all of these grateful thanks.

GLOSSARY

Angakok – Wise man of a settlement, a spiritual leader. Plural: **Angakut**.
Arnarkuagssoq – Goddess of the Sea, another name for **Sedna**.
Iglu – Stone and turf house.
Ilisiitok – Evil old man or woman. Plural: **Ilisiituk**.
Illuliaq – Traditional 'igloo'.
Inua – A soul, which the Inuit believed possessed all animate beings and inanimate objects.
Inuk – An 'eskimo'. The work means 'human being', a 'real man'. Plural: **Inuit**.
Inuit – Plural form of **Inuk**.
Inuktitut – Language spoken by Inuit.
Inuvialuit – Inuit living in the Mackenzie Delta region.
Joiking – Sami style of singing, very similar to that of the Inuit.
Kamiks – Boots of skin, often thigh length.
Kayak – Slender boat used for hunting at sea, made of seal skin stretched over bone or wooden framework. In Eurasia, known as **baidar**.
Knarr – Viking merchant ship.
Mattak, Muktut – The skin of walrus, whale or narwhal. A delicacy rich in protein and vitamins.
Nanuuk – A polar bear.
Nerrivik – Another name for **Sedna**. Also **Neqiviq**.
Nunavut – The territory containing all land and sea north of the tree line, east of the Mackenzie River, claimed by the Inuit as their homeland, to be governed by themselves within the Canadian Confederation under the supervision of Ottawa.
Polynya – An open channel of water.
Pulka – A small, boat-like sledge used by the Sami. Also known as an **akya** or **keris**.
Qallunaat – Inuit term for 'white man'. Also known as **Kabloonah**.
Qivitok – Half-savage victims of **Ilisiituk**, living wild in the mountains.
Sami – The people of Samiland, formerly called 'Lapps'.
Sedna – Goddess of the Sea and marine life. The most powerful of all the influences on the Inuit, with the exception of **Sila**.
Shaman – Spiritual leader, wise man of a settlement, also known as an **angakok**.

Sila – A spiritual presence, similar to the Chinese Tao. The most influential God in the Inuit world.

Skraelingar – Derogatory Viking word for the Inuit.

Tornat – Ministering spirits used by **angakut**.

Tupilak – Spirit, ghost. Plural: **Tupilek**.

Ulu – Woman's 'u'-shaped knife, used for flensing seal.

Umiak – Communal boat of skin, capable of carrying 10–12 people.

BIBLIOGRAPHY

During the past thirty years, hundreds of books have been written about the Arctic. The following is a selective bibliography of the most important titles. Each one will assist the reader to delve more deeply into specific aspects of the North.

Almgren, Bertil, and others. *The Viking.* AB Nordbok, Sweden, 1975.

Armstrong, Terence (with Brian Roberts, Charles Swithinbank). *Illustrated Glossary of Snow and Ice.* Scott Polar Research Institute, Cambridge, 1973.

Asp, Erkki. *The Lapps and the Lappish Culture.* University of Turku, Finland, 1980.
  The Social Consequences of Regulating the Watercourses in Lapland. University of Turku, Finland, 1981.
  The Skolt Lapps. University of Turku, Finland, 1982.

Baker, Dr Robin. *The Mystery of Migration.* Macdonald Futura Books, London, 1980.

Bhardarson, Ivar. *Det gamle Groenlands beskrivelse.* Ed. Finnur Jonsson, Copenhagen, 1930.

Berger, Thomas R. *Northern Frontier, Northern Homeland.* The Report of the Mackenzie Valley Pipeline Inquiry. Supply & Services Canada, Ottawa, 1977.

Birket-Smith, Kaj. *The Caribou Eskimos.* Nordisk Forlag, Copenhagen, 1940.
  Anthropological Observations on the Central Eskimos. Nordisk Forlag, Copenhagen, 1940.

Brower, Mayor Eugene. Address to Alaska Science Conference, Whitehorse, NWT, Sept., 1983.

Canadian Arctic Resources Committee (CARC). *Northern Perspectives.* Ottawa, no date.

Chantraine, Pol. *The Living Ice.* McClelland & Stewart, Toronto, 1980.

Creery, Ian. *The Inuit of Canada.* The Minority Rights Group, London, 1983.

Crisler, Lois. *Arctic Wild.* Secker & Warburg, London, 1959.

Cummings, Peter. *Canada: Native Land Rights and Northern Development.* IWGIA Document 26. Copenhagen, 1977.

Dalland, Oystein. *The Alta Case – Learning from the Errors Made in a Human Ecological Conflict in Norway.* Pergamon Press Ltd, London, 1983.

Danish Ministry for Greenland. *Groenland, 1982*. Arsberetning, Copenhagen, 1983.

Degerbol, Magnus. 'Animal Bones from the Norse Ruins at Gardar'. *Meddelser om Groenland* 76, 3, p. 183 44. Copenhagen, 1929.

Dene Nation, The. *Denendeh*. The Dene Nation, Yellowknife, 1984.

DIAND. *Government Activities in the North, 1982–83.*

Lancaster Sound Region, 1980–2000, The. Government Green Paper, Ottawa, 1982.

Dyson, John. *The Hot Arctic*. Heinemann, London, 1979.

Egede, Hans. *Det gamle Groenlands nye Perlustration eller Naturel-Historie etc.* 1741. ed. Louis Bobé, *Meddelser om Groenland*, 54, Copenhagen, 1925.

Relationer fra Groenland 1721–1736, ed. Louis Bobé, *Meddelser om Groenland*, 54, Copenhagen, 1925.

Efterretninger om Groenland, Copenhagen, ca. 1725.

Egede, Poul. *Relationer fra Groenland*, 1741. *Meddelser om Groenland*, 54, Copenhagen, 1925.

Efterretninger om Groenland, Copenhagen, ca. 1725.

Emmelin, Lars. Address, Nordic Scientific Conference, Ny Alesund, Svalbard, August, 1984.

Freuchen, Peter. *Arctic Adventure: My Life in the Frozen North*. Wm. Heinemann Ltd, London, 1936.

Book of the Eskimos. The World Publishing Co, Cleveland, 1951.

with Finn Salomonsen: *The Arctic Year*. Jonathan Cape, London, 1960.

Gad, Finn. *The History of Greenland*. Vol. I, II: C. Hurst & Co, London, 1970, 1973. Vol III: Nytt Nordisk Forlag, Copenhagen, 1975.

Gallagher, H. G. *Etok: A Story of Eskimo Power*. Putnam, New York, 1974.

Herbert, Wally. *Eskimos*. Collins, London, 1976.

Across the Top of the World: The British Trans-Arctic Expedition. Longmans, London, 1969.

Hertling, Knud (with Erik Hesselbjerg, Svend Klitgaard, Ebbe Munck, Olaf Petersen). *Greenland Past and Present*. Edvard Henriksen, Copenhagen, no date.

Hudson's Bay Record Society. *Andrew Graham's Observations on Hudson's Bay, 1767–1791*, Vol XXVII, Hudson's Bay Record Society, London, no date. *Northern Quebec and Labrador Journals and Correspondence, 1819–1835*, Vol XXIV. No date.

Illingworth, Frank. *Wild Life Beyond the North*. Country Life Ltd, London, 1951.

Inuit Circumpolar Conference. *The President's Report 1980–1983*. Nuuk, no date.

Inuit Tapirisat of Canada. *Inuit Nunagat – The Peoples' Land*. The Inuit Land Claims Commission, Ottawa, 1978.

Nunavut, Agreement in Principle Between the Government and the Inuit Tapirisat of Canada. Ottawa, 1976.

Inuit Today, and *ITC News*.

Irwin, Colin. 'Inuit Navigation, Empirical Reasoning and Survival'. *Journal of Navigation*, May, 1985.

Jacobi, Hans. *Usukutaq.* Jakobshavn Turistforening, Greenland, no date.

Jones, Mervyn. *The Sami of Lapland.* The Minority Rights Group, London, 1982.

Kaalund, Bodil. *The Art of Greenland.* University of California Press, Berkeley, 1983.

Keating, Bern. *The Northwest Passage.* Rand McNally & Co, Chicago, 1970.

Lauritzen, Philip. *Oil and Amulets.* Breakwater Books, St John's, 1983.

Lipton, Barbara. *Survival: Life and Art of the Alaskan Eskimo.* Newark Museum and Morgan and Morgan, New York, 1977.

Livingston, John. *Arctic Oil.* Canadian Broadcasting Corporation, Toronto, 1981.

Magnusson, Magnus. *Viking Expansion Westwards.* The Bodley Head, London, 1973.

Malaurie, Jean. *The Last Kings of Thule.* Jonathan Cape, London, 1982. E. P. Dutton, New York, 1982.

Manker, Ernst. *People of Eight Seasons.* AB Nordbok, Sweden, 1975.

Markham, Albert Hastings. *A Whaling Cruise to Baffin's Bay.* Sampson Low, Marston, Low & Searle, London, 1875.

Marsden, Walter. *Lapland.* Time-Life International, Amsterdam, 1976.

Mauss, Marcel. *Seasonal Variations of the Eskimo.* Routledge & Kegan Paul, London, 1979.

Marchuk, Guri. *Science and Siberia.* Novosti Press Agency, Moscow, 1983.

Mead, W. R. (with Helmer Smeds). *Winter in Finland.* Hugh Evelyn Ltd, London, 1967.

Milne, Allen R. (with Brian D. Smiley). *Offshore Drilling in Lancaster Sound: Possible Environmental Hazards.* Canadian Dept. of Fisheries and Environment, Sidney, B.C., 1978.

Mowat, Farley. *Sea of Slaughter.* McClelland & Stewart, Toronto, 1984.

Nansen, Fritjiof. *Eskimo Life.* Longmans, Green & Co, London, 1894.

National Geographic Society. *Alaska: High Roads to Adventure.* Washington, D.C., 1976.

Alaska's Magnificent Parklands. Washington, D.C., 1984.

Olivant, Simon. *Arctic Challenge to NATO.* The Institute for the Study of Conflict, London, 1985.

Paine, Robert. *Dam a River, Damn a People?* International Work Group for Indigenous Affairs (IWGIA), Copenhagen, 1982.

Peary, Robert E. *Nearest the Pole.* Hutchinson & Co, London, 1907.

The Discovery of the North Pole. Hodder & Stoughton, London, 1910.

Petersen, H. C. *Instruction in Kayak Building.* Vikingeskibshallen, Roskilde, Copenhagen/Groenlands Landsmuseum, no date.

Pimlott, Douglas. *Oil under the Ice – Offshore Drilling in the Canadian Arctic.* Canadian Arctic Resources Committee (CARC), Ottawa, 1976.

Rasmussen, Knud. *Across Arctic America: Narrative of the Fifth Thule Expedition.* Greenwood Press, New York, no date.

Rawlins, Dennis. *Peary at the Pole: Fact or Fiction?* R. B. Luce, Washington, 1973.

Ray, Dorothy Jean. *Artists of the Tundra and the Sea.* University of Washington Press, Seattle, 1961.

Resnick, Abraham. *Siberia and the Soviet Far East: Endless Frontiers.* Novosti Press Agency, Moscow, 1983.

Rich, E. E. *Hudson's Bay Company, 1670–1763*, Vol I. Hudson's Bay Record Society, London, no date.

Ries, Tomas. 'Defending the Far North', *International Defense Review* 7 (1984).

Ritchie, Carson. *Art of the Eskimo.* A. S. Barnes & Co, South Brunswick/New York, 1979. Thomas Yoseloff Ltd, London, 1979.

Scott, J. M. *Icebound.* Gordon & Cremonesi, London, 1977.

Smith, D. Murray. *Arctic Expeditions from British and Foreign Shores.* London, ca. 1877.
　Early Arctic Expeditions. London, 1877.

Smith, Frances C. *The World of the Arctic.* Lutterworth Press, London, 1960.

Smith, Norman. *The Unbelievable Land.* Canadian Broadcasting Corporation/Queen's Printer, Ottawa, 1971.

Smucker, Samuel M. *Arctic Explorations and Discoveries during the Nineteenth Century.* Miller, Orton & Co, New York, 1857.

Spence, Bill. *Harpooned: The Story of Whaling.* Conway Maritime Press Ltd, Greenwich, 1980.

Steltzer, Ulli. *Inuit: The North in Transition.* Douglas & McIntyre Ltd, Vancouver/Toronto, 1982.

Taylor, Col. Wm. J., Jr. *The Challenge to Nato's Northern Flank.* USICA, Washington, no date.

Valkeapaa, Nils-Aslak. *Greetings from Lappland.* Zed Press, London, 1983.

Whymper, Frederick. *Heroes of the Arctic.* Society for Promoting Christian Knowledge, London, 1875.

Williamson, Kenneth. *Bird Study*, Vol. 22. No. 2. Sept, 1975.

INDEX

240 *The Fourth World*

Sam Hall has had a long career as a journalist and has traveled to more than 50 countries for his work. As a Reuter
reporter for Independent Television News in London, he
covered the Nigerian-Biafran war and the Turkish invasion
of Cyprus. His reports for the important British nightly
news program *News At Ten* included coverage of the hostage
crisis in Iran and the 1982 siege of Beirut. For *The Fourth
World*, Hall traveled thousands of miles through the Arctic
over a period of years. ITN broadcast a series of his special
reports, and he also produced a documentary film, *Greenland: The Vikings Return*. He is now a reporter in London
with the TV AM program.

A NOTE ON THE TYPE

The text of this book was set in a film version of Ehrhardt,
a type face receiving its name from the Ehrhardt foundry
in Frankfort. The original design of the face was the work
of Nicholas Kis, a Hungarian punch cutter known to have
worked in Amsterdam from 1680-1689. The modern
version of Ehrhardt was cut by The Monotype Corporation
of London in 1937.

Composed in Great Britain